DAYS OF AWE
Jewish Holy Days, Symbols, & Prophecies for Latter-day Saints

Including a paper by Richard K. Scott discussing a possible Thursday crucifixion for Christ with supports From the Book of Mormon

by Gale T. Boyd

Copyright © 2002 and 2007 Gale T. Boyd

All rights reserved

Updated and revised March 2015

Originally formatted and prepared for publication by Ken Alford.

ISBN: 9781717816658

Copyright Notice

Charts, recipes, activities, and the Passover Haggadah found in Part IV may be photocopied multiple times for use in presentations.

Any other use of this text, photographs, or supplemental materials found herein constitutes breach of copyright.

Written permission is required for any other use of this text.

Disclaimer

This book is meant for a Mormon audience. It presupposes a belief that Jesus is the Messiah and that all the Old Testament prophets, including Moses, testified of that truth. This book is not meant as a conversion tool to convert followers of Judaism to Mormonism or Christianity. It is also not meant to ridicule or controvert any religious belief. The opinions expressed in this book are my own. I do not claim to represent The Church of Jesus Christ of Latter-day Saints.

Acknowledgments

Special thanks to Dr. Wayne Shute for his far-sightedness, vision, and close supervision of this work. Thanks also to Drs. Steven Liddle, Kent Hunter and Rob Jones for their excellent editing and suggestions. To the people who helped us get to Israel, stay in Israel, and to understand Israel and Judaism, many thanks. As sounding boards over the years, Carla G., Danny R., LDS friends in Israel and the U.S., and especially Puck. And my husband for often staying awake to listen to reports of my conundrums and for supporting my endeavors with tolerance and enthusiasm. The kids for toughing it out in foreign schools, being attentive through many lengthy Passovers, and ever appreciating the chicken soup and kugel.

Passover table setting photography by Stefan Halberg.

Cover photo by Justin Thornton via Dreamstime.com.

Coloring pages by Rivka Wilkins of Rivka's Renditions.

About the Author

Gale T. Boyd was born to Jewish parents in Washington, D.C. She was raised in Silver Spring, Maryland, and Pasadena, California. She attended the University of California at Santa Barbara and Brigham Young University, graduating with a B.A. in English.

She married Byron "Bud" Boyd, and together they have 6 children. As a family, they lived in Israel for 8 years, the island of Cyprus for 3 1/2 years, Ireland and Malaysia. They have traveled to many other countries.

Gale's interest in Judaica is matched only by her love for writing and teaching. Presently, she lives with her family in Utah.

TABLE OF CONTENTS

PROLOGUE xiv
INTRODUCTION. xvii
GLOSSARY. xviii
CHAPTER 1: JEWS AND JUDAISM 2
    WHO IS A JEW? 3
    GOD CHOOSES JUDAISM'S HEROES 3
    WHO IS THE MESSIAH? 4
    ANOTHER MESSIAH? 4
    JEWISH SCRIPTURE 5
    A COMPLEXITY OF LAW 6
    HAIRSPLITTING. 6
    THE SPIRIT OF JUDAISM 7
    LIVING AMONG ENEMIES 8
    A LEGACY OF SCHOLARSHIP 9
    NUMEROLOGY 9
    THE NURTURING GHETTO 10
    CHAPTER 1 ENDNOTES.. 11
CHAPTER 2: THE LAW OF MOSES 14
    A HOLY PEOPLE 15
    PROTECTION UNDER THE LAW 16
    COMPENSATING THE VICTIM 17
    NO JEWISH POLICEMEN 17
    THE IMPORTANCE OF MAKING RESTITUTION 18
    REFERRING BACK TO THE LAW 18
    CHAPTER 2 ENDNOTES.. 20
CHAPTER 3: WHAT IT MEANS TO KEEP KOSHER. 21
    WHAT ARE THE RULES? 21
    CHAPTER 3 ENDNOTES.. 24

CHAPTER 4: THE 13 CREEDS OF JUDAISM & THE NOAHITE LAWS	26
CHAPTER 5: BE THOU THEREFORE PERFECT	28
CHAPTER 6: THE SHAPE OF THE JEWISH YEAR	32
THE SABBATH QUEEN.	32
RAINS, HARVESTS, AND SEASONS	36
BORN OUT OF EGYPT	36
CHAPTER 7 ENDNOTES	38
CHAPTER 7: PESACH AND CHAG HAMATZOT	
(THE FEASTS OF PASSOVER AND UNLEAVENED BREAD)	39
THE ANCIENT RITE OF SACRIFICE	40
A MESSAGE FOR EGYPT	41
AN OBSERVANCE FOREVER	42
THE LAMB OF GOD	43
THE BREAD OF LIFE	44
DELIVERANCE.	45
ISRAEL FORGETS AND REMEMBERS	47
A WORLD OF TURMOIL AND CONTROVERSY	48
JESUS WAS BORN ON THE PASSOVER	49
THE LAST SUPPER	51
THE PATTERN OF THE LAST SUPPER	52
THE SACRAMENTAL BREAD	55
THE SACRAMENTAL WINE	55
WHY DID JESUS CELEBRATE PASSOVER ONE NIGHT EARLY?	56
JESUS WAS NOT CRUCIFIED ON FRIDAY	56
THREE DAYS, AND THREE NIGHTS.	57
A TRAGIC PASSOVER — 70 A.D.	57
PASSOVERS CELEBRATED IN PERIL.	58
PASSOVER PREPARATIONS	58
SAVING PRINCIPLES ARE TAUGHT BY THE FEAST	60
ELIJAH AND THE PASSOVER	61
SYMBOLS ESTABLISHED BY GOD.	62

CHAPTER 8 ENDNOTES...63
CHAPTER 8: *BIKKURIM* (THE FEAST OF FIRST FRUITS).............65
    THE SIGNIFICANCE OF "FIRST THINGS" 66
    A PERFECT OFFERING 67
    JESUS AS THE FIRST FRUITS 69
    CHAPTER 9 ENDNOTES...70
CHAPTER 9: COUNTING THE OMER 71
    A TIME OF TREPIDATION 73
    CHAPTER 10 ENDNOTES...75
CHAPTER 10: SHAVUOT (THE FEAST OF WEEKS)............................76
    A FESTIVAL OF REJOICING 77
    PENTACOST AND THE GIFT OF THE HOLY GHOST.................77
    SHAVUOT TODAY 78
    WORD AND SPIRIT — THE BLESSINGS OF ZION 79
    CHAPTER 10 ENDNOTES...80
CHAPTER 11: ROSH HASHANAH (THE FEAST OF TRUMPETS)........81
    PREPARING FOR THE BRIDEGROOM 82
    THE LAND OF THE LIVING 84
    AWAKE, AND ARISE 85
    A BLAST OF THE TRUMPETS...87
    MAY YOUR NAME BE WRITTEN IN THE BOOK OF LIFE 88
    THE END OF DAYS DRAWS NIGH 89
    CHAPTER 11 ENDNOTES...91
CHAPTER 12: YAMIM NORA'IM (THE DAYS OF AWE) 92
    HOW DOES ONE REPENT?..93
    CHAPTER 12 ENDNOTES...95
CHAPTER 13: YOM KIPPUR (THE DAY OF ATONEMENT) 96
    A DAY TO AFFLICT ONE'S SOUL..96
    BLOOD ATONEMENT 98
    COVERING SIN, CLEANSING SIN 100
    SEPARATION AND HOPE 101

CHAPTER 13 ENDNOTES..102
CHAPTER 14: SUKKOT (THE FEAST OF TABERNACLES)........................103
    THE FINAL INGATHERING 104
    THE SUKKAH 104
    WATER AND FIRE 106
    THE HOSANNA SHOUT 108
    CHAPTER 14 ENDNOTES...110
CHAPTER 15: THE SEVEN FESTIVALS 111
    OBSERVING THE FEASTS IS NOT ENOUGH................................113
    HEARERS OF THE WORD 113
SUPPLEMENTAL MATERIALS..116
APPENDIX A: FAMILY HOME EVENING PRESENTATIONS................118
    A SABBATH FAMILY HOME EVENING......................................119
    A PASSOVER FAMILY HOME EVENING 123
    A FIRST-FRUITS FAMILY HOME EVENING 127
    A WILDERNESS WALK FAMILY HOME EVENING.....................130
    A FEAST OF WEEKS FAMILY HOME EVENING (#1) 134
    A FEAST OF WEEKS FAMILY HOME EVENING (#2) 137
    A FEAST OF TRUMPETS FAMILY HOME EVENING 139
    A DAY OF ATONEMENT FAMILY HOME EVENING 141
    A FEAST OF TABERNACLES FAMILY HOME EVENING 143
    A PURIM FAMILY HOME EVENING 146
    A CHANUKAH FAMILY HOME EVENING 149
APPENDIX B: PASSOVER..152
    HOW TO PRESENT A PASSOVER FEAST...................................152
    FOR THE PRESENTER. 154
    A PASSOVER FIRESIDE 157
    HOW TO SET UP TABLES IN A LARGE HALL............................157
    HEBREW NAME GAME ....
    SETTING THE PASSOVER TABLE 159
    PASSOVER TABLE-SETTING CHECKLIST 160

SAMPLE PASSOVER MENU...162
HEBREW BLESSINGS FOR PASSOVER...163
PASSOVER MUSIC...165
APPENDIX C: A PASSOVER HAGGADAH
(FOR LATTER-DAY SAINT CELEBRANTS) 167
APPENDIX D: PASSOVER RECIPES..194
PREPARATION SUGGESTIONS 194
CHAROSET..195
IRANIAN CHAROSET...195
CARLA'S HAROSET 196
JEWISH MAMA'S CHICKEN SOUP 196
MATZAH BALLS 197
MATZAH STUFFING...197
PASSOVER POTATO PANCAKES ("LATKES")....................................197
POTATO KUGEL 198
CRUSTY CHICKEN BREASTS 198
GEFILTE FISH 198
ROAST LAMB SHOULDER ROLL 199
IRAQI MINTED SALAD...199
LEMON AND OIL DRESSING 200
DENISE'S SPINACH SALAD 200
POPPY SEED DRESSING 200
ZUCCHINI CASSEROLE..200
MATZAH CHOCOLATE TORTE 201
MATZAH APPLE TORTE 201
MATZAH SPONGE CAKE 202
COCONUT KISSES 202
BROWN SUGAR MACAROONS 202
MATZAH COOKIES 202
CINNAMON DATE PASSOVER ROLL 203
PASSOVER BANANA CAKE 203

APPENDIX E: FEAST OF WEEKS RECIPES (SHAVUOT/PENTACOST) 205
- SWEET KUGEL 205
- CHEESE BLINTZES. 206
- YOGURT COFFEE CAKE 206
- EUROPEAN JEWISH CHEESECAKE 207
- MIDDLE EASTERN MILK PUDDING 208

APPENDIX F: FEAST OF TRUMPETS RECIPES 210
- APPLE UPSIDE-DOWN CAKE 210
- APPLE KUGEL 211
- ROSH HASHANAH HONEY CAKE 211
- HONEY CAKE 212

APPENDIX G: FEAST OF TABERNACLES RECIPES 213
- PERSIAN FRUIT SALAD 213
- ACORN SQUASH WITH APPLE STUFFING 213
- PUMPKIN SPICE CAKE WITH ORANGE SAUCE 214
- ORANGE SAUCE 215
- GINGER-ALMOND SHORTBREAD 215
- FRESH FRUIT STRUDEL 215
- EDIBLE SUKKAHS 216

APPENDIX H: PURIM 217
- THE STORY OF ESTHER 217
- HAMENTASCHEN 218
- PURIM – GIFTS OF SWEETS (*MISHLO'ACH MANOT*) 219

APPENDIX I: CHANUKAH 220
- THE CHANUKAH STORY 220
- THE DREIDEL GAME 221
- CHANUKAH MENORAHS 222

APPENDIX J: HANUKKAH RECIPES 223
- CHANUKAH DOUGHNUTS (SUFGANIYOT) 223
- POTATO PANCAKES (LATKES) 224
- CHANUKAH POTATO PANCAKES (*LATKES*) 224

HONEY AND SPICE COOKIES	225
APPENDIX K: CHILDREN'S PICTURES	226
APPENDIX L: A TORAH SCROLL	237
APPENDIX M: *LAG B'OMER* BONFIRE ACTIVITY	238
APPENDIX N: MAKING A FLOWER HEAD WREATH	240
APPENDIX O: THE CRUCIFIXION MAY HAVE OCCURRED ONE DAY EARLIER by RICHARD K. SCOTT	241
BIBLIOGRAPHY FOR DAYS OF AW	

PROLOGUE

We arrived in Israel in August 1983, an American family of seven, off on a grand adventure, intending to live in the Holy Land indefinitely. We found a small apartment in a suburb of Jerusalem, and looked forward to experiencing a foreign culture. And foreign it was. We encountered unfamiliar systems of writing and speaking, weights and measures, money and banking, shopping and traveling, home life and education. And that's not all! Our days, weeks, months and years were transformed. Every measured unit on clock or calendar suddenly had religious significance. According to the Jewish calendar, the year was 5744, and the month was *Elul*. No longer did the day begin at dawn, but at sunset the day before. Each day then ended at sunset, and a new day began. We were measuring time the way Adam measured it; it was the Lord's time. Sabbath was on Saturday, the only day of rest (beginning Friday night). School and work consumed six days a week. No Wednesday nor Thursday existed, nor any other day of the week as we knew them; only the countdown to the next Sabbath – Day 1, Day 2, Day 3, Day 4, Day 5, Day 6, Sabbath.

We learned to love the bustle of Friday afternoons, as the entire country prepared for the coming Sabbath, everyone rushing to finish their preparations before the shops closed, and the buses stopped running. First to the *suq*, or open-air market, for fresh fruit, vegetables, cheeses, and sweets, then to the bakery for braided loaves of sweet Sabbath bread, called *challah*, then home to clean and do the cooking for the weekend. In every neighborhood the waning afternoon brought smells of the ethnic cooking of many lands — Jews had gathered to Jerusalem from all over the world.

Four Sabbaths after our arrival, we thought we had the rhythm of Sabbath preparation down-pat, when suddenly we were overtaken by a three-day

Sabbath. The triple Sabbath took us completely by surprise. When Day 5 (Thursday) arrived, the kids were up and ready for school, but there was none. Friday, the same. The two-day New Year (*Rosh HaShanah*) observance had occurred back-to-back with the Sabbath. We had known, in a vague, nebulous sort of way that we were gearing up for a holiday. No one was saying, "Hello, how are you?" any more. The typical greetings, even to complete strangers, were *shanah tovah* and *chatimah tovah* — "good year" and "good signature." It had been explained to us that "good signature" meant, "May your name be written in the Book of Life." It seemed strange that this very personal, very religious greeting was considered proper even in the office and the market place, but the religious spirit of the season seemed to permeate everything secular. We were still very culturally confused, barely beginning to grasp a little basic Hebrew. I thought I was in trouble at the super-market, when the clerk grabbed my receipt and took it to the manager. I followed the clerk dutifully, but had the feeling I was about to be arrested for something. The clerk and manager examined the receipt carefully and seriously, then they burst into broad smiles and thrust a bottle of wine at me, shouting, "*Shanah Tovah!*" I had spent enough money on groceries to win a gift of New Year's wine.

Since then, we have learned much about the Jewish holidays. We have grown to love the festivities that define the year in Israel, every holiday with its religious foundation. We have begun to grasp the rhythm of the holidays as they embrace the land and its harvests and lay out Biblical history in rich imagery.

But gradually, we have begun to understand that these holidays are much, much more than they appear on the surface, and that they have deep significance for us as Latter-day Saints. As we have immersed ourselves in Jewish culture and studied and observed the rituals of the Jewish holidays, we have begun to see in these Holy Convocations types and shadows of the Savior's future life, ministry, death, resurrection, redemptive powers, and Second Coming. We have also seen in the pattern of these Holy Convocations, the Lord's Plan of Happiness for his children, from beginning to end.

The Lord commanded the Israelites to keep these Holy Feasts forever. We, as members of The Church of Jesus Christ of Latter-day Saints are, by birth or adoption, Israelites. And although the Law of Moses has been fulfilled, might there still be a message for us in these Holy Feasts? I believe the answer is a resounding, "Yes!"

This book is an attempt to unfold to the view of the Latter-day Saint reader, the symbolism in the Gospel of Jesus Christ, as found in the celebration of the Jewish Holy Days. The book contains a history of all the Old Testament feasts, their ancient and current patterns of observance, their prophetic symbolism, and their relevance to each of us as Latter-day Saints.

Many Latter-day Saints sense the importance of the imagery in the Passover, which Jesus observed as the Last Supper. Sometimes Passover feasts are presented in wards, stakes, and for many years now, at

Brigham Young University. However, added information and cultural background often result in the ritual being presented in a new and more ethnically rich way, and the impact of the evening is far more meaningful.

INTRODUCTION

This book, and the accompanying appendices, will help those who wish to simulate the most familiar Holy Day, the Passover, to do so accurately and meaningfully. Materials can be printed out. They include recipes, proper setting of the Passover table, the booklet outlining the Passover ritual (*haggadah*), and a presenter's outline. In addition, the Appendices of this book contain instructions for teaching about the other Holy Days in the format of Family Home Evening lessons.

By following the instructions presented here, the reader will be better able to understand and feel the spirit and significance of the Jewish Feasts, and to see their significance in relation to our beliefs in the Lord, Jesus Christ. The Jewish Holy Days are rich with Messianic imagery.

Finally, I have added two other Jewish holidays, *Purim* and *Chanukah*, to the Family Home Evening lesson plans. Though they are not true "Holy Days" (were not dictated by Jehovah, nor commanded by the Lord to be observed), and though they do not contain Messianic imagery or prophecy, they are still very worthwhile learning about.

GLOSSARY

It is unusual for a glossary to be placed in the front of a book. However, there are many unfamiliar terms in this text, and it will serve you well to glance through this vocabulary list once or twice.

The Hebrew words that appear in this book are written in *italics*. Most of these words are included in this glossary. The use of Hebrew terms is not meant to intimidate you; they add to the ethnic flavor and the cultural and spiritual messages presented herein.

As for pronunciation, if you see a "ch" or a "kh" in a transliterated Hebrew word, pronounce it like an "h," but try to bring up a little spit from the back of your throat while doing so, for these sounds are gutteral.

Afikomon — Bread after dinner. A piece of unleavened bread which in the Passover ritual represents the Paschal Lamb. (ahf-ee-ko'-mon)

Ashkenazi — A Jew whose ancestors were scattered into Central or Eastern Europe. (Ahsh-ken-ah'-zee)

Aviv — "Spring"; the first lunar month of the ancient Jewish year. Now called *Nisan*. Passover always falls on the first full moon after the spring equinox (March 21st), with the day of sacrifice being the 14th of Aviv and the Feast of Unleavened Bread beginning the 15th of Aviv. (Also "Abib".) (Ah-veev')

Bar Mizvah — The time (at age thirteen) when a young man comes into manhood in the eyes of the Lord. He earns the right to read from the scriptures in synagogue, and takes upon himself other duties. A religious rite of passage. Girls now enjoy a similar rite in some congregations, called *bat mitzvah*. (Bar mitz'-vah)

Baytzah — The Hebrew word for egg. A roasted egg represents a festival offering in the days of the Temple. Also a symbol of mourning that no offering can be made until the Redemption. In jest, a symbol of the Jewish people — the more they're in hot water, the tougher they become. (Bay-tzah')

Bikkurim — A derivative of the Hebrew word *bekhor* (which means first-born son). First fruits. Now celebrated on the 16th of *Nisan*, First Fruits was commanded to be observed on the day following the first normal sabbath during Passover. The *Omer* is counted from this day. (Bee'-koor-eem')

Chag ha-matzot — Feast of Unleavened Bread. The first day of Passover is the sacrifice of the lamb; the remaining seven days are the Feast of Unleavened Bread. The two holidays have been combined to a one-week observance called Passover. (Chahg hah- mah-tzot')

Challah — Jewish sabbath bread, sweet and braided, or unsweetened in various shapes. A recipe is included on the accompanying disc. (Chah'-lah)

Chametz — Leaven; anything that causes bread products to rise. (Also *hametz*.) (Chah'-metz)

Chanukah or Hanukkah— Celebration of the cleansing and rededication of the Temple by the Maccabees around 166 BC, after it had been desecrated by a Greco-Persian army. There was only enough holy oil left to burn for one day, but the oil burned for eight, a great miracle. Called the Festival of Lights. (Chahn'-oo- kah)

Charoset — A sweet mixture of chopped fruit served as a symbolic Passover food, representing the mortar used by Jewish slaves in Egypt to make bricks; also representing the sweetness of hope. (Also haroseth, haroset.) (Chahr-oh'-set)

Chazeret — Hebrew for horseradish. A bitter herb and symbolic Passover food representing the bitterness of slavery and oppression (also hazeret). (Chahz-ehr'-et)

Chol hamo'ed — The intermediate five days of the Feast of Unleavened Bread during which work is not prohibited. The first and last day of Passover are High Sabbaths. Sukkot also has intermediate days of half-hearted work. (Chol ha-mo'-ed)

Diaspora — Any place but Israel. The Jews were dispersed upon the destruction of the Temple in 70 A.D. Since then they have lived in exile in various countries of the world. The Hebrew term is *galut*.

Gematria — Numerology. Attributing numerical values to Hebrew words and phrases to find spiritual symbolisms. (Gem-ah-tree'-ah)

Haggadah — Hebrew for "the telling"; a book which contains the pattern of the Passover ritual and feast. A haggadah (plural *haggadot*) can be a simple booklet or a beautifully illuminated book. (Hah'-gad-dah')

Halakha — Jewish law. Taken from the verb "to walk," it determines what is ethical and good as we walk through this life. (Hal-akh-hah')

Hyksos — "Shepherd Kings" — Semitic people who took over parts of ancient Egypt "without a fight," humiliating the Egyptians and breeding anti-Semitism.

Kabbala — Jewish mysticism. (Kahb-bah-lah')

Karpas — Parsley, onion or potato, served raw, as a Passover ritual food. These are spring vegetables, symbols of rebirth. These herbs also allude to backbreaking labor. (Kar'-pahs)

Khamsin — From the Arabic word for "fifty." The dry, hot, dust-laden winds from the south-east which blow about fifty days each year in the Holy Land. (Hebrew, *sharav*.) (Khahm-seen')

Kiddush — A chanted blessing over ceremonial wine. From the Hebrew word "kodesh," meaning holy. (Kihd-oosh')

Kosher — Fit to eat. Conforming to Jewish dietary laws, or laws of *kashrut*.

Knowledge — There are three types—wisdom, prophecy, and the commandments.

Lag B'omer — The thirty-third day of the *Omer*. A celebration of the suspension of the pestilence suffered among the many thousands of Rabbi Akiva's students. (Lahg' be-oh'-mehr)

Ma nishtanah — "*ma nishtanah ha-laylah ha-ze*" — a phrase and song meaning, "Why is this night different from all other nights?" Asked and sung during the Passover *seder.* (Mah' nish-tah-nah')

Maror — Bitter herbs. We use romaine lettuce to represent the bitter herbs. It is symbolic of the bitterness of slavery under the Egyptians. Eating it (especially with the *charoset*) endows a celebrant with the ability to transform bitterness into sweetness. Romaine is especially suited for its role as the bitter herb, because the leaf is sweet, but the stalk is bitter, much like Israel's experience in Egypt, which began happily but ended in bitterness. (Mah-rohr')

Matzah — Unleavened bread. For the Passover it is prepared with special haste (within eighteen minutes) and close supervision. The *matzah* symbolizes purity. As the *afikomon* eaten during the Passover meal, it symbolizes the Paschal Lamb. (Plural - *matzot*.) (Matz'-ah)

Messiah — Originally, anyone anointed and consecrated to do the work of the Lord. David's chosen and promised descendent, anointed to divine kingship on earth and the restoration of Israel. He will be the head of an age of universal peace, prosperity, and righteousness. The power of death will be limited, and mankind will return to its previously known longevity. Note that among some groups of Jews, the Messiah's kingship is divinely ordained, but the Messiah himself is not divine. Other groups see him as a warrior-king of divine origin who will come in glory from heaven (as prophesied by Zechariah and Malachi). It is not unusual to see bumper stickers in Israel that say, "We want Messiah Now!" (Hebrew, *moshiach*.)

Menorah — "Lamp." The seven-branched candelabra, used as the symbol of Israel. The menorah used at Hanukkah has eight branches, one of which holds a candle used to light the others (called a *shamash*). The Hebrew word for the Chanukah menorah is *chanukiah.* (Mehn-oh'-rah)

Midrash — Exegesis of scripture. It explains Biblical text from ethical and devotional points of view. (Mid'-rash)

Mikveh — A ritual bath where one is immersed to remove uncleanness. One goes to *Mikveh* as a new convert, or when periods of uncleanness end, or to devote oneself to a process of rededication as on the holiday of *Shavuot*. The concept of baptism by immersion taught by John the Baptist was not difficult for the Jews to understand. (Mihk'-veh)

Mishnah — A philosophical code of law credited to Judah the Prince around 200

It deals with women, agriculture, holy days, cleanliness and purity, and civil law. (Mish'-nah)

Mo'edim — "Holy convocations." The holy holidays are meant to be meeting times between God and man. (Moh-ed-eem')

Omer — A measure of grain or flour which equals about five pints. An offering of meal. The forty-nine days between Passover and the Feast of Weeks during which the barley harvest takes place. (Oh'-mehr)

Parve — A neutral food that can be eaten with either meat or dairy products. Fish is a parve food. (Also pareve, parveh.) (Pahr'-veh)

Paschah — The Greek word for Easter. (Pasha.) (Pahs'-chah)

Pesach — Passover. The Jewish holiday that celebrates the deliverance of the Children of Israel from captivity in Egypt. The offering of the Pascal Lamb on *Nisan (Aviv)* 14. The rest of the Passover holiday (seven days) is called "Chag ha-matzot," the Feast of Unleavened bread. The two festivals have been combined and called Passover, lasting one week. (Pay'-sach)

Pharisees — At the time of Christ the Pharisees were the largest Jewish Sect. They accepted both the *Torah* and the oral law, and believed in a merciful God and eternal judgment. They encouraged study and prayer in the synagogues. Jesus never criticized their beliefs, but he rained scathing criticism down upon their hypocrisy when they hid their personal unethical behavior behind a veil of piety.[1]

Pidyon HaBen — A rite performed when a first-born son is one month old, which absolves him from a lifetime of religious service. Literally, "redemption of the son." (Pihd-yohn' hah-behn')

---

[1] Ludlow, "Major Jewish Groups in the New Testament," *Ensign*, January 1975, 26.

Purim — The celebration of the Book of Esther, in the early spring. A Family Home Evening celebration of Purim, plus Purim recipes are found in the Presentations section of this book and on the accompanying disc. (Poo'-reem)

Rosh HaShanah — In the fall, a holiday marking the Civil New Year. Originally, the Feast of Trumpets, calling all to awake, arise, gather, repent, and be judged. (Rohsh' hah-shah-nah')

Sadducees — An aristocratic, priestly class of Jews which became cohesive while the Holy Land was in the process of being Hellenized, around 200 B.C. They rejected the Jewish oral law, and the concepts of resurrection and afterlife. In about 37 B.C. Herod killed about half the priests in the Sanhedrin. The Sadducees became very cooperative with the Romans, which (along with their philosophies, wealth, and corruption) made them unpopular with other Jewish sects. They disappeared completely when the Temple (over which they held control) was destroyed in 70 A.D.[2]

Sanhedrin — In ancient times, the Jewish senate or governing body with both political and religious power. The Sanhedrin "ruled as a Jewish law court in matters of faith, manners, and law in which Roman interests were not directly affected. . . . The Council consisted of members of the Sadducean aristocracy and more moderate Pharisees and scribes."[3]

Schmittah — Every seventh year in Israel, when the land enjoys a Sabbath year of rest. (Schmee-tah') The commandment says that the entire nation must observe it at once, and as it was with manna from heaven, double would be harvested the sixth year to prepare for the observance.

Scribes — At the time of Christ, secretaries for those who were illiterate. They were also legal counselors in temporal and spiritual matters.[4]

Seder — "Order." The Passover festival meal eaten the evening before 14th Nisan (in modern times, the 15th), the Jews counting their "days" from sundown to sundown. A "second seder" can be observed the second night, and a final seder at the end of the eight days (now seven days). (Say'-dehr)

Seder plate — A ceremonial plate upon which are served the six symbolic foods of Passover — horseradish, bitter herbs, *charoset*, lamb shank bone (or chicken neck), roasted egg, and sweet herbs.

---

[2] Ibid.
[3] Galbraith, Ogden and Skinner, *Jerusalem: The Eternal City*, 155.
[4] Ludlow, 26.

Sefirat Ha'Omer — The counting of the Omer, the forty-nine days between Passover and *Shavuot*, The Feast of Weeks. (Seh-fihr-aht' Hah-oh'-mehr)

Sephardi — A Jew whose ancestors were scattered into Spain or Portugal. Many then migrated to Mediterranean countries and are sometimes called Oriental Jews. (Sehf-ahr'-dee)

Shabbat — Sabbath. Saturday, the last day of the week, or the designated Sabbaths during holiday weeks. ie — The first day of Passover week is a Sabbath. (Yiddish — *shabbos*.) (Shah-baht")

Shofar — A ram's horn, designed for blowing as a signal to arise, awake, and gather, especially on Rosh HaShanah, the Feast of Trumpets. (Shoh'-fahr)

Shavuot — The Feast of Weeks; Pentecost, seven weeks after the Passover; a feast of first fruits; the first wheat harvest, or first fruits harvested in the promised land. (Shah-voo-oht')

Shemah — "Hear." The "Shemah is the central message of Judaism: "Hear O Israel, our God is one Lord."

Sin — Three Hebrew words denote three types of sin. "Heytah," used most often, means "to miss the mark." "On," means something distorted or twisted. "Passah" is the verb for "to rebel."

Sukkot — The Feast of Tabernacles. Jews build booths, called *Sukkot* in Hebrew, and eat and sleep in them to remember how they were succored by God during their sojourn in the wilderness. In the fall, at the final harvest. (Soo-koht')

Talmud — Rabbinical commentary. The Jerusalem Talmud (400 A.D.), also called the Yerushalmi, amplifies and extends passages of the Mishnah. The Babylonian Talmud, or Bavli (600 A.D.), is another commentary on the Mishnah written independently of the Yerushalmi. (Tahl'-muhd)

Tanakh — The *Torah*, the Prophets, and the Writings. The scriptures we would call the Old Testament. (Tahn-akh')

Tashlikh — A ceremony which takes place on the afternoon of the first day of *Rosh HaShana*, whereat people go to a body of water and symbolically shake their pockets as if to empty their sins into the sea (Micah 7:19). (Tash'-leekh)

Torah — The Law; the first five books of the Bible or five Books of Moses. Copied by hand with utmost reverence and care and kept in a synagogue's holy ark. The remainder of what we call "The Old Testament" comprises The Prophets and The Writings, all together called the "*Tanakh*." (Toh'-rah)

Yamim Nora'im — "Days of Awe;" Ten days of repentance between the Feast of Trumpets and *Yom Kippur*. (Yahm-eem' noh-rah-eem')

Yom Kippur — The "Day of Atonement." It refers to winning forgiveness for one's own sins, and is the climax of a ten-day period of repentance called the "Days of Awe" beginning with the Day of Judgment, *Rosh ha-shanah*, or new year (Feast of Trumpets). Repentance consists of casting sin aside and returning to righteousness. Occurring in the fall, it is a day of self-denial and rest. The highest holy day of the year. (Yohm' Kih-poohr')

Z'roah — Shankbone; placed on the Seder plate. Represents the Paschal lamb. Also represents the Lord's outstretched arm in liberating Israel. (Zeh-roh'-ah)

Zohar — (*Tzohar, tsohar*) Hebrew for splendor; shining radiance. A thirteenth century mystic commentary on the five books of Moses. Its basic tenet is that everything in the Torah has three-fold significance — the outward, the inner, and the innermost. (See the Family Home Evening presentation for the Feast of Weeks to see how a *tzohar*[4] was used in Noah's Ark.

PART I

JEWS AND JUDAISM

CHAPTER 1:
JEWS AND JUDAISM

Before we begin, it is necessary to understand a bit about Jews and Judaism. First of all, who are the Jews as far as lineage is concerned? Are they Semites? Hebrews? Israelites? Judahites? These terms tend to generate as much confusion as they do understanding. In Genesis we are given the genealogy of the Fathers, those who, through their birthright and righteousness, passed the priesthood down through the generations. The lineage is as follows: **Adam** — Seth — Enos — Cainan — Mahalaleel — Jared — Enoch — Methuselah — Lamech — **Noah** — **Shem** — Arphaxad — Salah — **Eber** — Peleg — Reu — Serug — Nahor — Terah — **Abraham** — **Isaac** — **Jacob**. (Special birthright promises are recorded in the Bible for some of these patriarchs; their names are in bold print.)

Anyone who is a descendant of Shem is a Semite. Some consider anyone who is a descendant of Eber a Hebrew. Others consider the descendants of Abraham, Hebrews, designating Abraham as one who "crossed over" from Ur to Canaan Genesis 14:13).[1] Anyone who is a descendant of Jacob is an Israelite. Strictly speaking, Jews are the descendants of Judah, one of the twelve sons of Jacob.

People who call themselves Jews today are ethnically and mostly the descendants of those who remained in the Southern kingdom of Judah, after the northern kingdom of Israel was conquered by Assyria (about 720 B.C.). The residents of the Kingdom of Judah were mostly Judahites and Benjaminites, but all the twelve tribes were represented. Lehi would have been considered a Jew because he was a citizen of the Kingdom of Judah, even though he was descended from Joseph. Also numbered among today's Jews are converts to Judaism and their descendants.

WHO IS A JEW?

The question, "Who is a Jew?" is still current and hotly debated. Should Jews be defined as an ethnic or a religious group? Jews have been persecuted both for their ethnicity and their religious beliefs. Adolph Hitler considered anyone with a Jewish grandparent Jewish, an ethnic definition. (In 1939 he ordered a Jewish census. The census forms had columns for all one's grandparents; the census-taker recorded whether or not they were Jewish.) Reflecting upon the sadness of Jewish history, one Rabbi stated that anyone crazy enough to want to be a Jew, is a Jew. The State of Israel sponsors a law called the "Law of Return." It allows any Jewish person, that is, anyone who has a Jewish mother,[2] to receive full Israeli citizenship the second he sets foot in Israel, unless he claims a belief in Mohammed (the Prophet of Islam) or in Jesus Christ. This law begins with an ethnic definition and ends with a religious one. Some rabbis subscribe to the principle, "once a Jew, always a Jew," claiming that even if a Jewish person converts to some other faith, he remains Jewish. This idea seems to favor an ethnic definition, but it also refers to the Abrahamic covenant, a covenant binding upon all of Abraham's descendants through Isaac and Jacob's birthright lineage. It was and is a covenant and lineage of blessings and royalty, of being a chosen people, of following One God. The phrase, "once a Jew, always a Jew," is another way of saying, "once a child of Abraham, always a child of Abraham."

GOD CHOOSES JUDAISM'S HEROES

One way to determine the character of a people is to look at its heroes. Whom do the people emulate, and why? Jews believe that God offered his covenants and commandments to all peoples, but that Abraham was the only man who chose to embrace them. There is no greater example of faith and obedience than Abraham. To the Jews, faith in the One God began with him. Like all covenants, the Abrahamic covenant required a commitment, bestowed a promise, and included a sign or token that the covenant had been made. The commitment for Abraham was to be a prophet to his followers and an ensign to the gentile nations — he sojourned all his life among heathen peoples. The promise from the Lord was earthly and eternal increase — through Abraham's seed, all nations would be blessed. The token was (and is) circumcision, a permanent, inalterable able sign of obedience and royal lineage. Abraham typified the message and mission of the Jewish people, that is, to bear witness against idolatry (whether those idols be statues or false ideas), and to testify of the One God.

As great as Abraham was, and as revered as he is, he is not considered Judaism's greatest prophet. That position belongs to Moses. Moses, the deliverer, the prophet, the lawgiver, who spoke with the Lord on Mt. Sinai, is Judaism's greatest spiritual inspiration. Through him, and under his administration, the nation of Israel was born, a nation of priests. A perfect law of ethics and justice was given through him, and scriptures were written that would guide a people and influence the world down to the present and into the future.

Elijah is especially revered because of his miracles and his role as the forerunner of the coming Messiah. A chair is reserved for him in the synagogue and at the Passover feast.

But the most evocative personage ever in the history and scripture of the Jews is David the King. Through his lineage will come the Messiah, and with the Messiah will come a restoration and glorification of Israel as an unconquerable kingdom. David's legacy and larger-than-life personality resonate through Israeli culture. Zionism, the yearning for Israel as the Jewish homeland, centers on David as its king — if not in person, then as its symbol. On Thursdays *bar mitzvah* ceremonies are held in Jerusalem at the Western Wall of the temple mount. The young man coming of age is hoisted onto the shoulders of his elders, as they sing, "David, King of Israel, lives, lives and continues." The song rejoices that David's legacy will be amplified in the Messiah.

WHO IS THE MESSIAH?

And who will Messiah be? According to the Jews, a descendant of David, a king just like he was, a hero in battle and in leadership. A warrior with divine attributes. Not the Only Begotten Son of God, but an inspired man of royal lineage who will lead the world into an age of peace, with freedom from strife, death, and disease.

ANOTHER MESSIAH?

Interestingly, the Jews believe in another personage they call "Messiah ben Joseph," meaning "Messiah, the Son of Joseph." Scholars and rabbis debate his identity, whether he will be the prophet who leads the Ten Lost Tribes out of the north, or someone else. He seems to be a modern figure, someone who will come before the Messiah, build the temple, and gather Israel. It is tempting for Mormons to identify him as Joseph Smith, Junior. Someday, we will know.

JEWISH SCRIPTURE

The scripture of the Jews, carefully copied from scribe to scribe, is essentially what we know as "The Old Testament." (Jews don't call it that, because an "Old Testament" presumes that there is a "New Testament," which they deny.) This collection of scripture is called the *Tanakh*, which is an acronym made from the letters beginning the Hebrew words, *torah, nevi'im,* and *ketuvim*, meaning "The Law, The Prophets, and The Writings."

When scriptures have been copied over the ages, they have been copied letter by letter. Thus, there has never been any room for supposition of meaning or substitution of words. Believing that the Lord gave the scriptures letter by letter, Jewish scribes dared not change a thing. Nephi testified that this standard of transcription worked, that the scriptures came forth from the Jewish scribes in their pure form.[3]

> "And the angel of the Lord said unto me: Thou hast beheld that the book proceeded forth from the mouth of a Jew; and when it proceeded forth from the mouth of a Jew it contained the fulness of the gospel of the Lord, of whom the twelve apostles bear record; and they bear record according to the truth which is in the Lamb of God.
>
> "Wherefore, these things go forth from the Jews in purity unto the Gentiles, according to the truth which is in God.
>
> "And after they go forth by the hand of the twelve apostles of the Lamb, from the Jews unto the Gentiles, thou seest the formation of that great and abominable church. . . for behold, they have taken away from the gospel of the Lamb many parts which are plain and most precious; and also many covenants of the Lord have they taken away."
>
> 1 Nephi 13:24-26

The Torah (the Law) consists of the five books of Moses: Genesis, Exodus, Leviticus, Numbers, and Deuteronomy. Herein lie the basic principles of the "Law of Moses." The Torah is greatly revered by Jews everywhere. A Torah scroll in danger should be defended even to the loss of one's own life. (This actually happened recently during the *al'aqsa intefadeh*, the first Palestinian uprising in the Holy Land. A Rabbi rescued a Torah Scroll from Joseph's Tomb while it was under attack, knowing it would cost him his life.) It is said that the Torah contains all the names of God (which comprise the entire text), and that all knowledge can be found within its pages. (The word *Torah* can also mean the whole philosophy of religion, or the entire gospel.)

A COMPLEXITY OF LAW

In addition to the written scripture, there is oral law (*mishnah*), ancient and extremely important. For example, there is little written in the *Torah* regarding the observance of *Rosh HaShanah* (New Year, the Feast of Trumpets), but the oral law is explicit regarding many aspects of this Holy Day. The oral law was expanded as points were discussed in more and more detail — such details as how to pray atop a wall or upon a horse, who was responsible for grain dropped into ant-holes, whether wooden legs or false teeth could be worn or carried on the Sabbath. (They can.)

Around the code of oral law there grew a vast body of commentary (*gemara*). Every rabbinical argument, every ruling, was preserved in the Jewish academies. Finally committed to paper, called the *talmud*, the commentaries also contained fables, history, folklore, and narrations regarding science. Often, the commentaries are complex, and need further, more modern commentaries to help us understand them.

HAIRSPLITTING

Why is it that the Book of Mormon prophets accused the Jews of "looking beyond the mark?" It's because there have always been Jewish scholars who have devoted their lives to studying and debating scripture and rabbinical commentaries. Day in and day out, the scholars debate, proposing problem after problem. Thus, what was given by the Lord has been "over-discussed." Details and points of view multiply over time and become what is known as *pilpul*, hairsplitting. Sometimes the letter of the Law is kept, but the spirit of the Law is lost.[4] Yet, there are many deeply spiritual Jews who manage also to keep the Law. (It is important to realize that this kind of situation can exist in any faith, including our own. We have been warned against zealously following tangents that lead us away from the center of our faith. An over-emphasis on the Word of Wisdom, on last-days prophecies, or any other gospel subject can cause us to "look beyond the mark.")

THE SPIRIT OF JUDAISM

Distilling the spirit of Judaism has been a quest for many. There are a myriad of sects and variations of religious practice today. Three are major. **Orthodox** Jews believe in following the letter of the law as found in scripture, and they are extremely careful to follow the direction of Moses and rabbinical law in their daily lives. **Conservative** Jews are strongly traditional, but not so strictly adherent to ancient laws. **Reform** Jews have adopted some of the patterns of worship found in Christian churches — liturgy in English, music and choirs — and leave the observance of the Law of Moses, including the dietary laws, to personal choice. The problem of how to adapt an ancient code to modern times is answered differently by each sect. (This situation cries out for direct inspiration from deity. A living prophet and willing followers can adapt modern practices to eternal truths, taking into account current social and cultural factors, while bowing to God's will.)

Zionists may not have any spiritual leanings at all, but center their fervor on the creation and upholding of Israel as the Jewish State. Members of all the sects can be Zionistic, but there are rabbis who call Zionism an apostasy, and their followers agree. Anti-Zionists feel that the Jewish State cannot be founded by anyone other than the Messiah himself. There are also **Ultra-Orthodox** sects that vary in their strictness, but outdo even the Orthodox in their observance of the commandments. These Ultra-Orthodox sects originated in Eastern Europe during the last few hundred years, and in Israel they still wear the traditional costumes of the *shtetl*s (Jewish ghettoes or towns) of their ancestors. These sects were founded to infuse worship with joy and spirituality, but gradually became stricter in their observance of the details of Mosaic Law than the Orthodox. It is a mistake to assume that strictly observant Jews live lives of rigid, serious, oppressed discipleship. Following Mosaic Law to the letter imbues every daily, mundane act with sacredness — these Jews eat, cook, dress, sleep, travel, read, and study with an attitude of careful devotion. Joy is the real goal of such devoted living. I have never seen more enthusiastic rejoicing anywhere than at an Ultra-Orthodox wedding, baby blessing (*brit*), or *bar mitzvah*.

Humanistic Judaism is the result of focusing attention on the affairs of this world and handling those affairs morally. There is very little information available to Jews regarding the afterlife, but vast information on ethics and charitable behavior. Thus, many Jews live ethically without concentrating on spiritual things, and might even consider themselves atheists. Nonetheless, they are confessed Jews and proud to be identified as such.

LIVING AMONG ENEMIES

Through the centuries, Judaism has been under constant attack as its adherents have been persecuted, forced, or tempted to assimilate into surrounding cultures. Abraham's people, Moses' people, David's people were encircled by pagans, whose rituals, ethics, and festivals were seductive, and certainly less demanding than following the One God.

During the three hundred years before the birth of Christ, **Hellenism** — the culture and philosophy of the Greeks — was forced upon the citizens of Israel by their conquerors.[5] A famous epigram states, "the Greeks worshiped the holiness of beauty, while the Jews worshiped the beauty of holiness." While much of Greek civilization sounds lovely, idolatry, superstition, sexual perversion, and infant sacrifice were also part of the package. The Jews fought back, both physically and culturally. The Jewish Maccabees triumphed over invading Greek armies, cleansing and rededicating the Temple. The Qumran society was established to escape the pagan influences brought by the Greeks. The Pharisaic Rabbis tried to stanch the inflow of Greek influence. However, the Sadducees were swayed by Greek philosophies, and elements of Greek philosophy show up later in Jewish mysticism.

The Holy Land into which Jesus was born was seething with controversy, not just between pagans and Jews, but among opposing Jewish sects. In addition, the Greek and then Roman legislators were often cruel masters, alternating between religious tolerance and ruthless oppression.

Jews have faced many situations where they have been scattered by their enemies. Perhaps the first was when the Assyrians took the northern kingdom of Israel. The second was when the Babylonians conquered the southern kingdom of Judea. Some Jews never returned to the Holy Land. By the time of Christ, there were about 1 million Jews in Alexandria, Egypt. Since Egypt was ruled by the Greeks, they spoke Greek, not Hebrew or Aramaic. And finally, there was the destruction of Jerusalem and the Temple in 70 A.D. by the Romans.

The few Jews remaining in the Holy Land were repeatedly vanquished (by the Ottoman Turks, European Crusaders, and others). In diaspora, they have been unwanted, misunderstood guests in Gentile societies. They have been forcibly converted (mostly by Christians), and bitterly oppressed by governments, states, and personal neighbors. Through it all, they have developed a wry sense of humor, an ability to laugh at their terrible misfortunes. ("God, if it is not yet time to redeem the Jews, please, at least redeem the Gentiles!") Through it all, most have tenaciously held on to their faith.

A LEGACY OF SCHOLARSHIP

During the Middle Ages brilliant and scholarly rabbis, such as Maimonides, both distilled and expanded Jewish philosophy. And after Maimonides (of the 12th century) an old strain of Jewish mysticism began to be amplified. In all ages, the quest of the mystic has been to directly experience things spiritual, to experience God. The mystics wrote prolifically through the Middle Ages, and laymen seemed to be able to access their writings, even though they were not meant for the uninitiated. The mystics sought for levels of spiritual meaning in the scriptures

and in religious practices. Jewish mysticism, *Kabbalah*, seeks an understanding of the following: creation, what heaven is like and how to get there, and the use of names to invoke power.

Dealing with the creation, the **Kabbalists** constructed an entire metaphysical universe of intermediate substances to bridge the gap between a God of spirit and the material world. Remember that mysticism developed when there were no prophets or temples. The vague memory of the visions and miracles of the prophets and of the temple rituals caused the mystics to seek the same answers that were known anciently (and are known today, among people who enjoy the blessings of prophets and temples). The Kabbalists began with sincere intent and pure motives, but often ended up with something akin to secret magical formulas. Though *Kabbalah* may be all the rage in modern Hollywood, it yields no answers for Latter-day Saints. The use of names becomes incantation, the mysticism becomes superstition, and the spiritualism can border on sorcery.

NUMEROLOGY

Some of the mystics, though certainly not all, embraced "**numerology**," that is, finding spiritual meanings in the numerical values of words. This is actually an expansion of what the Lord has done Himself in the scriptures —

There are no written numbers in Hebrew. Letters are assigned numerical values. Thus, A is 1, B is 2, and so on. That means that every word has a numerical value. Numbers are repeatedly used in scripture and have always had holy connotations: three is the number of attributes of the perfect Lord, seven is the number for wholeness — the week with its Sabbath.[6] Holy numbers appear in the observance of Holy Days, and they serve as symbols for spiritual truths. These structures were established by the Lord. The act of expanding the search, of looking for spiritual meaning in the numerical values of words and phrases, is called *gematria*. The practice can lead one in two directions — to an increased awareness of spiritual messages or to an increase of superstition.

THE NURTURING GHETTO

At times throughout history Jews have been awarded equal rights in the countries where they have lived. As this has occurred, they have exploded in intellectual and artistic achievement. In some societies the manifestations of their talents burst forth from the ghettos, small neighborhoods of Jews huddled within host societies. These ghettos were not dismal in every aspect. They provided hospitable, close-knit, supportive communities within which Judaism thrived. The movement of the Jews out of the ghettos and into society at large has caused some Jews to assimilate and lose their attachment to their faith. However, though the practice of Judaism varies from sect to sect, though Jews vary in their dedication to Mosaic Law, the spiritual message of Judaism has emerged from the ghettos unmarred.

It's remarkable to study the Passover ritual as it is practiced in far-flung Jewish communities throughout the world. There is so little variation in the order of the feast, it's amazing. Whether practiced in Yemen or New York City, the Passover ritual is intact. Whether fleeing from Spain or hiding from Hitler, dedicated Jews have kept their feasts. With the re-gathering to Israel occurring now, Jews have a center once again, the focus of their hopes for the future. All Jews look forward to the rebuilding of the Temple, and some are actively planning for it. The pilgrimage to the Temple in Jerusalem is one aspect of the feast days that Jews have had to ignore for many years. They look forward to the time when ". . . the mountain of the Lord's house shall be established in the top of the mountains, and shall be exalted above the hills; and all nations shall flow unto it (Isaiah 2:2)."

CHAPTER 1 ENDNOTES

[1] Those Arabs of Palestine who are descended Ishmael, son of Abraham and Hagar, would therefore be both Semitic and Hebrew, but not Israelite.

[2] Though most everything in Judaism functions under a patriarchal system, Jewish lineage is determined through the mother, because the identity of the father of a child might be difficult to determine.

[3] The Jews of Yemen were separated from the majority of Jewish communities for hundreds of years. Between 1948 and 1950 most Yemenite Jews were airlifted to Israel. They brought their Torah scrolls with them. When the scrolls were compared to those in Israel, they were found to be identical, except for a few minor spelling variations that did not affect meaning. (Ohr Somayach International, Issue 323, October 13, 2001.)

[4] The following is a good example of how the Law can be "kept" if there is enough scholarly discussion. This judgment was reported in the Jerusalem Post newspaper. Understand that Conservative and Reform marriages are not recognized when they are performed in Israel.

> "The Haifa rabbinical court has allowed a new immigrant from the U.S. who was twice married there to marry a *kohen*, or descendant of the priestly tribe, and save her son from *mamzerut*, or bastardy.
>
> "The court... decided that both her previous marriages -- one civil, the other Reform -- were invalid according to rabbinic law and the woman was, therefore, unmarried rather than a divorcee. According to *halakha* (Jewish law), a *mamzer* is a child born of an adulterous or incestuous relationship.
>
> "The woman's first marriage ended in civil divorce and the second marriage, from which the son was born, was not ended, because her Reform community in the U.S. does not carry out divorces.
>
> "The woman was represented by a lawyer from the Na'amat women's organization which yesterday expressed its satisfaction with the court's decision. Aside from giving the woman a second chance, the court had also saved the boy from a lifetime stigma, since as a *mamzer* he would be unable to marry a Jewish woman."
>
> Ya'acov Friedler, *Jerusalem Post*, January 26, 1989.

In a spiritual sense, I found this judgment to be disturbing. What do you think? How much time could we spend together debating this situation and what should be done about it?

The Jews sometimes find humorous their own propensity to "over-logic" everything. Here is one example:

"If one man saw a *koy*
> (an animal that was believed to be intermediate between a kid and a gazelle, and which, consequently, the rabbis were uncertain to classify as wild or domestic, or both or neither),

and said,
> "I vow to be a Nazarite if this is a wild animal,"

and another man said,
> "I vow to be a Nazarite if this is not a wild animal,"

and a third man said,
> "I vow to be a Nazarite if this is a domestic animal,"

and a fourth man said,
> "I vow to be a Nazarite if this is not a domestic animal,"

and a fifth man said,
> "I vow to be a Nazarite if this is both a wild animal and a domestic animal,"

and a sixth man said,
> "I vow to be a Nazarite if this is neither a wild animal or a domestic animal,"

and a seventh man said,
> "I vow to be a Nazarite if one of you six people is a Nazarite,"

and an eighth man said,
> "I vow to be a Nazarite if none of you seven people is a Nazarite,"

and a ninth man said,
> "I vow to be a Nazarite if all you eight people are Nazarites"

— then they are all Nazarites.

This joke is actually found in the Mishnah (Nazir 5:7) dating from about A.D. 200. For a more recent reference, please see *The Big Book of Jewish Humor*, Novak & Waldoks, Editors. 1981: Harper & Row Publications, New York. p. 56

---

[5] For an excellent description of Greek influences in pre-Christ Jerusalem see *Jerusalem: The Eternal City,* by Galbraith, Ogden, and Skinner, 134-151.

[6] There is a number sign given for the "beast" in Revelation 13:18. The number is six hundred, three- score and six. Three sixes in a row. Seven is the holy number, the week with its' Sabbath, the world with its holy aspects, a symbol of completeness in the Lord. Six, then, is the evil number, the week without a Sabbath; the material world without holy influence. And six-six-six would be like saying "ever and eternally incomplete."

CHAPTER 2:
THE LAW OF MOSES

If we were to play the game "Tell Me the First Thought That Comes Into Your Mind," and I were to give you the cue "The Law of Moses," your response would be quick. You would probably say, "an eye for an eye, and a tooth for a tooth." And if I were to ask you what that means, you would say, "It means that if I put out your eye, you get to put out mine." You would go on to explain that Jesus brought us a new law that would teach us to love one another rather than to take revenge. Interesting. I have spent the last several decades in Sunday School classes, trying to correct this erroneous perception of the Law of Moses.

Firstly, who gave the law? Was it Moses? No, it was the Lord. And who was the Lord? He was Jehovah, god of the Old Testament, who would be known on earth as Yeshu or Y'shua — Jesus. Would Jesus have given a law of retribution and revenge to his Chosen People? We know he gave them a "school-master" law, meant to train them to be a treasure unto him. But a law of vengeance would be a poor teaching tool to prepare them for anything godly.

Secondly, was the Golden Rule first taught by Christ during his ministry? Was the Law of Moses devoid of commandments to love one's neighbor? Consider this verse from Leviticus, one of the five books of the Bible which contain the Mosaic Law:

> "**Thou shalt not avenge**, nor bear any grudge against the children of thy people, but **thou shalt love thy neighbor as thyself**: I am the Lord."
>
> Leviticus 19:18 *(emphasis added)*

"And one of the scribes came, and having heard them reasoning together, and perceiving that he had answered them well, asked him, Which is the first commandment of all?

"And Jesus answered him, The first of all the commandments is, Hear O Israel; The Lord our God is one Lord:[1]

"And thou shalt love the Lord thy God with all thy heart, and with all thy soul, and with all thy mind, and with all thy strength: this is the first commandment.

"And the second is like, namely this, Thou shalt love thy neighbour as thyself. There is none other commandment greater than these.

"And the scribe said unto him, Well, Master, thou hast said the truth: for there is one God; and there is none other but he:

"And to love him with all the heart, and with all the understanding, and with all the soul, and with all the strength, and to love his neighbour as himself, is more than all the whole burnt offerings and sacrifices.

"And when Jesus saw that he answered discreetly, he said unto him, Thou art not far from the kingdom of God."

Mark 12:28-34

So let's begin again. Pretend you know nothing about the Mosaic Law, and let's build from there —

A HOLY PEOPLE

When Jesus came, when he finished his atonement for our sins, He <u>fulfilled</u> the types given in the Law of Moses, and He ended blood sacrifice. Jesus said,

"Think not that I am come to destroy the law, or the prophets: I am not come to destroy, but to fulfill.

"For verily I say unto you, **Till heaven and earth pass, one jot or one tittle shall in no wise pass from the law**, till all be fulfilled.

"Whosoever therefore shall break one of these least commandments, and shall teach men so, he shall be called the least in the kingdom of heaven: but whosoever shall do and teach them, the same shall be called great in the kingdom of heaven."

Matthew 5:17-19 *(emphasis added)*

The Laws of Reparation or **Restitution** outlined in the Law help us to understand the process of repentance. When we injure someone, we restore as best we can and ask forgiveness. Jews restored fourfold, often more, to insure that restitution was complete. This is a basis for charity; making restitution leads us on the path to developing Christ-like love. The Law contains policies of justice, generosity, liberty and equality that were practically unknown outside ancient Israelite society. It differed from the systems of other societies in that it wiped out class distinctions, prohibited harsh and unjust punishments, and guaranteed compensation for victims. This legal system has provided a foundation for every just legal system since then in the Judeo-Christian world.

PROTECTION UNDER THE LAW

One of the priorities of the Law of Moses was **protection**. Most important, was the protection of the society as separate and holy. That is why the death penalty (or banishment or just reparation)[2] was mandated for the following crimes and sins: Idolatry, premeditated murder, kidnaping, witchcraft, sexual perversion, adultery, desecration of the Sabbath, disobedience to parents, robbery (looked upon as a sort of military intrusion, different from simple theft). All of the above crimes and sins, if left undisciplined and unchecked, can ruin a society, family by family. The part about disobedience to parents might have startled you. You are probably running to show your children right now. There were always caveats in the Law to guarantee humaneness. The parents had to accuse the child, and they had to throw the first stone. The Lord knows how much parents love their children. There is no record of this punishment ever being carried out. But the children knew the commandment existed; they knew how important it was to be obedient to God-fearing parents. And the parents were aware of their responsibility to teach their children righteousness. (Read the Book of Samuel to see how the priest, Eli, was disciplined for not reining in his sons.)

Protection for the poor, for women and children, for widows, and for servants,[3] was also guaranteed and provided for under the Law of Moses. Provisions for the poor were many. Gleaning, as described in the Book of Ruth, was an excellent system. The farm owner left the corners of his field unharvested. Also, when the rest of the field was harvested, anything that was dropped was left for the poor to glean. (This system is being experimented with in modern times.) Women, under the Law, were absolved from the strenuous details of ritual worship. Marriage was considered sacred. Levirate marriage, where the brother of a deceased man took responsibility for his wife and household, guaranteed that widows would be cared for. (Note that this often necessitated a polygamous marriage.) The stewardship of husbands and fathers were outlined, so that everyone in a household would be cared for and protected.

The legal system of the Law of Moses included protections for the accused. Confessions were not considered enough to declare a person guilty. Witnesses were required. Witnesses had to take part in punishments, thereby making them take their jobs very seriously. The accused had to have a friend in court. This is one of the requirements that proves the trial of Jesus was illegal — since he had no friend in court, the case should have been thrown out.

(For a good summary of Jewish court law, read *The Illegal Trial of Christ*, by Steven W. Allen, 2005, Legal Awareness Series, Inc., Mesa, Arizona.)

COMPENSATING THE VICTIM

And now, back to "an eye for an eye." Remember, that under the Mosaic Law, someone who injures another person or his property is accountable to the victim, not the state.[5] This is infinitely more fair than our current penal system, where the victim is often uncompensated. Harrowing up in his mind what suffering a similar injury would be like, the perpetrator was expected to fully extend himself to compensate the victim. Usually, he would pay money, as we do in civil suits, but he might also work off his debt by indenturing himself to the victim, perhaps part time while continuing his normal duties and family life. His servitude could only last six years, however, for in the Sabbath year, he was freed. This encouraged forgiveness on the part of the victim. If the criminal refused to make reparations, or if his offense was against the community, he could be whipped, but lashing was limited. The infamous "cat-o-nine-tails" of the Romans, which laid open the back, was certainly not a Jewish invention. Only deliberate murderers were surely put to death. Many others chose exile to a non- Israelite society, and other capital crimes could be compensated for by making reparation with money or labor.[6]

NO JEWISH POLICEMEN

Offenses were brought before the court, and witnesses were provided. Policemen were not necessary under this system. Nor were prisons or dungeons. When we read of the clandestine trial of Jesus Christ, we see that wicked men had taken the Law into their own hands and bent it to fit their own will. The system, however, was righteous, having been instituted by the Savior himself. Though the laws of blood sacrifice were fulfilled and done away with by Christ, the other laws as given to Moses continued in their efficacy and desirability. The Law of Moses was and is a law of charity. The 613 commandments are called *mitzvot*, a word with two meanings. It means both "laws" and "good deeds." The laws are meant to guide men through this life in kindness; they are laws of ethics. So what was the "new law" instituted by the Savior? It was to extend ourselves in charity past our own capacity to love and forgive, and surpassing our own capacity, to cry unto him for that gift of charity that only he can give, thus blessing the victim, and the repentant sinner.

THE IMPORTANCE OF MAKING RESTITUTION

One important lesson for the Latter-day Saint in the Law of Moses, is the importance of making restitution during the process of repentance. Why is it so difficult to repent of the "sin against the Holy Ghost," murder, or adultery? It is because making restitution is nearly impossible. The sin against the Holy Ghost is to deny the Christ once we have a sure knowledge of him; the Lord says it is equivalent to crucifying him anew. It is impossible to restore what we have destroyed. In the case of murder, one cannot restore a life. In the case of adultery and fornication, one cannot restore stolen virtue. The Lord taught the Israelites that there is no such thing as a "victimless crime." Any shortcoming we might manifest influences or harms others. We are encouraged by our leaders to constantly, daily repent. As we do so, we bless the lives of others around us, restoring damaged testimonies, feelings, and sensitivities.

REFERRING BACK TO THE LAW

Section 98 of the Doctrine and Covenants dictates laws governing persecutions and afflictions and the Saints' response to them. The pattern and instructions given to early members of The Church of Jesus Christ of Latter- day Saints exactly follows the Law of Moses. In verse 32 it says, "Behold, this is the law I gave unto my servant Nephi, and thy fathers, Joseph, and Jacob, and Isaac, and Abraham, and all mine ancient prophets and apostles." This reference helps us to see Moses as a **restorer**, and not an originator of the law. He was reclaiming a people whose ancestors had been taught and trained by prophets from the beginning of time. Everything those prophets taught, every law they gave, pointed to Christ and prepared them to be his people.

CHAPTER 2 ENDNOTES

[1] This is called the *shemah* ("hear"). It is the basis of the Jewish faith and is recited all the time.

[2] There were designated places of asylum or sanctuary for those who were suspected of a crime to flee to. John the Baptist's father, Zacharias, was actually killed holding onto the horns of the altar, a designated place of sanctuary where, by law, he should have been safe.

[3] Some people wonder why Moses, and then Jesus, did nothing to abolish slavery or indentured servitude. The Law of Moses demanded that masters look upon their servants as real people rather than property, to protect and to nurture them, to be certain they enjoyed the right to establish families of their own (without threat of separation), and eventually to make them independent.

[4] The laws of cleanliness decreed that ill people had to isolate themselves, and those attending to them also needed a period of quarantine. When the plague rolled through Europe during the Middle Ages, most Jews escaped death because of their health laws. In some instances, however, this backfired. The gentiles, seeing that they were dying like flies and the Jews weren't, blamed the plague on the Jews and put the Jews to death.

[5] See W. Cleon Skousen's treatment of the Law of Moses in *The Third Thousand Years,* 346-360.

[6] There was one circumstance where a punishment dismemberment was called for, and it's certainly very colorful reading. Find it in Deuteronomy 25:11.

CHAPTER 3:
WHAT IT MEANS TO KEEP KOSHER

Included in the Law of Moses are dietary laws which dictate what foods are fit to eat and how they must be prepared. These laws are called *kashrut*, meaning fit, proper, or correct. The word "kosher" (*kasher*) comes from the same root. Non-kosher, forbidden, or unclean foods are called "treyf," which means "torn." It is supposed that this word is used for unclean foods, because animals that have been torn by other animals are considered unclean. There is much discussion regarding the laws of *kashrut*. They appear to be ancient laws of health unneeded today because of improvements in food processing, refrigeration, and delivery. There are even Jews that feel this way and ignore the law. But health was not mentioned when the law was given, although following the law did ensure good health.[2] However, close examination of the requirements of the law, with health as the main focus, turns up some unexplainable details. For instance, camels and rabbits provide healthy meat, but they are "treyf." In truth, the main purpose of the dietary laws was **separation**. An observant Jew could not eat at the same table as Greeks or Romans and still keep the dietary laws.[3] Thus, the observant Jew was protected from the pagan influences of those societies.[4] The dietary laws also force the observant Jew to watch his own behavior constantly, thus causing him to be careful about his choices each day, each hour. This careful living gives sacredness to the acts of eating and preparing food, thereby imbuing each day with a feeling of hour to hour dedication to that which is sacred.

WHAT ARE THE RULES?

The general rules of *kashrut* are as follows:

1. Certain animals are considered unclean and can never be eaten; neither can their milk, eggs, or organs. Both rennet (used to harden

cheeses) and gelatin may contain products from unclean animals, so they are not kosher.[5] Many unclean animals seem to have unclean diets themselves. Shellfish, for instance, which are unclean, are "bottom-feeders" in the ocean. Poisons in the seas seem to collect in shellfish first. Pigs, which are unclean, eat swill. The pig is considered more "treyf" than any other animal, because it manifests many of the traits of a clean animal, so it seems truly counterfeit. In Leviticus 11:3 and Deuteronomy 14:6 it states that clean animals must both chew the cud and have a cloven hoof. Therefore, sheep, cattle, goats and deer are kosher. Sea creatures may be eaten if they have both fins and scales (Leviticus 11:9 and Deuteronomy 14:9). Birds that are unclean are all birds of prey. Chickens, ducks, geese and turkeys are all kosher. A few insects are listed as kosher in Leviticus, including the locust (Leviticus 11:22).[6] However, insects and creeping things (including rodents, reptiles, and amphibians) are never eaten now, because their identities are difficult to determine from the scriptures.

2. Animals, birds and mammals that are fit to be eaten must be killed in accordance with Jewish law. Animals are slaughtered very humanely. This has made hunting a decidedly non-Jewish pastime. (Biblical characters known as hunters are not admired by Jews. Lehi's family probably had a special dispensation from the Lord in order to hunt, and perhaps a promise that their hunt would be humane.)

3. The blood of animals is not kosher.[7] All the blood must be drained from the meat or broiled out before eating. (Fish are exempted from this rule.) Most of the process takes place during slaughtering. After that, either by broiling, salting or soaking, one has seventy-two hours to complete the process before cooking, freezing, or grinding the meat. Eggs that contain blood spots are not kosher.

4. Certain parts of clean animals are not kosher. This includes the sciatic nerve and its surrounding blood vessels. (In honor of Jacob, whose leg was made lame when he wrestled with an angel.) It's so difficult and time-consuming to remove the nerve, that most kosher butchers ignore the hind quarters of the beef or cattle, passing it on to non-kosher butchers and just using the forequarters. The fat surrounding the vital organs is not kosher to eat.

5. Meat products cannot be eaten with dairy products. Certain foods are considered neutral (*pareve*) and may be eaten with either meat or dairy products. These neutral foods are fish, eggs, vegetables, fruit, and grains. Kosher products are labeled with a symbol, and may add the letters m, d,

or p, for meat, dairy or pareve. After eating a meat meal, it is customary to wait a number of hours before eating dairy products. After eating dairy products, it only takes a half an hour to digest the food and prepare to eat meat. Some Jews happily become vegetarians.

6. Utensils used to prepare or serve meat products may not be used for dairy products, and vice versa.[8] Utensils that come in contact with heated non- kosher foods may not be used for kosher foods. Jewish families that keep kosher will have meat dishes and utensils and another set for dairy foods. Families with enough money will have an entirely different set of dishes for Passover use.

7. Grape products are problematic. Notice in Doctrine and Covenants section 27, that the Lord counsels Joseph Smith not to use wine for the sacrament, because he would have to purchase it from his enemies. In the ancient world, Jews faced a similar problem. Any wine they purchased may have been consecrated for some pagan rite. Thus, they must purchase wine made by Jews for Jews. Baking powder is a problem, because it contains cream of tartar, a by-product of wine making.

Rabbinical supervision is required for the slaughter of kosher animals and every process remaining for meats and all other kosher products. Foods that pass muster carry stamps of approval on the packages. Passover requires another stamp of approval; foods labeled "kosher for Passover" do not contain leaven. *Matzah* crackers can be purchased for everyday use, but require closer supervision and a rabbinical seal to be kosher for Passover.

This all sounds very elaborate and difficult, to be sure. But the only reason for this is that the rest of the world does not keep kosher. If everyone were Jewish, it would be easy.[9]

CHAPTER 3 ENDNOTES

[1] Many of the details in this chapter come from "Judaism 101: Kashrut: Jewish Dietary Laws, found at the following web site: www.jewfaq.org/kashrut.html

[2] Modern science continues to prove that the laws of *kashrut* produce good health. It's much the same situation as we have with the Word of Wisdom — the dangers of drinking alcohol, coffee and tea continue to be uncovered, but were largely unknown when the law was given.

[3] When we lived in Israel, we had many Jewish friends. Some would not partake of any food while visiting us. Some would eat packaged foods, such as pretzels, served on disposable plates. Some would eat anything we offered. Once we had a luncheon for my husband's business associates, catered by a kosher restaurant. They arrived with all the food, but before bringing it into the house, they covered every surface of my kitchen with plastic sheeting.

[4] "Assimilation" has been as big a threat to Judaism as persecution, hence the Lord's desire to keep them somewhat separated from the societies in which they lived. One Mosaic law, that traveling is forbidden on the Sabbath, provides us with a good example. Jews walked to synagogue and were allowed to take one thousand steps before reaching "home" (a place of rest and refreshment). Jews would limit themselves to 999 steps to be sure the law was not broken. This meant that the synagogue needed to be close by. Homes clustered around the synagogue, forming a ghetto of Jewish residents. Within the ghetto was all the neighborhood support needed to help a person be a good Jew. As soon as Jews became willing to drive on the Sabbath, they enabled themselves to move out of the ghetto and into the surrounding gentile neighborhoods, opening themselves up to the temptation to live like gentiles. Some Rabbis say the breaking of this single, simple law (traveling on the Sabbath) has decimated the Jewish people.

[5] Haribo, AG, the German candy company, has been attempting to recreate its famous gummi bears as a gelatin-free product. This has entailed considerable effort and experimentation. A recent Associated Press article described the company's trials — "The first time we made it, we got a marmalade you could spread on bread, and at the other extreme was something you could fill a swimming pool with and drive a truck across." (Quoting Neville Finlay, a UK exporter, from the article by Hans Greimel) In the meantime, a rabbi had to "oversee production and inspect every ingredient. . . . Every cooking vessel, collection bin and conveyer [had to be] scrubbed down with boiling water to wash away impurities."

[6] This is a big disappointment for Sunday School teachers who dearly want to say that John the Baptist, who lived on locusts and honey, was really eating carob. He wasn't. Grasshoppers are kosher.

[7] After Jesus' death there was a controversy among his early followers. Some wanted to require adherence to certain Mosaic Laws. The apostles disagreed for a while, and then decided to release new converts to Christianity from all but a few Mosaic requirements: "But that we write to them, that they abstain from pollutions of idols, and from fornication, and from things strangled, and from blood (Acts 15:20). Some of our own missionaries are cautioned against eating blood products in countries where they are popular.

[8] On King George Street in Jerusalem, near the City Tower, there is a row of fast food eateries. Out front on the cobblestone plaza there are tables and chairs set out. I went into one eatery and bought a hamburger, sat at a table out front, and ate it. When I finished, I went next door and bought an ice cream cone. I went back to my exact same seat and began to eat the cone. The doors to both restaurants flew open and both managers popped out at once. They came right for me and escorted me to a table right in front of the ice cream shop — the table where I was sitting was a "meat table!"

[9] Of course it is easiest to keep kosher in Israel, where even the laundry soap and brooms are certified.

CHAPTER 4:
THE 13 CREEDS OF JUDAISM & THE NOAHITE LAWS

Just as we have thirteen Articles of Faith, Judaism has thirteen creeds, written by Moses Maimonides (1135-1204). Maimonides was the greatest Jewish philosopher of the Middle Ages. Born in Cordoba, Spain, his Hebrew name Shlomo ben Maimon, he was by trade a doctor, but he devoted himself to furthering the study and practice of Judaism and helping the Jewish community in Cairo, Egypt. He felt that Aristotelian philosophy was compatible with the Jewish tradition and tried to demonstrate that. He wrote *The Guide for the Perplexed*, finished in 1190, which drew on Aristotle's works. He completed the *Mishnah Torah* around 1178. It has become one of the most important Jewish law codes. Maimonides is quoted so often that a joke exclaims, "This is according to Maimonides; that's my-monides, not your-monides!" His creeds are condensed into simple sentences in the following list.

1. There is a creator.
2. He is one.
3. He is incorporeal.
4. He is eternal.
5. He alone must be worshiped.
6. The prophets are true.
7. Moses was the greatest of all prophets.
8. The entire Torah was divinely given to Moses.
9. The Torah is immutable.
10. God knows all the acts and thoughts of man.

11. He rewards and punishes.
12. Messiah will come.
13. There will be a resurrection.

The Jews feel that the laws given on Sinai are immutable laws. That is, they are God's laws for all peoples. They are the laws of true righteousness. However, to expect all societies to pay attention to and align themselves with those laws is too much even to consider. However, Judaism has distilled some laws of basic decency from which all societies can be judged, no matter what their chosen religion or form of government. Societies that fail to follow these suggested rules of behavior are wicked societies and tempt the wrath of God. Since Noah was the father of all peoples, these laws are called the Seven Laws of the Sons of Noah, or the Noahite Laws. The *Talmud* says that non-Jews who practice these laws will be known as righteous and will enjoy bliss in the hereafter.

1. To have only one God and not to worship idols.
2. To lead a moral life and not to commit adultery or incest.
3. To be a useful member of society and not to commit murder.
4. To be honest and not to steal.
5. To have respect for God and not to blaspheme.
6. To have law courts and to practice justice.
7. To be kind to animals and not to be cruel to them.

CHAPTER 5:
BE THOU THEREFORE PERFECT

The commandment to be perfect is found in many scriptures:

(The Lord speaking to Abraham) —
"I am the Almighty God; walk before me, and be thou perfect."

Genesis 17:1

"Thou shalt be perfect with the Lord thy God."

Deuteronomy 18:13

". . . .Be perfect, be of good comfort, be of one mind, live in peace; and the God of love and peace shall be with you."

2 Corinthians 13:11

"But let patience have her perfect work, that ye may be perfect and entire, wanting nothing."

James 1:4

"Therefore I would that ye should be perfect even as I, or your Father who is in heaven is perfect."

3 Nephi 12:48

We, as Latter-day Saints, seem to be especially intimidated by the commandment to be perfect, when we, of all people, should understand and rejoice in the concept. We know we can't be perfect without Christ; we know we have sincere faith and a more complete comprehension of him than most; yet, we have created an impossible yardstick against which we measure our progress. How often do we equate our progress solely with our works? We count our efforts as if we were using a scorecard:

> "Pay tithing — check! Hold Family Home Evenings — check! Live the Word of Wisdom — check! Family Prayer morning and night — well, we're trying."

Too often we come up short and begin to despair that we'll ever make the grade. There's always a loose end someplace, always a failing. Perhaps we need to look at our quest for perfection from a different angle.

In Hebrew, and in the scriptures, two words are used for the word "perfect." They are *tam* and *shalum*. Look at the second word; the consonants are the same as for the Hebrew word *shalom*, which means "peace." A little Hebrew lesson is in order here. Hebrew verbs, and their associated nouns, adjectives and adverbs, have three root letters, all consonants. The root letters of *shalom*, then, are shin, lamed, mem, sh-l-m. Words change parts of speech and shades of meaning with changes in the vowels which separate the consonants. The related words sometimes teach a Biblical lesson, as with the word "Adam." In Hebrew, *adam* is Man, *dam* is blood, *adamah* is soil, and *adom* is red. Relatives of the word *shalom*, meaning peace, are *shalum* — whole or complete, *leshalem* — to pay for or ransom. Therefore, to be perfect means to be whole and complete, at peace, ransomed. The word *tam* is another Hebrew word for wholeness, and carries the secondary meanings of flawless, unblemished, simple, innocent and artless. The Lord is commanding us to be whole. Although we are judged upon our works, wholeness is a collection of <u>attributes</u>, those attributes which God himself has.

Numerology (*gematria*) comes into the picture here. The attributes of God which we must attain are 3 and 7, the numbers which represent perfection and wholeness. Three are the most important attributes of God: Love, Mercy, and Justice. The concept of justice without mercy was a frightening one to the Jewish mystics, almost more intimidating than evil. It is the mingling of perfect justice with love that creates mercy. This triangle of attributes can be associated with the family structure — father, mother, child. We as Christians can associate the concept of "three" to the Godhead, three individuals who are one in purpose, reigning in perfect justice, love and mercy.

Seven are the divine attributes which contribute to wholeness and perfection. These seven attributes are represented by seven Patriarchs, called "the seven shepherds." The first three attributes are those which God has — love, justice, and mercy. Abraham is the shepherd manifesting the attribute of abundant love. Isaac represents justice. Jacob is the shepherd of mercy.

The fourth attribute is Kingship, symbolized by David and his royal house. The fifth attribute is prophecy, with two shepherds, Moses and Aaron. (We can divide this attribute and manifest the two priesthoods, Melchizedek and Aaronic.) The sixth attribute, then, would be priesthood. The seventh attribute is covenant and righteousness in the face of temptation; this includes enduring to the end, and is typified by Joseph.

If we measure ourselves against this yardstick, we may fare better than we did before. **Love, Justice and mercy** are part and parcel of charity, without which all else is vain. Forgiveness, patience and unselfishness have to be included. If we live the two main commandments, to love the Lord with all our being, and love others as ourselves, we are mastering the first three attributes. The fourth, **kingship**, is ours through the covenants we make. We are raised up as the Children of Abraham, part of his royal house. We are promised thrones in heaven through our temple covenants. **Prophecy** is ours through the constant companionship of the Holy Ghost, reliance on our ancient and latter-day prophets, patriarchal blessings, priesthood blessings, scriptures. **Priesthood** is ours, both Aaronic and Melchizedek, with their attendant power to bless and guide our lives. **Enduring to the end in righteousness** is our opportunity, and the one attribute that leans most upon our works and service and obedience.

And we know the Good Shepherd, who is at the head of these dedicated seven under-shepherds. With his help, because of him, and through him, these attributes are attainable, by degree, until we become truly whole. I am comforted by this list. The gospel and the true Church offer us access to these attributes, access that cannot be found anywhere else. These are peaceful, comforting concepts. As the psalmist said:

> "Mark the perfect man, and behold the upright: for the end of that man is peace."
>
> Psalm 37:37

NOTE:
These concepts come from the Jewish mystical writings of the Middle Ages, notably the *Zohar* (by Moses b. Shem Tov de Leon), and the writings of Jacob and Isaac Kohen, and Joseph Gikatilla. (Scholem, Gershom, *On the Mystical Shape of the Godhead: Basic Concepts in the Kabbalah*. 1991: Schocken Books, NY.)

PART II

THE SEVEN FEASTS OF THE LORD

CHAPTER 6:
THE SHAPE OF THE JEWISH YEAR

To understand any culture, one must understand its calendar with its holiday milestones. In the Holy Land, every calendar event is religious. But so is each ordinary day. The Jewish day is shaped in accordance with scripture:

> "And God called the light Day, and the darkness he called Night. And the evening and the morning were the first day."
>
> Genesis 1:5

> ". . . from even unto even, shall ye celebrate your Sabbath."
>
> Leviticus. 23:32

The Lord said, "even unto even." So be it. The day begins at sundown and ends at sundown. And since Israelites are observant and dedicated to doing everything right (under the watchful eye of the rabbis), the day begins <u>exactly</u> at sundown. In the days of Christ the *Sanhedrin* (Jewish senate) announced the arrival of sundown. Special witnesses noted the appearance of the first stars, and they reported to the High Priests. Now, the exact time of sundown is listed on the front page of Jewish newspapers and found online. This is especially important as the Sabbath approaches.

THE SABBATH QUEEN

We gained a new appreciation for the Sabbath while we lived in Israel. We had always "kept" the Sabbath. But we had never "exalted" it, nor had we "revered" it the way observant Jews do. Never had we called the day "Sabbath Queen." Never had we avoided driving a car or carrying an umbrella. Never had we sung songs to welcome the Sabbath, as they do in Israeli kindergartens. Never had we wished strangers on the street, *Shabbat Shalom,* "Sabbath peace." Never had we seen a classified ad ending with a telephone number and the initials "N.S." — "Not *Shabbat.*" Never had we seen a city like Jerusalem, where neighborhoods are organized into ghettos, set apart by the residents' dedication to Sabbath-keeping. Never had we seen streets barricaded to keep Sabbath drivers out.

Never had we seen a people that spent the entire week anticipating and preparing for the Sabbath. *Yom Kippur,* The Day of Atonement, is the highest Holy Day of the year, and yet the weekly Sabbath is considered holier still. I can remember when refugees were being airlifted from Ethiopia into Israel. The airlift had to be completed quickly. The Israeli government knew it would be halted when the world found out about it. The Rabbis declared a special dispensation, a matter of life and death, for the planes to keep arriving even on the Sabbath. A life or death situation is considered the only valid reason for breaking the Sabbath. (In addition, the Holy Days are considered Sabbaths, including the first and last days of Passover week and the beginning and end of the Feast of Tabernacles. Rosh HaShanah, as mentioned above, brings a two-day Sabbath to Israel, but only one day in the *diaspora.*)

> "Wherefore the children of Israel shall keep the Sabbath, to observe the Sabbath throughout their generations, for a perpetual covenant.
>
> "It is a sign between me and the children of Israel for ever: for in six days the Lord made heaven and earth, and on the seventh day he rested, and was refreshed."
>
> Exodus 31:16, 17

This, then, is the shape of the week. Six days and a Sabbath with the six days of labor spent in joyous anticipation that the Sabbath is approaching. This is, perhaps, the most important structure in the Jewish calendar. The number seven appears repeatedly in larger intervals and greater Sabbaths. Every seventh year, *schmittah,* is a Sabbath for the land. The fields must be allowed to rest. The Lord dictated that the whole country should observe the holiday at once (as opposed to rotating crops through portions of a field). He promised he would bless the Israelites with double the harvest during the sixth year, so they could lay aside food for the seventh. This echoes the pattern followed by the Israelites in the wilderness, when they received a double portion of manna on the sixth day, meant to sustain them through the Sabbath. After seven-times-seven years there is a year of jubilee, when all debts are forgiven. Remember that the number seven represents wholeness and perfection. The entire calendar is structured to encourage the Children of Israel towards that goal.

When the Israelites dwelt in Egypt, the year began in the fall. It was a logical time to begin again, because all over the Mediterranean world, it was the season of the final harvest and the beginning of a new natural cycle. The Jewish civil year still begins in the fall at *Rosh HaShanah* (the Feast of Trumpets). Years are counted from this festival for the dating of legal documents and the calculating of Sabbath and jubilee years. *Rosh HaShanah* represents the time of the world's creation, and Jewish years are reckoned from that time (3761 B.C.).[1]

When the Lord instituted the Passover, as the Israelites fled from Egypt, he commanded that the calendar be changed. The Exodus began during the month of *Nisan* (or *Aviv*), and now this is the first month of the religious year.

> "And the Lord spake unto Moses and Aaron in the land of Egypt, saying,
>
> "This month shall be unto you the beginning of months: it shall be the first month of the year to you."
>
> Exodus 12:1-2

The Jewish months, beginning with Nisan in the spring, are *Nisan, Iyar, Sivan, Tammuz, Av, Elul, Tishri, Heshvan, Kislev, Tevet, Shevet, and Adar.* (See the zodiac chart below.) You may see some strange names for these months in the Old Testament. Those original names were Canaanite. The current names (above) were adopted after the Babylonian captivity.

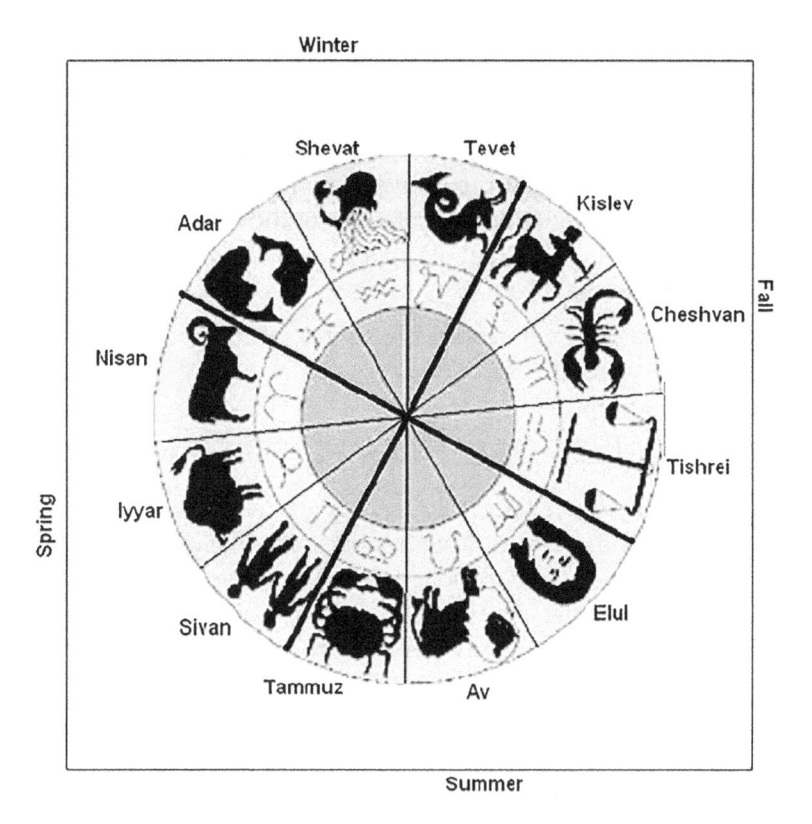

Notice that this Zodiac chart rotates counter-clockwise, because Hebrew is written from right to left.

Notice also, that the civic new year (Trumpets/Tishrei) and the religious new year (Passover/Nisan) divide the year exactly in half—the "meridians of time."

    The Jewish calendar is a "luni-solar" calendar. The months are based on the phases of the moon (beginning with new moons), and they have an average length of 292 days. The Jewish year usually contains twelve months (about 354 days). The calendar has a nineteen year cycle with leap years on the third, sixth, eighth, eleventh, fourteenth, seventeenth, and nineteenth years. During leap years one extra day is added to the month of *Adar*, and a thirteenth month (*Adar sheni*) is added to the calendar. This lunar reckoning causes the holidays to fall on different dates each year (that is, on our calendar), yet to stay in the same season. (The Qumran society may have calculated their months from "dark moons" instead of new moons, moving their holidays, and further separating them from Judean and Pharisaic culture.)

— 35 —

Anciently, chosen witnesses observed the sky and reported to the *Sanhedrin* when the new moon appeared. Then the *Sanhedrin* officially announced the news. As the Jews were dispersed to faraway lands, this method of announcing new months became difficult to carry out. Though the Sanhedrin went through the motions of interviewing witnesses, it did possess its own closely-guarded calculations of the moon's phases. Around 360 A.D. Rabbi Hillel, the Great Patriarch, published these calculations. This eliminated the need for

the witnesses and diminished the control of the Sanhedrin. This one act sped the demise of the Sanhedrin.[2]

RAINS, HARVESTS, AND SEASONS

The cycle of the Jewish holy days aligns with the cycle of yearly rains, harvests, and seasons. The Mediterranean countries have four seasons, but only two kinds of long-lasting weather. Spring-like weather and autumn-like weather may span only days, while winter and summer last half-a-year each. When they speak of the weather, Israelis claim to have only two seasons. Summer is hot and dry. It brings six months of relentless sunshine and tests the land and whatever grows from it. Winter is rainy. Surprisingly, Jerusalem receives about the same amount of rainfall as London. It simply all falls at once. (We witnessed many driving rainstorms that lasted an entire week.) The winter rains last from mid-October through mid-April. The October through December rains are called the "former rains." The January through March rains are called the "latter rains." They are separated by the long dry period. When the Lord changed the first month of the year to *Nisan* (*Aviv*), he put Passover at the beginning of the cycle. Thus, the year was transformed to portray a chart of the Plan of Salvation:

```
               Rains -------- Dry Period -------- Rains
Pre-existence /Birth ---------- Earth life, testing --------------------- Salvation
Passover (birth) -------- Exodus, wilderness, testing -------- Promised Land
```

BORN OUT OF EGYPT

The Israelites were tested in Egypt just as we were in the pre-mortal world. No, the societies were not the same, but the choice was. The Israelites chose to leave the known for the unknown, the womb for the wilderness, just as we consented to venture from Paradise into the

"Lone and Dreary World." The Israelites were literally born from the womb of Egypt, through the waters (of the Red Sea), just as we are born from the waters of the womb. Then they crossed the wilderness, facing choice after choice to test their faith.[3] The more righteous of their descendants eventually inherited the Promised Land, just as we hope to attain a kingdom of glory in the world to come.

Symbolically, Passover occurs just as the dry season begins, and the land itself launches into a wilderness period. Other holy days occur during this dry season that symbolize the help our Heavenly Father gives us to find our way back to him. In the fall, when the life-giving rains begin again, holy days occur which are symbolic of final repentance, final judgment and the ushering in of the Millennium. The construct of the year with its holy milestones looks like this:

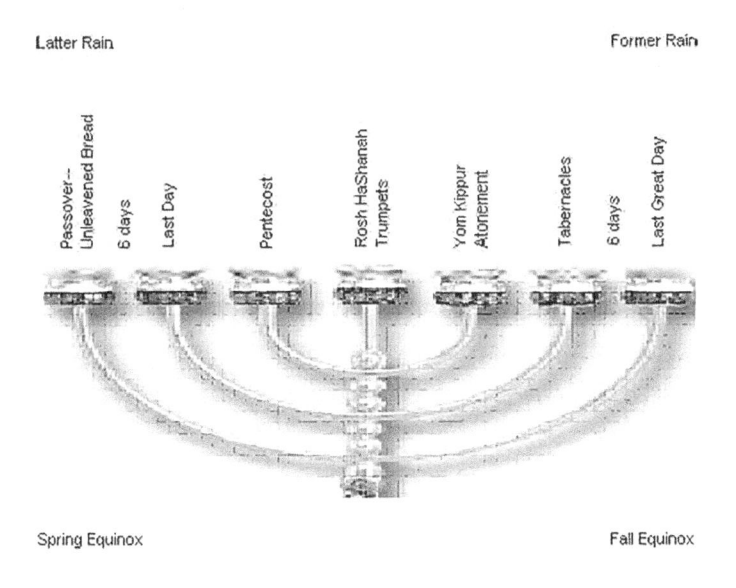

Latter Rain — Passover–Unleavened Bread — 6 days — Last Day — Pentecost — Rosh HaShaneh Trumpets — Yom Kippur Atonement — Tabernacles — 6 days — Last Great Day — Former Rain

Spring Equinox — Fall Equinox

The holy milestones established by the Lord are called *mo'edim*, or holy convocations. They are "solemn appointed times." Literally, they are appointments between God and Man with the Temple (at Jerusalem) as the meeting place.[4] The milestones correspond to major events in the life of Christ,[5] and to principles of perfection (or wholeness) to which we must adhere in order to make our way towards salvation. Each milestone requires that we present ourselves before the Lord in an act of accountability. By laying our offerings at his feet, we show him what we have accomplished with the gifts he has given us. In turn, he promises us abundance, protection, and exaltation.

CHAPTER 7 ENDNOTES

[1] According to the Jews, if you add the current year to the year of Adam's creation (3761 B.C.), you will arrive at the current Jewish year (give or take a few months, because their calendar year begins in the fall). Thus, the year 2007 would be the Jewish year 5768. Some scholars argue that there has been a 250-year error in the Jewish calculations, so the year should be closer to 6000 A.D.

[2] Howard, *Feasts of the Lord*, 40.

[3] The Mormon pioneers, under the leadership of the "modern Moses," Brigham Young, called themselves "The Camp of Israel." Their migration to the Rocky Mountains followed the same pattern as the Exodus. They crossed the Missouri River by miraculous means. (The river froze solid enough for heavy wagons to traverse it.) They journeyed through the wilderness to a promised place of sanctuary, facing tests and receiving spiritual sustenance on the way.

> "Behold, I say unto you, the redemption of Zion must needs come by power; therefore I will raise up unto my people a man, who shall lead them like as Moses led the children of Israel. For ye are the children of Israel, and of the seed of Abraham, and ye must needs be led out of bondage by power, and with a stretched-out arm. And as your fathers were led at the first, even so shall the redemption of Zion be. Therefore, let not your hearts faint, for I say not unto you as I said unto your fathers: Mine angel shall go up before you, but not my presence. But I say unto you: Mine angels shall go up before you, and also my presence, and in time ye shall possess the goodly land (D&C 103:15-20)."

[4] Howard, 42.

[5] It is significant that when the original civil New Year in the autumn (first of Tishrei) is used as the beginning of the year, then the Passover month of Nisan is the "Meridian of Time" for that year, Passover being the time of Christ's birth. When the month of Nisan becomes the first month of the year, as commanded at the institution of the Passover, then the autumn holidays fall at the "Meridian of Time." Fall is the season of the Second Coming imagery.

[6] Winter, *The High Holy Days*, 15.

CHAPTER 7:
PESACH AND CHAG HAMATZOT (THE FEASTS OF PASSOVER AND UNLEAVENED BREAD)

The spring month of Nisan, by commandment, had now become the first month of the year. The spring rains would have already blessed the Promised Land, and it would be blooming exuberantly, with wild red poppies dancing, and fig trees bringing forth their fruit. The rains represent blessings from heaven. Now, with the establishment of the Passover, the latter rains would come to symbolize for us the first coming of the Messiah. When future kings would reign in Israel, their subjects would count the number of years of their rule from the month of Nisan. We count our own years from the birth of our King, Jesus the Messiah.

Israel herself was about to be born into the world, a nation of believers — separate, chosen, and holy. The Lord called them his "firstborn." Down through the ages Passover would relive this "delivery;" The Passover presents in rich symbolism the message of deliverance and redemption. Just as we choose to avail ourselves of Christ's atonement, the Israelites had to choose to trade the yoke of the Egyptians for the yoke of the Lord.

The basic patterns of the Passover ritual were dictated to the Israelites just prior to their escape from Egypt (Exodus 8-13). The rituals, however, were already familiar. It was a coming together of three ancient rites: the rite of circumcision, the offering of grain, and the offering up of the firstlings of the flocks. All the symbolisms of these rites were joined in order to teach of the atoning sacrifice of the Messiah to come. Passover would occur at the time of the first barley harvest in the Promised Land. Offerings given in the Temple would show gratitude for the seasonal rains. The grain offerings would be of fine meal and oil without corrupting leaven. Only the circumcised could attend a Passover meal — circumcision signifying commitment to the Abrahamic Covenant. In other words, the Passover (which the Savior would transform into the sacrament) was meant for the covenant people in commemoration of deliverance. At each Passover service (*seder*), when the Children of Israel would retell the story of their redemption from Egypt and slavery, they would begin with Abraham and the Covenant.

THE ANCIENT RITE OF SACRIFICE

Sacrifice was the most ancient of rites. As Jehovah, Christ had commanded Adam and Eve to "worship the Lord their God, and . . . offer the firstlings of their flocks, for an offering unto the Lord" (Moses 5:5). At the time, Adam did not understand the purpose of this commandment, but wishing to be obedient in all things, he did as the Lord commanded. When Jehovah was satisfied that Adam had shown his willingness to obey, and that the sacrifice was prepared and offered properly, he sent a messenger to Adam to further instruct him.

"And after many days an angel of the Lord appeared unto Adam, saying: Why dost thou offer sacrifices unto the Lord? And Adam said unto him: I know not, save the Lord commanded me.

> "And then the angel spake, saying: This thing is a **similitude** of the sacrifice of the Only Begotten of the Father, which is full of grace and truth.
>
> "Wherefore, thou shalt do all that thou doest in the name of the Son, and thou shalt repent and call upon the name of the Son forever."
>
> Moses 5:7-8 *(emphasis added)*

Undoubtedly, Adam was instructed in the exact pattern of the ordinance: that the animal should be a first-born male, without blemish, to be slain with the shedding of blood but with no bones broken, and that this sacrifice should be performed in a spirit of humility and repentance.[1] Thus, from Adam's time onward, believers would perform this ritual looking forward to the redeeming sacrifice of the true Messiah. Through the practice of the ordinance of blood sacrifice, men were living a parable, performing an allegory, meant to prepare them to recognize and receive the Christ when he should come.

However, because of the strength of tradition and the tenuous nature of man's spiritual sensitivity, ordinances may continue where true meanings have been lost. This was the case with the Israelites in Egypt. They had dwelt in Egypt for at least four hundred years. Joseph and Jacob had passed away. No other prophet appeared to teach them what Adam, Abraham, Joseph, and Jacob knew about the divine nature of the coming Messiah (Jacob 4:5). They practiced circumcision as the representation of God's covenant with Abraham. They laid grain and meal offerings upon the altar in the spring in thanks for the first harvest of the year. They offered the firstlings of their flocks to the One God as they always had. Yet worship and religious practices were difficult and often dangerous. In slavery they lost the ability to make choices, to raise up inspired leadership, or even to perform basic ordinances in safety. They were truly in dire straits.

The Lord had to do more than take the Israelites out of Egypt. Beginning with the Passover and extending through the journey in the wilderness, he had to train them to be citizens of a great and peculiar nation, ready to conquer societies that were more advanced materially and politically. At the same time, each individual had to be converted — personally born into the kingdom. The Lord began by sending Moses, himself a type of the Savior.

The family of Israel, that is, Jacob's sons and their heirs, were the Lord's "chosen people," inheritors of the promises made to Abraham. They were brought into Egypt for two purposes, to protect the family from famine, and to influence the Egyptians, whom the Lord favored. (He had sent Abraham and Joseph to bless them; in the future Egypt would protect the infant Christ; and at the end of days Egypt will be blessed rather than cursed.)

In Egypt the family of Israel burgeoned into a huge, healthy population. After Joseph's death, however, Egypt became increasingly idolatrous. Egyptians also harbored a grudge against the Semites, because of the humiliating triumphs of the Semitic Hyksos ("Shepherd Kings") over Egypt. Fearing a large Semitic population might join with their enemies, Egypt began to oppress the Israelites (Exodus 1:9,10).

A MESSAGE FOR EGYPT

The edicts of Moses against Egypt, including the ten plagues, were meant as much to <u>teach</u> the Egyptians as to convince them to release Israel. The Talmudic sages maintained that each plague brought against Egypt corresponded to a crime committed against the Israelites, measure for measure. Some plagues were meant to overcome superstitious beliefs nurtured by the Egyptians. For instance, the first plague was against the Nile, which Egyptians regarded as a God. Egyptians also venerated the frog and the bull.[2] Pharaoh himself was revered as a god. Symbolically, he was forced to sacrifice his first-born son so that Israel could be free. Jewish tradition has it that the Egyptians were polluted with sin and addicted to witchcraft and lusts of the flesh.[3] But the Israelites themselves were superstitious, believing that magic animals would warn Egypt if Israel tried to escape. (Luckily, the animals were quiet as the Exodus began.) In all of the miracles performed by the Lord in Egypt and through the Exodus, there was a desire to manifest the power of the God of Israel to the heathen nations as a testimony of the One God. The Lord was as interested in saving the heathen as in saving the Israelite.

Jewish tradition also says that the miracles performed in Egypt had only a partial influence on the Israelites; not all the Israelites followed Moses into the wilderness.[4] Not all were moved to paint the lintels of their hovels with the Blood of the Lamb. Those who were obedient had only a basic understanding of what they were doing, since the symbolisms of the Passover were essentially new to them. The miracles, the plagues, and the Passover commandments were the very beginning of their re-education in the gospel.

AN OBSERVANCE FOREVER

The Children of Israel were commanded to observe the Passover as "a feast to the Lord throughout your generations; . . . a feast by an ordinance forever" (Exodus 12:14). One observance was not enough, nor was it enough to observe it through the forty years in the wilderness. By the time of Christ there had been hundreds of Passovers, and still the imagery had not been fully grasped. Exodus 10:2 says, "And that thou mayest tell in the ears of thy son, and of thy son's son, what things I have wrought in Egypt, and my signs which I have done among them; that ye may know how that I am the Lord." Why continue hearkening back to this one event? Why repeat this teaching exercise over and over? Because in the pattern and story of the Passover and the Exodus, is found the type of the life, mission, and redemptive power of the Savior, and the spiritual history of the earth. Not until the End of Times will the full import of the imagery fall into place.

Nephi said, **"Behold, my soul delighteth in proving unto my people the truth of the coming of Christ, for, for this end hath the law of**

Moses been given, and all things which have been given of God from the beginning of the world, are the typifying of him (2 Nephi 11:4)." The Passover was indeed designed to typify Christ:

> "Speak ye unto all the congregation of Israel, saying, In the tenth day of this month they shall take to them every man a lamb, according to the house of their fathers, a lamb for an house . . .
>
> "Your lamb shall be without blemish, a male of the first year: ye shall take it out from the sheep, or from the goats:
>
> "And ye shall keep it up until the fourteenth day of the same month (Nisan): and the whole assembly of the congregation of Israel shall kill it in the evening."
>
> Exodus 12:3, 5-6

THE LAMB OF GOD

The lamb selected for sacrifice was kept for four days to be examined carefully for purity and for the family to become attached to it — this sacrifice would be made with a broken heart. The Lamb was to be "without blemish, a male of the first year," just as Christ would be the Only Begotten Son of the Father, a man without flaw. The lamb was to be fully consumed, but no bones were to be broken, just as the Savior's life would be fully consumed on the cross, but none of his bones would be broken. The Passover lamb was to be killed between 3:00 and 5:00 p.m. on the afternoon of the fourteenth day of Nisan, which would ultimately be the day and time of Christ's crucifixion.

> "And they shall take of the blood and strike it on the two side posts and on the upper door post of the houses, wherein they shall eat it."
>
> Exodus 12:7

The Israelites surrounded their doorways with the blood, and stayed safely inside their houses. The blood of the lamb became a protection for the household from the destroying angel — typifying the eternal saving role of the Blood of the Lamb. Those with faith enough to make use of the Blood, having faith that the Lord knew what he was doing, and that Moses was indeed a prophet, saved themselves and their families. Thus, the Blood of the Lamb, Jesus Christ, saves us with our families from sin and the eternal consequences of sin. Ether said (speaking of Zion), ". . .

for it is they whose garments are white through the blood of the Lamb . . . (Ether 13:10)." Moroni said, "And again, if ye by the grace of God are perfect in Christ, and deny not his power, then are ye sanctified in Christ by the grace of God, through the shedding of the blood of Christ, which is the covenant of the Father unto the remission of your sins, that ye become holy, without spot (Moroni 10:33)."

The blood was applied to the lintel with a branch of hyssop. Hyssop was a healing herb used to treat leprosy; in the future Jesus would be the healer of lepers. It was also the sponge used to offer vinegar to the dying Christ. The people were to eat the feast girded for travel, standing, and ready to leave, symbolizing instant willingness to follow the Lord and his prophet. During the night the destroying angel passed over the houses that were marked according to God's command. The following day the Exodus began.

THE BREAD OF LIFE

The fourteenth of Nisan was the Passover, the offering of the Lamb, then on the fifteenth, the seven-day Feast of Unleavened Bread began, and on that day the Israelites were delivered from bondage. Unleavened bread, the "bread of affliction," became a symbol of haste (to obey the commandments), since the Israelites had no time to add leaven or to allow the bread to rise. The hot sun baked the flat loaves in the wilderness. The *Zohar* calls it "celestial bread," the antidote to Egyptian bondage, decay, and corruption.[5] The unleavened bread suggests purity of heart, moral courage, and eagerness to serve the Lord. Leaven came to represent the "evil impulse," in the sense of fermenting passion. The Apostle Paul said in 1 Corinthians 5:6-8:

> "Your glorying is not good. Know ye that a little leaven leaveneth the whole lump? Purge out therefore the old leaven, that ye may be a new lump, as ye are unleavened. For even **Christ our passover is sacrificed for us**. Therefore let us keep the feast, not with old leaven, neither with the leaven of malice and wickedness, but with the unleavened bread of sincerity and truth"

At Passover all leaven must be purged from the homes of the believers during a thorough spring cleaning. Jewish moralists say that when we remove leaven from our homes, we should also remove evil inclination from our hearts. As we traditionally remove leaven from our homes by the light of a candle, we must remove evil by the light of conscience, the "lamp of the Lord." As the leaven represented decay, it was forbidden to offer it in the grain or meal offering; the offering was to represent the pure in heart. Interestingly, Christ called the doctrines of the Pharisees and Sadducees leaven, and warned His followers against them (Matthew 16:6). Though the unleavened bread is called the "bread of affliction," it represents the "living bread" — both the manna in the wilderness and the Savior Himself. Unleavened bread must be pierced and striped to keep it from puffing.

DELIVERANCE

The Exodus began on 15 Nisan, as the Lord delivered his covenant offspring Israel from the womb of Egypt, foretelling the birth of Christ on the same date in the meridian of time. The Israelites had been protected by the blood of the Lamb, and now they crossed the water into the wilderness.

> ". . . and inasmuch as ye were born into the world by water, and blood, and the spirit, which I have made, and so became of dust a living soul, even so ye must be born again into the kingdom of heaven, of water, and of the Spirit, and be cleansed by blood, even the blood of mine Only Begotten; that ye might be sanctified from all sin, and enjoy the words of eternal life in the world to come, even immortal glory;
>
> "For by water ye keep the commandment; by the Spirit ye are justified; and by the blood ye are sanctified;. . .
>
> "And now, behold, I say unto you: This is the plan of salvation unto all men, through the blood of mine Only Begotten, who shall come in the meridian of time."
>
> Moses 6:59-60, 62

The Only Begotten Himself was the deliverer of the Children of Israel, just as He is the deliverer of all who will lay hold upon His atoning sacrifice and thereby become His children. Nephi said —

> "And **the God of our fathers**, who were led out of Egypt, out of bondage, and also were preserved in the wilderness by him, yea, the God of Abraham, and of Isaac, and the God of Jacob, **yieldeth himself**, according to the words of the angel, as a man,

into the hands of wicked men, to be lifted up . . . and to be crucified. . . and to be buried in a sepulcher. . . ."

1 Nephi 19:10

At the time of the Exodus the Lord designated the Levites as his "firstborn" among his firstborn nation, and he claimed them for his service:

"And I have taken the Levites for all the firstborn of the children of Israel.

"And I have given the Levites as a gift to Aaron and to his sons from among the children of Israel, to do the service of the children of Israel in the tabernacle of the congregation, and **to make an atonement** for the children of Israel: that there be no plague among the children of Israel, when the children of Israel come nigh unto the sanctuary."

Numbers 8:18

The Levites then became another type of Christ. Levites entered the Lord's service at age thirty. Christ performed his first public miracles and began His ministry on Passover, when He turned thirty years old.

Other tactile images were established with the Passover in addition to the Lamb and the unleavened bread — the eating of bitter herbs, as a reminder of the bitterness of slavery; the eating of a sweet blend of chopped fruit, as a reminder of the sweetness of hope even in oppression; the eating of sweet herbs, as a reminder of the rebirth of the world in spring; the shank-bone of a lamb, as a reminder of God's outstretched arm, which led and protected Israel; and covenantal cups of wine, as a reminder of Israel's obedience and the Lord's promises to deliver Israel from slavery and from Egypt, to take them as His people, and to give them the Promised Land for an inheritance. Thus, the Passover is at once a commemoration and a promise of deliverance, both temporal and spiritual. Each year, on Passover and during the Feast of Unleavened Bread, the children of Israel recite the story of the oppression, the plagues, and the deliverance. The recitation is a reminder that the Lord was, is, and ever will be a God of miracles, willing to save His children. Nephi followed this pattern of telling the Passover story when he recited to his wayward brothers:

"And it came to pass that I, Nephi, spake unto them, saying: Do ye believe that our fathers, who were the children of Israel, would have been led away out of the hands of the Egyptians if they had not hearkened unto the words of the Lord?

"Yea, do ye suppose that they would have been led out of bondage, if the Lord had not commanded Moses that he should lead them out of bondage?

"Now ye know that the children of Israel were in bondage; and ye know that they were laden with tasks, which were grievous to be borne; wherefore, ye know that it must needs be a good thing for them, that they should be brought out of bondage.

"Now ye know that Moses was commanded of the Lord to do that great work; and ye know that by his word the waters of the Red Sea were divided hither and thither, and they passed through on dry ground.

"But ye know that the Egyptians were drowned in the Red Sea, who were the armies of Pharaoh.

"And ye also know that they were fed manna in the wilderness.

"Yea, and ye also know that Moses, by his word according to the power of God which was in him, smote the rock, and there came forth water, that the children of Israel might quench their thirst. . . .

"And he loveth those who will have him to be their God. Behold, he loved our fathers, and he covenanted with them, yea, even Abraham, Isaac, and Jacob; and he remembered the covenants which he had made; wherefore, he did bring them out of the land of Egypt. . . .

"And they did harden their hearts from time to time, and they did revile against Moses, and also against God; nevertheless, ye know that they were led forth by his matchless power into the land of promise."

1 Nephi17:23-29, 40, 42

ISRAEL FORGETS AND REMEMBERS

The Israelites kept the Passover all the years they were in the wilderness and then as they settled in Canaan, the Promised Land. But by the time King Hezekiah ruled Judah (726 B.C.), the Passover had slipped away, due to the spiritual carelessness of the people and their rulers. King Hezekiah cleansed and repaired the temple and ordered priesthood holders to purify themselves. He sent messengers to all the tribes, urging them to rededicate themselves and keep the feast. Some did humble themselves, but others "laughed them to scorn" (2 Chron: 30). It took the priests and Levites extra time to purify themselves, so the feast was celebrated a month late. The priests had to offer sacrifices for many of the people, since most had not cleansed nor sanctified themselves. Hezekiah's own prayers on their behalf moved the Lord to accept their offerings. Eventually, the citizens of the southern kingdom of Judah were carried away to Babylon, while the northern kingdom of Israel had already been conquered by Assyria. Groups of faithful Jews tried to keep the feasts wherever they were located, but the Temple could not be central as it was meant to be. Without the Temple, no offerings, no animal sacrifices could be made. When the Jews returned from Babylon, the Temple was rebuilt, and the former, temple-centered practices of worship were renewed.

A WORLD OF TURMOIL AND CONTROVERSY

The two hundred years leading up to the birth of Christ were full of turmoil and controversy. No prophet had taught in Judea since Malachi. Under the Maccabee family the Jews had repeatedly thwarted the advances of a Greco- Persian alliance, cleansing the desecrated temple over and over. Greek influence was profound and disturbing. A gymnasium (where male Greek athletes competed) was built that overlooked the temple, an insult to observant Jews. The culture of the Greek gymnasium became popular with the worldly, just as the sports culture is popular in our day and age. Only men competed, but they did so in the nude. Jewish athletes were humiliated by their obvious physical difference from gentile athletes — they bore the sign of the Abrahamic covenant. Thus, there was a temptation to go without, or even to try to reverse, circumcision. Greek philosophy, culture, and language spread everywhere, though dedicated Jews, especially the Pharisees and their followers, resisted and refused to learn Greek. The Pharisees forcefully upheld the old law, but in setting themselves above and apart, lost the sensitivity to keep the spirit of the law. (See Matthew 23:2-10.) Many were outwardly observant, but privately sinful. The Sadducees, Israel's aristocracy, embraced Greek culture and philosophy to the point that they no longer believed in a resurrection from the dead. For the Jewish people, reliance on the sages among the Pharisees, Sadducees and Scribes replaced reliance on the prophets.

Rome conquered Judea in 65 B.C. and later set up Herod to govern. Herod was hated by his subjects not only for his ruthlessness, but because he was an Edomite (a descendant of Esau, and therefore not of Israel) who claimed to be Jewish. In 37 B.C. he murdered about half the members of the Sanhedrin. The Sadducees, already Hellenized, became very beholden to the Romans for their survival, position, and prosperity. Priesthood positions could be purchased from the heads of state, so corruption abounded. The Essenes separated themselves from the swirl of corruption and Greco-Roman influence and established a retreat at Qumran. Zealots, who believed in Israel's <u>national</u> salvation, set up rival groups bent on breaking the grip of Roman rule. Into this world of conflict and controversy was born the Savior.

JESUS WAS BORN ON THE PASSOVER

December 25th was not the date nor the season of Christ's birth. Our December celebration of the birthday of Christ is based on pagan winter solstice festivals, which reveled in the knowledge that the days would grow longer and bring warmer weather. We know from reading Doctrine and Covenants 20:1 that The Church of Jesus Christ of Latter-day Saints was organized on April 6th. Since then, our modern prophets have upheld this time of the year as the season of our Savior's birth. This is soon after the spring equinox of March 21st, and Passover occurs at the first full moon after the equinox. The last trickles of the latter rains would have been falling. The hills would have been fresh and lush for grazing. The breezes would have been mild, and shepherds would have been watching over their flocks by night, including the baby lambs birthed in early spring. The imagery of deliverance, the symbol of the Lord's firstborn Israel being delivered on 15 Nisan, establishes the connection with Jesus' spring birth. He was born at Passover.

Passover was an opportune time for the Roman authorities to take a census of Jews, since it was the most well-attended pilgrimage festival of the year, the other two being Shavuot (the Feast of Weeks) and Sukkot (the Feast of Tabernacles). These festivals required that every able male appear at the Temple in Jerusalem to offer sacrifices.[6] At Passover a count could be made of the lambs sacrificed at the Temple, and by multiplying by ten (the suggested number of celebrants sharing a lamb at the Passover meal), an approximate count of the population could be reached. Josephus tells us that during the days of Cestius, 256,500 lambs were sacrificed. The Romans approximated 2,750,200 souls were in Jerusalem at the time of the feast.[7]

Picture the walled city of Jerusalem at the time of Jesus' birth — just over a mile square — crowded with pilgrims. They must have camped all over the hillsides round about. We know that the families of Mary and Joseph were observant Jews, and that they made pilgrimage in caravans that included their family and friends, because there is an account of one of their pilgrimages in the New Testament.

> "Now his parents went to Jerusalem every year at the feast of the passover.
>
> "And when he was twelve years old, they went up to Jerusalem after the custom of the feast.
>
> "And when they had fulfilled the days, as they returned, the child Jesus tarried behind in Jerusalem; and Joseph and his mother knew not of it.
>
> "But they, supposing him to have been in the **company**, went a day's journey; and they sought him **among their kinsfolk and acquaintance**."
>
> <div align="right">Luke 2:41-44 <i>(emphasis added)</i></div>

We must then revise our imagined pictures of the first Christmas, with Mary and Joseph making the lonely journey south from Nazareth with only a donkey to ease the way. Instead, we must visualize them journeying in caravan with all their extended family and trusted friends. We must visualize the hills blooming with spring wild-flowers, and then add hundreds of thousands of people with their beasts of burden, sacrificial animals, and provisions traveling to, or camping around, Jerusalem. Bethlehem is just an additional few miles to the south, and surely the distance between Jerusalem and Bethlehem would have been crowded with travelers and tents (the poor would have camped in the open). Joseph could never have expected "room in the inn." He must have hoped that Mary's condition, or the special nature of the child she was carrying, would yield the miracle of a little space and protection. The sheep-fold, however humble, was a fitting place to bring forth the Lamb of God.[8]

The passage from Luke quoted above records the pilgrimage when Jesus was twelve. That Passover, while in Jerusalem, Jesus turned thirteen, the age when Jewish boys begin to read from the *Torah* before the congregation. After the pilgrimage, unable to find Him among the company in their caravan, Mary and Joseph returned to Jerusalem and found Him teaching in the temple. It is doubtful He would have been invited to participate, if He were younger, but He was *bar mitzvah* age, prepared to become a "Son of the Covenant." Jewish boys study carefully and diligently for the time when they are qualified by their age and knowledge to read in the synagogue and discuss the holy writings with the elders. This is the age when Jewish boys become men in the sight of the Lord. Jesus made this transition and began to teach on His own volition, to do the work of His Heavenly Father, to go about "His Father's business."

On the Passover of His thirtieth year Jesus performed his first public miracle. He entered his public ministry at the age of a Levite, as the Levites were appointed upon the deliverance from Egypt to be a type of the Firstborn (Numbers 3:12;8:18). In John 2:23 we read, "Now when he was in Jerusalem at the Passover, in the feast day, many believed in his name, when they saw the miracles which he did."

Jesus cleansed the temple twice before Passover at the beginning and end of His ministry. It was a fitting time of year for cleansing: the homes of the observant were scrupulously cleaned in preparation for the holiday, and the minds, bodies, and spirits of the pilgrims were also required to be cleansed.

THE LAST SUPPER

At every Passover meal there is an officiator. He is also considered the sacrificer. Usually, it was he who took the lamb to the Temple as a Passover offering. Up to his final Passover, Jesus would have participated in ceremonial meals where the patriarch of the family would have offered the sacrifice and officiated at the feast. But Jesus' final Passover was different. Jesus separated Himself from his family at this time (although his mother was in the city for the Feast), for He had a strong desire to observe the feast with His apostles. This would be His last opportunity to teach His apostles, and the lesson would be profound. The importance of the moment emphasizes the importance of this holy day and its rites. During this teaching session He would cleanse the apostles from the blood of their generation through the washing of feet (D&C 88:138-141), fulfilling the type of the traditional purging of leaven from the home, and the evil inclination from the heart. Washing of the hands was already part of the Passover ritual. He would teach his apostles that the symbolic foods and practices of the ceremonial ritual represented Him, the True Messiah. From then on the types would not look forward to His coming, but backward in remembrance. Thus, He would institute the Sacrament. At this one and only Passover, Christ would be the officiator, the sacrificer... and the sacrifice:

> "For such an high priest became us, [who is] holy, harmless, undefiled, separate from sinners, and made higher than the heavens, Who needeth not daily, as those high priests, to offer up sacrifice, first for his own sins, and then for the people's: for **this he did once, when he offered up himself**."
>
> <div align="right">Hebrews 7:27 <i>(emphasis added)</i></div>

Again, we must make changes to the pictures we've created of the Last Supper, with Christ and his apostles seated in chairs around a western-style table. The slave crouched in the field to eat, but the free men of the Mediterranean world reclined. There may have been no table at all, or a table very low to the floor, surrounded by pillows. Such Middle Eastern tables were often in the shape of a "U", and were sometimes suspended from the ceiling. (A server could walk into the center to serve the celebrants.) Jesus and the apostles would have reclined on the pillows on their left sides, with their feet pointing outward.[9] It would have been a simple thing for John to lean upon the breast of the Savior (Luke 13:23), if he were reclining at the Savior's right. Tradition holds that John was the youngest apostle. At the Passover dinner, this is usually the seat of the youngest son — he sits to the right of the officiator to ask the Passover questions, one of which takes on poignant meaning here: "Why is this night different than all other nights?" The place of honor at a Passover meal is to the left of the officiator — on this night, the seat of Judas Iscariot. It was a simple thing for Judas to dip in the sop (meat with broth) with Jesus. Christ Himself would have been in the center, the seat of the officiator. This knowledge also enlightens us as to why there was a dispute among the Apostles as to the seating arrangements for the evening.

THE PATTERN OF THE LAST SUPPER

The *mishnah* indicates that the basic pattern of the Passover meal was in place by this time, including questions asked by the children, the reciting of psalms, and recounting of the Deliverance from Egypt. The basic structure of the Passover ritual meal is this:

A *seder plate* is set out displaying symbolic foods explained during the evening.
- The foods are a *z'roa*, a lamb shank bone (or chicken neck, representing God's outstretched arm), a little *charoset*, (chopped fruit mixture, representing the sweetness of

hope and the mortar used to make bricks for Pharaoh), *karpas* (sweet herbs, representing the bounties of spring), *maror* (bitter herbs, representing the bitterness of slavery and oppression), *chazeret* (also bitter herbs, usually horseradish), *baytzah* (a roasted egg, representing rebirth and a festival offering).

- The envelope holding the three *matzot* (unleavened bread) is also set out.
- Wine enough for five covenantal cups is set out.
- A dish of salt water is set out to represent the tears of affliction.
- A cup is poured to welcome the spirit of Elijah the prophet, the forerunner of the Savior.
- During the evening psalms are sung; they are songs of redemption and deliverance, both temporal and spiritual.

The table is set and the candles are lit.

Kadesh:
The first of four cups of wine is poured.

{"I will bring you out of Egypt."}

(Each cup of wine represented a promise made by the Lord to Israel.) A blessing is recited to sanctify the feast day.

Urechatz:
The hands are washed.

Karpas:
Sweet herbs are dipped in salt water, then eaten.

Yachatz:
The middle of the three *matzot* is removed from its envelope. It is broken in two pieces by the officiator. The larger piece is wrapped and hidden. It becomes the *afikomon*.

Maggid:
The second cup of wine is poured.

{"I will deliver you from slavery."}

The story of the deliverance from Egypt is told.

Some groups begin with the Abrahamic covenant and give a history of the Israelite people down through the Exodus.

Rachtzah:
The hands are washed in preparation for the meal.

Motzi:
A prayer is said before breaking bread.

Matzah:
The matzah is blessed.

Maror:
The bitter herb (usually horseradish) is tasted.

Korech:
A combination of matzah, bitter herbs, and charoset is eaten.

Shulchan Orech:
The meal is served and eaten.

Tzafun:
A child (or youngest adult) discovers the *afikomon*. He redeems it for a gift from the officiator. It is broken, passed and eaten.

Barech:
The third cup of wine is poured, and the grace after the meal is recited.

{"I will redeem you."}

An extra cup is poured for Elijah, the door is opened, and he is welcomed into the household.

Hallel:
The fourth cup of wine is poured, followed by psalms of praise.

{"I will take you as my children."} A prayer is said.

Nirtzah:
The service concludes with a hymn. Recreational songs may be sung.

In ancient times a fifth cup of wine may have been taken, representing the covenant, "I will restore you."

Nowadays, this comes in the form of a toast: "Next year, in Jerusalem."

THE SACRAMENTAL BREAD

As you can see in the outline of the ritual, unleavened bread (*matzah*), the bread of affliction and purity, is broken, blessed and passed several times during the meal. Three pieces of unleavened bread had been placed between napkins or in a special pouch near the officiator for use in the ceremony. At one point in the ritual, the officiator removes the middle matzah and breaks it in half. He wraps one half of the broken bread in a white linen cloth and hides it. Later it is found ("resurrected") and redeemed with a gift, then broken and passed to the company.[10] It was this bread which Christ broke and passed to his disciples, saying, "This do in remembrance of me," "This is my body. . . ." The symbolism could not be more certain, and surely must have been profound for those present. Later, upon the destruction of the Temple, it became impossible to offer up the sacrificial lamb, or to eat a sacrificial lamb at the Passover meal. It had been customary to eat a piece of lamb as the final food of the evening as a token of the sacrifice. This special piece of unleavened bread, then, took the place of the lamb. Called by the Greek name, *afikomon,* the bread then represented the lamb; it was the bread of the sacrament, the bread of life. Certainly, the message was clear to the apostles, when Jesus took this piece of bread and declared Himself to be the fulfillment of this symbolic ritual. The fact that matzah is "pierced and striped" to keep it from rising, adds to the imagery of the afflicted Christ.

THE SACRAMENTAL WINE

When we partake of the sacramental "wine," we remember Him, even as we look forward to his second coming. (See *A Haggadah for Mormon Celebrants* accompanying this book.) We partake of the Sacrament to renew the covenants we made at baptism — we were born through water into a wilderness of testing, where hopefully, the Blood of the Lamb will save us and lead us to eternal life. Christ partook of some of the covenantal cups of wine required at the meal, but declined one or more cups, which represented covenants He would not fulfill until the Kingdom of God is permanently restored on earth. Unfulfilled is the covenant of restoration — Jehovah promised that He would restore His children to the promised land forever.

This cannot happen until the ushering in of the millennium.

WHY DID JESUS CELEBRATE PASSOVER ONE NIGHT EARLY?

The close followers of Jesus called themselves Nazarene Jews. The Nazarenes, Essenes, Samaritans, and others celebrated the feast days as they were dictated in Exodus, where fourteen Nisan was the day of sacrifice and Passover meal, and the fifteenth through twenty-first were the seven-day Feast of Unleavened Bread. But there is compelling evidence that by the time of Christ the ruling Pharisees had combined the Passover and the Feast of Unleavened Bread into one, seven-day celebration (as it is now celebrated in modern times).[11] That means Jesus and his followers would have been following the God-ordained schedule dictated in Exodus, while the majority of citizens and pilgrims in Jerusalem would have had their Passover meal and ritual observance one day later. Because Jews calculate their days from evening to evening, Jesus could have shared the Passover meal with His apostles on the eve of the 14th, then been crucified on the following afternoon of the 14th, and then been taken down as twilight ushered in the Pharisaic Passover on the 15th. (See John 18:28 — The Chief Priests and Pharisees would not enter the Praetorium to judge Jesus for fear of becoming unclean for their Passover beginning the 15th of Nisan.) Because of the disparity in times of worship, Christ would have celebrated his sacrifice with his apostles on the given day of Passover, and then he would have been crucified at the same time as the lambs were sacrificed in the Temple.

JESUS WAS NOT CRUCIFIED ON FRIDAY

It is certain that the Savior was crucified on **Thursday** afternoon, 14 Nisan.[12] The first and last day of Passover are Sabbaths, and they are called "high sabbaths." In John 19:31, we read about the Jews' anxiety over leaving the crucified on their crosses as the Passover high Sabbath approached:

> "The Jews therefore, because it was the preparation, that the bodies should not remain upon the cross on the Sabbath day, (**for that Sabbath day was an high day**) besought Pilate that their legs might be broken, and that they might be taken away."

Therefore, it was not the Friday-night-to-Saturday Sabbath the Jews were up against. As was said by those who gathered clandestinely at the house of Caiaphas, "Not during the feast, lest there be a tumult among the people (Matthew 26:5)." That year of Christ's crucifixion there were actually two Sabbath days in a row — Friday, the Pharisaic Passover High Sabbath (beginning Thursday evening), and Saturday, the weekly Sabbath, beginning Friday evening. Research by the Society for the Advancement of Nazarene Judaism has shown that there were no Friday night Passover Sabbaths from 25—35 A.D, and therefore, no high Sabbaths that fell on the normal Sabbath day.[13]

THREE DAYS, AND THREE NIGHTS

Having died late Thursday afternoon, Christ <u>actually was</u> in the grave for a full three days and three nights, of which Jonah was a type, and rose on Sunday morning, the first day of the week. (The Book of Mormon account of three full days of darkness helps substantiate this.) Thus, is the Passover imagery fulfilled in Christ — the unfolding of the Plan of Salvation, deliverance and redemption, the saving value of the Blood of the Lamb, the bread of life, the covenant and the sacrament, death, and finally, resurrection.

A TRAGIC PASSOVER — 70 A.D.

I mentioned above that 256,500 lambs were sacrificed at the time of Cestius. Cestius reported to Nero in Rome. It was Passover, 70 A.D., and Titus was closing in on Jerusalem. Josephus says Roman troops had already annihilated over one million Jews elsewhere in the country.[14] The work of destruction and dispersion was entering its final phase. To add to the confusion and danger, groups of Jewish zealots contended with one another. Pilgrims trying to offer sacrifice at the temple were caught in the crossfire. Then Titus laid siege to Jerusalem, trapping over two million pilgrims and citizens inside the tiny city:

> "Now this vast multitude is indeed collected out of the remote places, but the entire nation was now shut up by fate as in a prison, and the Roman army encompassed the city when it was crowded with inhabitants. Accordingly, the multitude of those that therein perished exceeded all the destructions that either men or God ever brought upon the world."
>
> Josephus, *Wars of the Jews*, VI, IX: 4.

PASSOVERS CELEBRATED IN PERIL

Since the dispersion, Jews have lived in peril through many centuries and in many societies. Passovers have been observed in utmost secret; discovery meant death or forced conversion. During the middle ages "blood libel" — the idea that Jews murdered Christian babies and used their blood to make unleavened bread — caused Jews brave enough to celebrate Passover at all, to serve chicken instead of lamb, the chicken bones looking less like human bones. In Israel many of our neighbors served chicken, and placed a chicken neck bone on the *seder plate*. (The use of chicken is also common because the temple has been destroyed and no lamb can be sacrificed. Beef is avoided, because cows are sacrificial animals, as well as objects of pagan worship.)

During World War II, Jews trapped in the Warsaw ghetto managed a bit of egg and cracker for their Passover meals. Rations were indeed meager, but a special spirit imbued the ritual. The Passover means even more when celebrated in captivity, poverty, or danger. By bringing to mind the miraculous deliverance from Egypt, it provides a renewal of faith in the possibility of freedom and safety.

After the temple was destroyed, the Passover became more than ever a holiday centered in the home. Since there can be no sacrificial lamb (the Falashas in Africa and Samaritans still perform the sacrifice, while mainstream Jews wait for the temple to be rebuilt), the *afikomon* becomes even more important. Inherent in the ceremony is the plea for all mankind to enjoy peace and freedom.

PASSOVER PREPARATIONS

As Passover approaches, "Spring cleaning" begins. After living in Israel for so long, I became convinced that spring cleaning must have originated with the Jews. In every home a flurry of preparation begins. Furniture is piled out in front of the house, as the plastered walls receive a new coat of whitewash. Carpets, which warmed the cold tile floors during the winter, are cleaned, rolled up, and put away. Every inch of the house is cleansed, and any food product that contains leaven is taken from the house, save for a few crumbs of bread to be searched out as part of the ritual preparations. If the household cannot afford a separate set of dishes for Passover, the every-day china dishes are boiled. Shopping is done, guests invited, family gathered. Hotels offer first and second night *seder* meals, trying their best (and succeeding) to be gourmet in spite of so many dietary restrictions. The sacred week begins with a high Sabbath, and leavening "disappears" from the entire country. In the supermarkets, unacceptable foods are either banished from the shelves or covered over with butcher paper, so they cannot be touched. On the butcher paper are little notices

— "Forbidden, not kosher for Passover!"[15]

In a Jewish home the first family ritual occurs the evening before the first *seder* meal. The family searches the house by candlelight for any traces of leaven. Mother and Father know that leaven will be found, since Mother has deliberately left those few crumbs of bread in an otherwise thoroughly cleansed house. The search for leaven is led by the father, who carries a wooden spoon in one hand and a few feathers in the other. He uses the feathers to sweep the crumbs into the spoon. He also recites a prayer for the occasion. He wraps the spoon and its contents in a piece of paper tied with cord and burns the entire package at the synagogue the next morning. At the end of the search and again at the end of the ritual at the synagogue, the following verse is recited: "Any kind of leaven in my possession which has escaped my notice, and which I have not removed, shall be regarded as non-existent or as mere dust of the earth."

Leavening can be defined as anything that ferments, rises, or causes to rise. Damp flour will ferment and rise on its own, even without added leavening. That's why *matzah* crackers are ground into meal for Passover cakes and cookies. Once flour has been baked, it won't rise again. Baking powder and soda are leavenings. Traditional American gelatin is suspect at any time of the year, because it has typically been made from hooves of pigs and horses. *Ashkenazic* and *Sephardic* Jews differ in their opinion of rice and legumes. (When damp, do they rot or ferment?) In Jewish shops, foods marked "kosher for Passover" have a special Rabbinical stamp on them, meaning they have been prepared and processed under strict Rabbinical supervision. Even matzah crackers might not be kosher for Passover; they must be prepared within eighteen minutes to prevent them from rising, and the process must be supervised and certified.

To the basic Passover ritual already in place at the time of Christ have been added recreational songs, prayers for Jews and oppressed people worldwide, and prayers and wishes for the gathering of the Jewish people, the safety of Israel, the building up of Jerusalem as a holy city, and the coming of the Messiah. Some families, especially the very orthodox, go to great length in retelling Jewish history from Abraham through the present. Stories about great rabbis are told, as well. The evening feast and ritual can go on for many hours. A Passover seder combines learning, fun, and religious observance.

SAVING PRINCIPLES ARE TAUGHT BY THE FEAST

Thus, the Passover teaches us of the saving power of God. As it recalls the physical deliverance from slavery and the worldly culture of Egypt, it reminds us that we can be delivered spiritually, as well. We can be delivered from the chains of sin, out of the world, into grace. As we wander the wilderness in search of the promised land, we can be upheld by God's outstretched arm. We can be protected, nurtured, taught, and healed.

As the Passover speaks of deliverance and redemption, it also predicts exact events. Jesus, our Savior, would be born in a stable at the Passover season and become the Lamb of God. He would be the Only Begotten of the Father. He would become the great, atoning sacrifice, pure and undefiled. He would be pierced and striped, and crucified. He would be buried, but he would rise again. The sacramental bread would become a symbol of his flesh. The sacramental wine would become a symbol of the blood he shed for us. And what about the cup of wine that Jesus declined to drink? He promised his apostles that he would not drink of the fruit of the vine until he would drink it new in the kingdom of God, when it is established on the earth (Luke 22:15-20, Matthew 26:27-29). The exact event that Jesus was pointing to at the Last Supper is described in the Doctrine and Covenants. The event is still future:

> "Behold, this is wisdom in me, wherefore, marvel not, for the hour cometh that I will drink of the fruit of the vine with you on the earth, and with Moroni, whom I have sent unto you to reveal the Book of Mormon, containing the fulness of my everlasting gospel, to whom I have committed the keys of the record of the stick of Ephraim.
>
> "And also with Elias, to whom I have committed the keys of bringing to pass the restoration of all things spoken by the mouth of all the holy prophets since the world began, concerning the last days.
>
> "And also John the son of Zacharias, which Zacharias he (Elias) visited and gave promise that he should have a son, and his name should be John, and he should be filled with the spirit of Elias;

"Which John I have sent unto you, my servants, Joseph Smith, Jun., and Oliver Cowdery, to ordain you unto the first priesthood which you have received, that you might be called and ordained even as Aaron;

"And also Elijah, unto whom I have committed the keys of the power of turning the hearts of the fathers to the children, and the hearts of the children to the fathers, that the whole earth may not be smitten with a curse;

"And also with Joseph and Jacob, and Isaac, and Abraham, your fathers, by whom the promises remain;

"And also with Michael, or Adam, the father of all, the prince of all, the ancient of days;

"And also with Peter, and James, and John, whom I have sent unto you, by whom I have ordained you and confirmed you to be apostles, and especial witnesses of my name, and bear the keys of your ministry and of the same things which I have revealed unto them;

"Unto whom I have committed the keys of my kingdom, and a dispensation of the gospel for the last times, and for the fulness of times, in the which **I will gather together in one all things, both which are in heaven, and which are on the earth;**

"And also with all those whom my Father hath given me out of the world."

D&C 27:5-14 *(emphasis added)*

This fulfillment of events predicted during the Last Supper will be a pilgrimage feast and a great sacrament service that **we** could qualify to attend.

ELIJAH AND THE PASSOVER

And what about Elijah? Since he ascended into heaven, Israel has awaited his return.[16] Their traditions have told them that the Messiah would follow Elijah so closely, that it would be as if the Messiah were clinging to Elijah's cloak. This part of the Passover ritual would also be fulfilled by an exact event. During Passover (on the festival of *Bikkurim*), on April 3, 1836, the Prophet Joseph Smith and Oliver Cowdery received the following vision in the Kirtland Temple:

". . . another great and glorious vision burst upon us; for Elijah the prophet, who was taken to heaven without tasting death, stood before us, and said:

"Behold, the time has fully come, which was spoken of by the mouth of Malachi — testifying that he (Elijah) should be sent, before the great and dreadful day of the Lord come — . . . .

"Therefore, the keys of this dispensation are committed into your hands; and by this ye may know that the great and dreadful day of the Lord is near, even at the doors."

D&C 110:13-14, 16

SYMBOLS ESTABLISHED BY GOD

The Lord originally established this imagery in order to prepare the Children of Israel to recognize and receive Him. He has fulfilled the symbols he created by saving us temporally and spiritually. He has used these symbols to prophesy of exact events. He was born at Passover; He died on Passover; He was the Passover. In truth, then, a celebration of the Passover encompasses both Christmas and Easter, with a complete dedication to things spiritual — the material world has never been allowed to intrude upon this holiday. Its rich messianic images, shared in an atmosphere of familial togetherness and rejoicing, can be a special blessing to Latter-day Saints.

CHAPTER 8 ENDNOTES

[1] Brandt, "The Priesthood Ordinance of Sacrifice" *The Ensign,* December 1973.

[2] Birnbaum, *Encyclopedia of Jewish Concepts,* 146.

[3] Birnbaum, 270.

[4] The Midrash says 80% of the Israelites stayed behind in Egypt.

[5] Birnbaum, 75.

[6] Women could attend, but were not required to do so, because their duties at home were important and unpredictable.

[7] Josephus, *Wars of the Jews,* VI, IX:3.

[8] The "stable" where Jesus was born would not have been a wooden structure, but a hollow in the natural limestone of the hills.

[9] Edersheim, *Life and Times...,* 559.

[10] The rabbis have tried to determine the symbolism of the three *matzot*. The strongest tradition suggests that they represent (in descending order) the Priests, the Levites, and the Israelites. Another tradition suggests that they represent Abraham, Isaac, and Jacob, the Three Patriarchs. If the three matzot represent the levels of priesthood, then the middle matzo would represent the Levite. During the Exodus, the Levites were chosen to represent God's firstborn; sacrifice is a Levitical ordinance (under the supervision of the High Priest). Jesus performed a Levitical ordinance when he offered himself as the ultimate sacrifice for our sins. If the three matzot were to represent the Godhead, then God the Father would be the top piece of unleavened bread, Christ would be the middle piece, and the Holy Ghost would be the bottom piece. How fitting that the middle matzo should be pierced, striped, wrapped in linen and hidden away (buried), then resurrected at the offering of the third cup of wine in the Passover ceremony (the third day). Then the bread is blessed and passed as a representation of the Lamb, thus becoming the sacramental bread.

[11] Lingle, "The Timing of Pesakh."

[12] Edersheim, *Life and Times...,* 553.

[13] See also "On What Day Was Christ Crucified?," Elder Charles F. Watkins, *Improvement Era,* 1899.

[14] Josephus, *Wars of the Jews,* Book VI, Chapter IX, section 3.

[15] A week is a long time to go without one's favorite foods. Not only the leavened foods were stripped from the shelves or covered up, but any food not labeled "Kosher for Passover" by a supervising rabbi. When we lived in Israel, I would stock up on forbidden foods just before the holiday (pretzels, bread, chips, etc.), hoping they would last us through the week. One year, however, I ran out

of canned cat food in the middle of the week. I knew in my heart of hearts that no rabbi would spend his time certifying cat food, and that no pet food company would hire a rabbi to do so. I practiced a few phrases of Hebrew and set out for the supermarket. As I had expected, the cat food was nowhere to be found. I approached the manager, and in my practiced Hebrew said, "There's no cat food."

"It's not kosher for Passover," he replied. "But. . . my cat's a Christian."

The manager laughed heartily and went dutifully down into the basement to fetch some food for my "Christian" cat.

[16] Elijah (also called Elias) was on the minds of the people when Jesus and John the Baptist were teaching. There were many incidents recorded in the Gospels when people thought Jesus or John the Baptist might have been Elijah (Matthew 16:14; Mark 8:28; Luke 9:19; Mark 6:15; Luke 9:8; John 1:21). They were already looking for his return, as well as the coming of the Messiah.

CHAPTER 8: *BIKKURIM* (THE FEAST OF FIRST FRUITS)

A few days after Passover begins, another symbolic Jewish holiday occurs. It is called *Bikkurim*, First Fruits. The word *Bikkurim* derives from the word *bekhor*, which means "first-born son." *Bikkurim* is currently celebrated on the 16th of Nisan, which now is the second day of Passover week. But originally the commandment was to celebrate it on the day after the first Sabbath occurring during Passover Leviticus 23:11). The rabbis have debated this one: Which Sabbath? — the first day of Passover is a high Sabbath, but then the regular Sabbath occurs during the week of the feast. The rabbis settled on celebrating the day on the sixteenth. Now that Passover and the Feast of Unleavened Bread have been combined into a seven-day holiday, the sixteenth is the day after the high Sabbath beginning the holiday week. But what happened the year of Christ's crucifixion? Jesus was crucified on Thursday. The regular Jewish Sabbath was Saturday. He rose the day after that Sabbath (on Sunday, the third day) and became the First Fruits of the resurrection. Therefore, Jesus rose as the first fruits were commanded to be offered — the day after the first regular Sabbath during Passover week.

Passover occurs when the first barley harvest of the season is brought in. Yet while the Temple stood and offerings could be made, the flour baked in haste to make matzah was from the past year's harvest of grain. No new grain could be used until the First Fruits offering had been made. Thus, this offering opens the door to the harvest. This is the offering of the first perfect sheaves of barley. The offering of the sheaf guarantees a bounteous future harvest for the rest of the year. Christ, the First Fruits of the resurrection, guarantees that all of us will be resurrected, perfectly restored both body and spirit:

"For I delivered unto you first of all that which I also received, how that Christ died for our sins according to the scriptures;

"And that he was buried, and that he rose the third day according to the scriptures. . . .

"But now is Christ risen from the dead, and become the firstfruits of them that slept."

1 Corinthians 15:3-4, 20

THE SIGNIFICANCE OF "FIRST THINGS"

In setting up types and symbols, the Lord has emphasized the importance of "first things." The Israelites knew that all "first things" belong to the Lord:

> The first fruits of all major crops (barley, wheat, grapes, figs, pomegranates, olives, dates — called the "seven species" in Deuteronomy 8:7-8)
>
> All first bread dough (the heave offering). All first-born animals.
>
> All Israelites (since they covenanted to act as the "firstborn of mankind").
>
> The Levites, who were considered the firstborn among the Israelites; they inherited no land in Canaan, but were assigned to administer priestly duties.
>
> Every first-born son of Israelite families.

It is true that first-born sons in Jewish families rarely devote their efforts full-time to the Lord's service. They participate even now as infants in an ordinance made to acknowledge their role as the first fruits from the womb, and to absolve them of the responsibility of serving. This ordinance is called the *Pidyon HaBen* — the "redemption of the son." Anciently, at one month of age, all first sons except Levites were presented at the Temple, redeemed, and released from lifetime service to the Lord.[1] The presentation of the first born of Mary and Joseph, then, was somewhat ironic:

> "And when the days of her purification according to the law of Moses were accomplished, they brought him to Jerusalem, to present him to the Lord;
>
> "(As it is written in the Law of the Lord, Every male that openeth the womb shall be called holy to the Lord;)

"And to offer a sacrifice according to that which is said in the law of the Lord, A pair of turtledoves, or two young pigeons."

Luke 2:22-24

Mary and Joseph kept the religious law by presenting the infant Jesus to be redeemed from lifetime service, yet His lifetime service redeemed us! The apostles and Book of Mormon prophets have called us, the followers of Christ, the First Fruits of Mankind through the Spirit:

"Wherefore, beloved brethren, be reconciled unto him through the atonement of Christ, his Only Begotten Son, and ye may obtain a resurrection, according to the power of the resurrection which is in Christ, **and be presented as the first-fruits of Christ unto God**, having faith, and obtained a good hope of glory in him before he manifesteth himself in the flesh."

Jacob 4:11 (emphasis added)

At the end of the last days, when Zion has been established and the wicked are groaning under the weight of pestilence and war, the Lord will call up and anoint 144,000 high priests for one last foray into the world to do missionary work. These men will be the very elect, sealed, protected from the extreme danger and wickedness of the world of that future day. They are also called first fruits:

"These are they which were not defiled with women; for they are virgins. These are they which follow the Lamb whithersoever he goeth. These were redeemed from among men, being the firstfruits unto God and to the Lamb."

Revelation 14:4

A PERFECT OFFERING

In order to insure the perfection of the priest's first fruits offering, the grain for the offering was not gleaned from the fields of the land. Instead, a special field of barley was grown under the supervision of the *Sanhedrin*, the Jewish senate.

The field was close to the Temple in Jerusalem. Seeds were sown in winter, during the former rains. The field was never watered by hand, nor was it fertilized by the hand of any farmer. The field would be watered only by the natural rains. (Jesus himself grew up this way, nurtured by the Spirit, waxing strong in grace and truth without needing to be taught by man.) On *Bikkurim* a three-man harvesting team chosen from among the Sanhedrin came down from the Temple to reap pre-chosen bundles of barley. A crowd would watch the harvesting.

It was a joyous occasion, and the priests would ask rhetorical questions of the crowd to guide them through the harvesting. Thus, common consent became part of the harvesting process. The pattern of this ritual resonates in the nature of Christ's mission to become the first fruits of the resurrection. Before we came to this earth, when we were all spirit children dwelling with our Father in heaven, Jesus was pre-chosen to be the first fruits of the resurrection, and we consented to his mission. His perfect offering guaranteed a perfect future harvest — the resurrection of us all.

The priests would harvest one "ephah" of barley — about two-thirds bushel. The grain would then be taken to the Temple and threshed in the Temple court. The grain was threshed with rods rather than the usual ox-drawn sledges to keep from injuring the grain. The grain was then parched over an open flame, then winnowed to remove the chaff. It was then milled and sifted very fine. Then it was presented to the Lord.

For the presentation to the Lord, one *omer* (about five pints) of barley flour was mixed with three-fourths pint of olive oil. A small amount of frankincense (fragrant resin) was sprinkled on top. The priest waved the offering before the Lord, burned a small amount on the altar, and then gave the rest to the Levites.[2]

While this special first-fruits offering was made by the priests, each family was to bring its offering also. Before the Passover pilgrimage, each family would glean barley from the family field. As the barley ripened, the family would do as the priests would do — that is, tie the chosen sheaves with cords <u>to set them apart</u>, and to keep them protected, just as the Lord would protect the Savior until it was his time to be offered up. The grain was then harvested and taken along on the pilgrimage to Jerusalem:

> "And now, behold, I have brought the firstfruits of the land, which thou, O Lord, hast given me, And thou shalt set it before the Lord the God, and worship before the Lord thy God."
>
> Deuteronomy. 26:10

JESUS AS THE FIRST FRUITS

This is the same pattern that Christ followed, when He made His last pilgrimage to the Holy City. He knew He would be offered up; He was set apart, bound by His covenant with the father. As the grain offering would be waved before the Lord by the priest, Jesus would rise from the grave, the First Fruits of the resurrection. When Christ rose from the grave on this day, the Elect followed him. The Elect were harvested from the far fields of the land. The Bible says that they "appeared unto many" in their risen state.

As the offering of grain on *Bikkurim* guaranteed a perfect harvest for the rest of the year; as the offering of the Savior guaranteed a perfect harvest for the Lord, since all of us will be resurrected; so Elijah's coming—with the restoration of the sealing power—would guarantee a perfect harvest of sealed families for the Lord. Therefore, it is fitting that Elijah restored the sealing keys to Joseph Smith on *Bikkurim*. The Lord again exactly fulfilled the imagery of his ordained Holy Day.

The sheaf of grain, called a "wave offering," was called in Hebrew, the *Omer*. Since the destruction of the Temple, such offerings have ceased, and nowadays the holiday of *Bikkurim* is hardly noticed. However, this day is the beginning of the "counting of the Omer," called *Sefirat Ha'Omer*. This is the beginning of counting seven times seven weeks, as commanded, until the Feast of Weeks, *Shavuot*, which is held on the fiftieth day.

At the end of the Passover week, and after *Bikkurim*, there is another special day. This, the seventh day of the Feast of Unleavened Bread, is another high Sabbath, concluding with the "Feast of Messiah" — a festive meal complete with matzah and four cups of wine. The festivity is designed to greet the Messiah and to offer a glimpse of the Messianic age. Sephardic Jews celebrate "Mimouna" at this time, enjoying family parties with sweets for all.

CHAPTER 9 ENDNOTES

[1] Howard, *Feasts of the Lord,* 84.
[2] Howard, 78-79.

CHAPTER 9:
COUNTING THE OMER

This forty-nine day countdown to the Feast of Weeks (from *Bikkurim*) is very important, both temporally and spiritually. This is the reaping season which began with the first barley harvest at Passover. The countdown takes place during a season of agricultural insecurity. Breezes usually blow from the west in

Israel, coming rain-laden or refreshing from the Mediterranean Sea. About fifty days a year the winds change direction, coming from the east.[1] Winds from the east are hot and dry and can disrupt the growing period and the harvest. Therefore, the days of the *omer* are counted in trepidation.

Earlier, I mentioned the importance of numbers and numerology in Judaism. The *omer* is counted for seven-times-seven weeks, or forty-nine days.

> "The forty-nine days of the Omer period correspond to the forty-nine gates of repentance, and these in turn correspond to the forty-nine letters in the Hebrew names of the twelve tribes. It is through these letters and gates that we must make our return to God Almighty. The festival of *Shavuot* is the fiftieth gate. This is the gateway of God's >repentance,' when God himself returns, as it were. That is to say, He returns to us in love. . . . During the forty-nine days of the counting of the Omer we have to cleanse ourselves of our impurity and return to God. Then God will return to us on *Shavuot*."[2]

The concept of gates differs from the concept of a straight and narrow path, in that the children of God wander from gate to gate, rather than following a straight path. This certainly seems true to life, as we reach milestones (or gates) in our quest for truth and worthiness, yet we all seem to have to blaze a trail of our own. We wander. But the path becomes straighter and narrower the closer one gets to true enlightenment, the closer one draws unto God himself:

> "For strait is the gate, and narrow the way that leadeth unto the exaltation and continuation of the lives, and few there be that find it, because ye receive me not in the world neither do ye know me.
>
> "But if ye receive me in the world, then shall ye know me, and shall receive your exaltation; that where I am ye shall be also.
>
> "This is eternal lives — to know the only wise and true God, and Jesus Christ, whom he hath sent. I am he. Receive ye, therefore, my law."
>
> D&C 132:22-24

This counsel and plea from the Doctrine and Covenants contains a favorite Jewish word, "law." As we proceed through the wilderness, we hopefully learn lessons and pass checkpoints (or gates) of spiritual progress. As we become more and more enlightened, more familiar with the ways of the Lord, we seem to perceive new laws of behavior and righteousness, more exacting and demanding than those we have already mastered. Thus, the directive, "Receive ye, therefore, my law," is a continuing. eternal process, leading to wholeness.

As the *omer* is counted in trepidation, so we climb in trepidation from ignorance to spiritual enlightenment. So the Israelites wandered from Egypt (worldliness) to Mount Sinai, where they received the great spiritual gift of the *torah*. The six hundred thirteen commandments contained therein would shape them into God's people determined to draw nigh unto the Lord.

At the festival of *Shavuot*, or Feast of Weeks, Jews go through a ritual immersion in living water, called a *mikveh*. This is similar to our baptism, but is for periodic cleansing after times of uncleanness, as well as initiation into the faith. We are baptized once, but ritual immersion is repeated whenever necessary. *Shavuot* is the culmination of a period of rededication that began with the Passover, or the trek into the wilderness. At the moment of immersion, one is connected with the "highest levels of God's loving kindness and abundant mercy, and [one can] attain awesome levels of perception of God." *Shavuot* is the attainment of illumination, the "wellspring of holiness and purity for Israel."[3]

Rabbi Akiva was the greatest Torah sage of his generation. During Rabbi Akiva's lifetime twenty-four thousand of his disciples died in a terrible epidemic. It is believed they were being punished for their lack of respect for each other. This epidemic occurred during the counting of the Omer. As a result, the counting of the Omer has been imbued with even greater trepidation. The period has become one of semi-mourning. Very orthodox Jews do not hold weddings or festivities during this period. And some do not shave or receive haircuts. However, history records that on the thirty-third day of the Omer, the epidemic was suspended. The day has become a joyous holiday. One of Rabbi Akiva's later students was Rabbi Shimon bar Yochai, who wrote the *Zohar*, meaning "The Shining Light." The Zohar is a mystical writing which illuminates the secret teachings of the *Torah*. In Israel bonfires are lit in every neighborhood, in honor of this great rabbi and the relief from the plague, and potatoes and onions are roasted in the flames. Neighbors enjoy the mild weather of the season, as they gather around the bonfires. The holiday is called *Lag B'omer*, literally the thirty-third of the Omer. (Haircuts may be given on *Lag B'omer*, and three-year old Orthodox Jewish boys receive their very first haircut on that day.)[4]

A TIME OF TREPIDATION

Remember that Christ was killed on the Passover, and rose on *Bikkurim*. As Israel was counting the Omer until the Feast of Weeks, the followers of Christ went through a period of intense danger and trepidation. The period began in confusion. The apostles were shocked, dismayed, and terrorized by Jesus' crucifixion and did not yet fully understand resurrection. Many followers had scattered to protect themselves from those wicked priests of the Sanhedrin and from the Roman authorities. They were taught and encouraged by the Savior Himself, but they had not yet received the permanent comforter, the Holy Ghost. They had not yet come together as a church. As the Jewish holidays mark exact events with significance to us as Christians, the counting of the Omer marks this period of wandering and defining.

The counting of the *Omer* has significance for us in its symbolism. As Passover and *Bikkurim* symbolize the birth, mission, death and resurrection of the Savior, this knowledge brings us to a desire to repent. The repentance process is a wilderness process. We wander whithersoever it is necessary to leave the world behind and find the mount where the Lord is. There, we are immersed, baptized, and enter the gate beyond which lies the path to the kingdom. When we are baptized, we are accepted into the fold of the believers, God's church, and we then qualify for enlightenment through the permanent gift of the Holy Ghost, which gift is represented in the symbolism of the Festival of Shavuot.

CHAPTER 10 ENDNOTES

[1] Winds from the east are called *khamsin* (for "fifty" — the number of days they can be expected each year — or *sharav*). During *khamsin* in Jerusalem, the normally cool nights are sultry, and the weather brings on depression. Sensitive people are cautioned to stay indoors. The sky looks smoggy, but is actually sand laden, and one must clean the grit out of one's nostrils once in a while.

[2] Breslov Research Institute, "Counting the Omer...," www.breslov.org, April 2001.

[3] Ibid.

[4] Rabbi Moshe Newman, ed., Ohr Somayach International, "What is *Lag B'omer?*." http://ohr.edu, 1998.

CHAPTER 10:
SHAVUOT (THE FEAST OF WEEKS)

The forty-nine days of the *Omer* have now been counted in trepidation. The harvest has gone well. The land has offered up its fruits — barley, wheat, dates, grapes, figs, olives, and pomegranates, called the "Seven Species." The first wheat harvest is at hand, and it is time to make another pilgrimage to Jerusalem and the Temple. This is the Feast of Weeks, a First Fruits festival. (The New Testament calls the holiday "Pentecost," a derivative of the Greek word meaning "fifty," because *Shavuot* is the fiftieth day after Passover.) While we make an offering of wheat and the Seven Species, we pray for the Lord to pour out His spirit upon us. This He did for our ancestors: The Passover season had reached its conclusion, they had wandered through the wilderness to Sinai, and there the Lord was waiting to bless them.

The Jews believe that the event at Sinai was their greatest gift, for this was the giving of the *Torah*, what we call the Law of Moses. This was a **blessing of law and spirit**. Rabbis say that Passover was a rebirth for the Israelites in that they traded the yoke of Egypt for the yoke of the Lord, and that *Shavuot*, The Feast of Weeks, was the birth of the nation:

> "In the third month, when the children of Israel were gone forth out of the land of Egypt, the same day came they into the wilderness of Sinai. . .
>
> ". . . and there Israel camped before the mount.
>
> "And Moses went up unto God, and the Lord called unto him out of the mountain, saying, Thus shalt thou say to the house of Jacob, and tell the children of Israel;
>
> "Ye have seen what I did unto the Egyptians, and how I bare you on eagles' wings, and brought you unto myself.

"Now, therefore, if ye will obey my voice indeed, and keep my covenant, then ye shall be a peculiar treasure unto me above all people: for all the earth is mine:

"And ye shall be unto me a kingdom of priests, and an holy nation."

Exodus 19:1-6

A FESTIVAL OF REJOICING

When the Children of Israel obtained the Promised Land and built a Temple in Jerusalem, they made Shavuot a most colorful festival. After pouring into Jerusalem from near and far, they paraded to the Temple in joyous processions. Oxen, with boughs and flowers woven into their horns, would be at the head. The people would follow, carrying elaborately decorated baskets full of the first fruits of the land. One offering at the Temple would be from the first fruits of the wheat harvest. But since this is a feast of fulfillment, the wheat was baked into bread, the full finished product of leavened loaves. Two long, flat loaves of wheat bread were taken to the priests. Because of the leavening, they were not burned upon the altar, but were eaten by the priests.

The bringing of the First Fruits of the land to the Temple symbolizes to us the offering we make of ourselves, as the first fruits of God's children, a covenant people, ready to hear and obey. We add to the Father's glory when we bring forth good fruit. Thus, we are commanded to be joyful on this day, as we are a holy nation.

PENTACOST AND THE GIFT OF THE HOLY GHOST

What is the exact event prophesied by the Feast? It is found in Acts:

"And when the day of Pentecost was fully come, they were all with one accord in one place." (In Jerusalem for the Shavuot festival, fifty days after Christ rose from the dead.)

"And suddenly there came a sound from heaven as of a rushing mighty wind, and it filled all the house where they were sitting.

"And there appeared unto them cloven tongues like as of fire, and it sat upon each one of them.

"And they were filled with the Holy Ghost, and began to speak with other tongues, as the Spirit gave them utterance.

"And there were dwelling at Jerusalem Jews, devout men, out of every nation under heaven.

"Now when this was noised abroad, the multitude came together, and were confounded, because that every man heard them speak in his own language.

"And they were all amazed and marveled, saying one to another, Behold, are not all these which speak Galileans?. . .

"But Peter, standing up with the eleven, lifted up his voice, and said unto them, Ye men of Judea, and all ye that dwell at Jerusalem, be this known unto you, and hearken to my words:

". . . this is that which was spoken by the prophet Joel;

"And it shall come to pass in the last days, saith God, I will pour out of my Spirit upon all flesh: and your sons and your daughters shall prophesy, and your young men shall see visions, and your old men shall dream dreams."

Acts 2:1-7, 14, 16-17 *(parenthetical comments added)*

Peter goes on to bear testimony of Christ who was crucified and resurrected. As a result, three thousand souls entered the waters of baptism. Thus, as Israel was born a holy nation on *Shavuot*, the First Fruits unto God, so the Lord's Church was born on this day with the Gift of the Holy Ghost, the First Fruits unto God <u>in Christ</u>.

SHAVUOT TODAY

Today, *Shavuot* is a one-day holiday in Israel and two days in the diaspora. It is a Sabbath, so no work can be done. However, it differs from a normal Sabbath in that cooking and baking, transferring of fire, and carrying can be accomplished. If *Shavuot* falls on a regular Sabbath, then the normal prohibitions against cooking and other work take effect.[1] The fruits of the land are a huge part of the *Shavuot* holiday. Two loaves of *challah* are on every family's table, representing the two loaves offered in the Temple. Dairy foods are eaten on this day — blintzes, cheesecakes, cheese "kreplach." Fruit salads and dried fruit are served, and the little girls wear wreaths of flowers in their hair.[2] It is traditional to decorate homes and synagogues with flowers, tree boughs, and greens for the holiday — The sages taught that the trees of the land are judged by God on Shavuot.[3]

Tradition holds that on the morning Israel was to present itself at Sinai before the Lord, the people overslept. Therefore, the custom is to stay up all night and study the *Torah* on the first night of *Shavuot*. In some congregations, Rabbis lecture deep into the night. On the second night of

Shavuot the Book of Ruth is read before studying the Torah. The Book of Ruth takes place during the harvest season. Boaz was righteous and left the corners of his field unharvested for the poor to glean the leftovers. This is a story of conversion, of family loyalty, and of loving kindness. True to the spiritual meaning of *Shavuot*, we share the bounties of the land (and of the gospel) with the less fortunate. The Book of Ruth also gives the lineage of David, who ruled Israel at its greatest, thus emphasizing nationhood.

WORD AND SPIRIT — THE BLESSINGS OF ZION

The combination of spiritual outpouring and nationhood resonates in the giving of the Torah at Mount Sinai, and the bestowal of the Holy Ghost fifty days after Jesus rose from the dead. The images also resonate into the future. In the Last Days, Zion will be established. The Holy Spirit will fill the hearts of its inhabitants, creating harmony. During the millennial reign of Jesus Christ, two great capitals, Old and New Jerusalem, will be the seats of his power. The law, of which the *Torah* scripture is the type, will proceed forth from the mountains of Jerusalem, of which Sinai is the type. The righteous of Judah and other tribes will have already gathered there, the first-fruits of Israel. The Word, of which the outpouring of spirit is the type, will proceed forth from the Mountain of the Lord's house in New Jerusalem. The righteous will have already made pilgrimage there, a gathering of the first-fruits of the Church and those who have sought Zion's protection. Governing all will be Christ himself, the promised descendant of David.

CHAPTER 10 ENDNOTES

[1] The basis for judging whether a task is proper for Sabbath, is that nothing can be done that is similar to tasks undertaken for building the Temple. Only holy objects can be carried. No fire can be kindled, including an electric light, heating element, or gas flame. Therefore, a stove cannot be lit. In Israel accommodations are made for observant Jews. Some apartment buildings have "Sabbath elevators." They run themselves on Sabbath and stop automatically at every floor. No one in the elevator has to push a button. Lights come on automatically as darkness falls. Observant Jews cook for Sabbath the day before, or slow-cook their food, so that the oven just has to be turned off on the Sabbath. Hotels in Israel serve only cold food on Sabbath.

[2] I struggled to comprehend these traditions at first. A note came home from the kindergarten (in Hebrew), and it looked to me like I was supposed to send a "dry, silly savage" to school with my child. My neighbor helped me translate more effectively — the children were bringing dried fruit for a first-fruits salad. The flower wreaths were even more problematic. It took me several Feast of Weeks holidays to get them right. My instructions are included in Appendix A in the Shavuot Family Home Evening — Gift of the Holy Ghost.

[3] The purpose in life for living things other than humans is to "fulfill the measure of their creation." Thus, Jesus cursed a "wicked" fig tree that bore leaves but no fruit (Matthew 21:19). Christ atoned not just for the sins of Mankind, but for all living creatures, plants included.

CHAPTER 11:
ROSH HASHANAH
(THE FEAST OF TRUMPETS)

Rosh HaShanah means "head of the year," or New Year. The name is recent, since about 200 A.D. The holiday is actually the Feast of Trumpets (*shofarot*). It is also called *zikhron teruach* — The Memorial of the Blowing of Trumpets. It occurs on the first day of the Jewish month of *Tishrei*, at the new moon. Not much is written in the scriptures about this holiday; most of the information regarding its traditional patterns of observance come from oral transmission. The commandment to keep the holiday is found in Leviticus, and it is referred to as a solemn but joyous time in the Psalms:

"And the Lord spake unto Moses, saying,

"Speak unto the children of Israel, saying, In the seventh month, in the first day of the month, shall ye have a sabbath, a memorial of blowing of trumpets, an holy convocation.

"Ye shall do no servile work therein: but ye shall offer an offering made by fire unto the Lord."

Leviticus 23:23-25

"Sing aloud unto God our strength: make a joyful noise unto the God of Jacob.

"Take a psalm, and bring hither the timbrel, the pleasant harp with the psaltery.

"Blow up the trumpet in the new moon, in the time appointed, on our solemn feast day.

"For this was a statute for Israel, and a law of the God of Jacob."

Psalm 81:1-4

Rosh HaShanah is considered the birthday of the world and of mankind. It begins the civil year. Legal documents dated in Jewish years are dated from Rosh HaShanah. It is the beginning of the year for counting sabbatical years of rest and jubilee years. (Jewish years date from the Creation of the World, and the Creation is celebrated on *Rosh HaShanah*.) It is also the "day of the Lord," when God's enemies are destroyed and the believers are saved. (See Isaiah, chapters 4 and 5.)

Rosh HaShanah has often been celebrated for two days because of the difficulties inherent in telling exactly when the new moon has appeared.[3] It was, however, a one-day celebration in Israel until the twelfth century, when French immigrants pushed others to follow their two-day traditional celebration. Ever since then, it has been a two-day holiday in Israel. At present, Reform Jews everywhere celebrate *Rosh HaShanah* for only one day. Since 300 A.D. the rabbis have forbidden the first day of the celebration to fall on Sunday, Wednesday, or Friday to keep the high holy day of *Yom Kippur* from falling on the day before or day after the Sabbath. This edict also keeps the last day of *Sukkot* (*Shemeni Atzeret*) from falling on a Sabbath.[4]

PREPARING FOR THE BRIDEGROOM

Rosh HaShanah is the first of three autumn holy convocations, the other two being *Yom Kippur* (the Day of Atonement), and *Sukkot* (The Feast of Tabernacles). While Passover, *Bikkurim*, Counting the *Omer*, and *Shavuot* (Feast of Weeks) celebrate the late rains and early harvests, testifying of the life, mission, sacrifice, and resurrection of Jesus Christ (his first coming), plus the later gift of the Holy Ghost, these latter holidays typify his atonement, judgment, and second coming. They occur as the former rains just begin, when the final harvests are gathered in. These latter feasts are full of wedding symbolisms — the marriage of Israel, the bride, to her eternally faithful husband, the Lord. For this marriage, the bride must be worthy; it is a sacramental marriage, an eternal covenant. Judgment is an important aspect of the symbolism. Remember the parable of the Ten Virgins? Imagine they were prepared during the spring holidays — they had received a witness of the divine mission of the Messiah, had made covenants, and had become part of the nation of believers. Their receiving of the Holy Spirit can be considered a mid-journey milestone in their wilderness experience and time of testing (symbolized by the Feast of Weeks). That is essentially when their lamps were lit. Their long wait into the night for the bridegroom can be associated with the rest of the wilderness period, which typifies our time of testing before the second coming, or our inheritance of heaven. Those who were prepared and kept their lamps lit with ample spiritual oil went in unto the bridegroom. The others were left out of the ceremony and the union, even though they had originally gotten off to a good start.

The month of *Elul* precedes the month of Tishrei, and it is a preparatory month for the holy convocations that lie ahead. Just as there are fifty days between Passover/Bikkurim (typifying the resurrection) and *Shavuot* (typifying the bestowal of the spirit and birth of the Church), there are fifty days between the first of *Elul* (the beginning of final preparations) and the end of the Feast of Tabernacles. Thus, the seven-times-seven symbolism repeats itself.

Elul is a word that is really an acrostic. It comes from the Bible, Solomon's Song of Songs: "I am my beloved's and my beloved is mine." During the Elul preparations, the twenty-seventh psalm is read in the synagogues:

> "**The Lord is my light and my salvation**; whom shall I fear? the Lord is the strength of my life; of whom shall I be afraid?
>
> "When the wicked, even mine enemies and my foes, came upon me to eat up my flesh, they stumbled and fell.
>
> "Though an host should encamp against me, my heart shall not fear: though war should rise against me, in this will I be confident.
>
> "One thing have I desired of the Lord, that will I seek after; that **I may dwell in the house of the Lord all the days of my life, to behold the beauty of the Lord, and to enquire in his Temple.**
>
> "For in the time of trouble he shall hide me in his pavilion: in the secret of his tabernacle shall he hide me; he shall set me up upon a rock.
>
> "And now shall mine head be lifted up above mine enemies round about me: therefore will I offer in his tabernacle sacrifices of joy; I will sing, yea, I will sing praises unto the Lord.
>
> "Hear, O Lord, when I cry with my voice: have mercy also upon me, and answer me.
>
> "When thou saidst, Seek ye my face; my heart said unto thee, Thy face, Lord, will I seek.
>
> "Hide not thy face far from me; put not thy servant away in anger: thou has been my help; leave me not neither forsake me, O God of my salvation.

"When my father and my mother forsake me, then the Lord will take me up.

"Teach me thy way, O Lord, and lead me in a plain path, because of mine enemies.

"Deliver me not over unto the will of mine enemies: for false witnesses are risen up against me, and such as breathe out cruelty.

"I had fainted, unless I had believed to see the goodness of the Lord in the **land of the living.**

"**Wait on the Lord**: be of good courage, and he shall strengthen thine heart: wait, I say, on the Lord."

Psalm 27 (emphasis added)

There are certain important themes which run through this psalm. It is called a Psalm of David, and therefore we tend to look at all the references to "enemies" as political. Certainly, the armies of Israel's enemies were a constant and dangerous threat. But the theme is light and salvation, and therefore, wickedness and the wiles of Satan are more to be feared. Inherent in the message is a plea for righteous judgment and qualification to be accepted into the Lord's kingdom. The author is willing to separate himself from his father and mother in order to qualify. This is the marriage process, when one leaves his parents and cleaves unto his spouse.

THE LAND OF THE LIVING

Notice near the end of the psalm, the reference to the "land of the living." This phrase is found in the Doctrine and Covenants:

". . .also in thy ministry in proclaiming the gospel in the land of the living, and among thy brethren."

D&C 81:3

The "land of the living" is the community of the saved. Salvation is not seen as the moment of judgment only, but as something to be attained and qualified for on a daily basis. Therefore, "waiting on the Lord" connotes not just an act of patience, but a process of service and constant repentance. Remember that all ten virgins in the parable were qualified to begin with, and they were all patient, still waiting when the bridegroom finally arrived; but five failed to continue in worthiness until that judgment day. Brigham Young addressed the concept of continual salvation:

> "It is present salvation and the present influence of the Holy Ghost that we need every day to keep us on saving ground. When an individual refuses to comply with the further requirements of Heaven, then the sins he had formerly committed return upon his head; his former righteousness departs from him, and is not accounted to him for righteousness: but if he had continued in righteousness and obedience to the requirements of heaven, **he is saved all the time**, through baptism, the laying on of hands, and obeying the commandments of the Lord and all that is required of him by the heavens — the living oracles. He is saved now, next week, next year, and continually, and is prepared for the celestial kingdom of God whenever the time comes for him to inherit it."
>
> *Journal of Discourses*, 8:124 (emphasis added)

During the month of *Elul*, the month of preparation, there is a recitation of the *selihot*, the divine attributes of God — "The Lord, the Lord, God, merciful and gracious, long-suffering, and abundant in goodness and truth; keeping mercy unto the thousandth generation, forgiving iniquity and transgression and sin; and acquitting."[1] These qualities are saving qualities to be emulated by mankind in preparation for judgment. Achieving these qualities in ourselves reconciles us to God.

AWAKE, AND ARISE

For many, this is a time of reawakening. Often in the scriptures we are commanded to awake and arise, to remember the Lord and follow his paths:

> "Hearken unto me, ye that follow after righteousness, ye that seek the Lord: look unto the rock whence ye are hewn, and to the hole of the pit whence ye are digged.
>
> "Hearken unto me, my people; and give ear unto me, O my nation: for a law shall proceed from me, and I will make my judgment to rest for a light of the people.
>
> "My righteousness is near; my salvation is gone forth, and mine arms shall judge the people; the isles shall wait upon me, and on mine arm shall they trust.

"Hearken unto me, ye that know righteousness, the people in whose heart is my law; fear ye not the reproach of men, neither be ye afraid of their revilings.

"**Awake, awake**, put on strength, O arm of the Lord; awake, as in the ancient days, in the generations of old...."

Isaiah 51:1, 4-5, 7, 9 (emphasis added)

The Feast of Trumpets was designed and designated to awaken men to repentance and gather them into the "land of the living." The signal for men to awake, arise, and gather was sounded by blowing the *shofar* against the background heralds from the silver trumpets of over one hundred priests. The shofar is a ram's horn that is chosen and finished to fit certain criteria. It is reminiscent of the ram provided as a substitute for Isaac when Abraham was about to offer him as a sacrifice. It actually can be the horn of any kosher animal, except the ox or the cow (which hearken back to Egyptian deities). The horn must be curved, the curve symbolizing a bent will. It must have no impairment of sound. It must have no split or hole. This horn is notoriously difficult to blow, especially repeatedly. Nonetheless, it is blown repeatedly in a certain pattern of blasts after each morning service, and after the reading of Psalm 47:

"O clap your hands, all ye people; shout unto God with the voice of triumph.

> "For the Lord most high is terrible; he is a great King over all the earth.] "He shall subdue the people under us, and the nations under our feet.'
>
> "He shall choose our inheritance for us, the excellency of Jacob whom he loved. Selah.
>
> "**God is gone up with a shout, the Lord with the sound of a trumpet**.
>
> "Sing praises unto God, sing praises: sing praises unto our King, sing praises.
>
> "For God is the King of all the earth: sing ye praises with understanding.
>
> "God reigneth over the heathen: God sitteth upon the throne of his holiness.
>
> "The princes of the people are gathered together, even the people of the God of Abraham: for the shields of the earth belong to God: he is greatly exalted."

After the destruction of the Temple in 70 A.D., the blowing of the shofar was continued. However, when the Sanhedrin was finally dissolved, so that there was no temple and no judgment seat, the blowing of the shofar was discontinued.

A BLAST OF THE TRUMPETS

The great rabbi, Sa'adiah Gaon (892-942 A.D.) gave the following symbolisms for the blowing of the shofar at the Feast of Trumpets.[2] First, Israel proclaims **God's kingship** on this day, and the blowing of the shofar is consistent with coronation day ceremonies. Second, this holy day introduces a ten-day period of penitence, so the blowing of the shofar calls the people to **repentance**. Third, the practice hearkens back to **Mount Sinai** — the horn was blown when the *Torah* was given. Fourth, the horn is symbolic of the warning of **the watchman on the tower**. The watchman watches for the enemy, but also for the Lord of the vineyard to come for his harvest. Fifth, this is the call to battle, to the **reclaiming of Israel's glory** (which will be hers during the millennial reign of the Messiah). Sixth, it is reminiscent of the ram provided for Abraham's **sacrifice in obedience**. Seventh, the blast of the horn causes **fear and trembling** — this is the time for man to prepare to meet God. Eighth, the blowing of the shofar evokes **the ultimate day of judgment**. Another name for *Rosh HaShanah* is *Yom HaDin*, the Day of Judgment. It is a time for seeking God through repentance and receiving pardon through his justice and mercy. Ninth, the horn signals **the final ingathering** of exiles:

> "And it shall come to pass in that day, that the great trumpet shall be blown, and they shall come which were ready to perish in the land of Assyria, and the outcasts in the land of Egypt, and shall worship the Lord in the holy mount at Jerusalem."
> Isaiah 27:13

> "And he shall send his angels with a great sound of a trumpet, and they shall gather together his elect from one end of heaven to the other."
> Matthew 24:31

Tenth, the sound of the trumpet is connected to **the resurrection**:

"In a moment, in the twinkling of an eye, at the last trump: for the trumpet shall sound, and the dead shall be raised incorruptible, and we shall be changed."

1 Corinthians 15:52

Moses Maimonides, perhaps the greatest Jewish philosopher, wrote the message of the shofar's sound:

"Awake, you sleepers, from your sleep and you slumberers awake from your slumber. Reflect on your deeds and repent, and remember your Creator. Look to your souls and mend your ways and actions, those who forget the truth because of the empty vanities of life, who all their years go astray following vanity and folly which neither profit nor save. Let each one of you abandon his evil way and thoughts which are not good."

Note how similar were the words of Nephi's brother Jacob in the Book of Mormon:

"O my brethren, hearken unto my words; arouse the faculties of your souls; shake yourselves that ye may awake from the slumber of death; and loose yourselves from the pains of hell that ye may not become angels to the devil, to be cast into that lake of fire and brimstone which is the second death."

Jacob 3:11

MAY YOUR NAME BE WRITTEN IN THE BOOK OF LIFE

Rosh HaShanah is considered the day of judgment for every person, group, and nation of the earth. Although the judgment is symbolic of the great and last judgment, each celebration of the holiday during the interim is considered a yearly ruling and portent of one's fate for the coming year. On Rosh HaShanah, God gives every citizen of the world a signature in one of his three books, one for the righteous, one for the unrighteous, and one for the fence-sitters whose judgment is delayed until they can repent:

"And now I say unto you, all you that are desirous to follow the voice of the good shepherd, come ye out from the wicked, and be ye separate, and touch not their unclean things; and behold, their names shall be blotted out, that the names of the wicked shall not be numbered among the names of the righteous, that the word of God may be fulfilled, which saith: The names of the wicked shall not be mingled with the names of my people;

"For the **names of the righteous shall be written in the book of life**, and unto them will I grant an inheritance at my right hand..."

Alma 5:57-58

Many current traditions uphold the original messages and symbolisms of the Feast of Trumpets. Since this is a season of judgment, the story of Abraham is read. (At question is the judgment of Ishmael. Why was he allowed to survive, when his descendants have been a scourge for Israel? Because he was innocent at that time, so God had no reason to curse him.) White garments are worn, and the *Torah* scroll is wrapped in white. The white is reminiscent of a death shroud as well as a symbol of purity. No bitterness is allowed into the holiday observance, so sweet foods are eaten, such as bread and apples dipped in honey. Sweet fruits and round loaves of *challah* are also considered suitable holiday fare. On the first day of Rosh HaShanah in the afternoon a special ceremony is conducted on the shores of bodies of water. Called the *tashlikh* ceremony, it derives its symbolism from Micah 7:19 — "He will turn again, he will have compassion upon us; he will subdue our iniquities; and thou wilt cast all their sins into the depths of the sea." Whoever desires to participate goes to the body of water and shakes his pockets, as if to empty his sins into the sea. For half the day Jews make supplication unto the Lord, and they pray for the realization of the kingdom of God on earth. This is important for the beginning of the fall holy-day season, which begins with judgment, continues in bitter repentance, and ends with the symbolism of the establishment of the millennial reign.

THE END OF DAYS DRAWS NIGH

This festival ensures that once a year, Jews are forcefully reminded that the "end of days" is drawing nigh, and that repentance should not be postponed. It is a wake-up call that people of all faiths would benefit from heeding. Are we, as Latter-day Saints, awake? Are we casual in our religious devotion? Are there faults or difficulties in our relationships to God and Man that need tending to? The structure of Judaism is such that the fabric of life is constantly unraveled and examined for weaknesses in the tiniest details, then woven again with new strength and beauty. This is the summoning call of the Feast of Trumpets. We should listen, awake, arise, and obey.

Again, in these latter days, the Lord has fulfilled the imagery of an ordained high holy day — the gold plates were delivered to Joseph Smith on *Rosh HaShanah*, the Feast of Trumpets. The message of the Book of Mormon is that the final gathering of the righteous is nigh, and that no man should procrastinate the day of his repentance.

CHAPTER 11 ENDNOTES

[1] Winter, *The High Holy Days,* 3.

[2] Winter, 32-33.

[3] The Sanhedrin had mathematical calculations to judge when a new moon would occur, but these were not relied upon until 359 A.D.

[4] Branches are carried on Shemeni Atzeret, the Last Great Day, an activity forbidden on the Sabbath.

CHAPTER 12:
YAMIM NORA'IM
(THE DAYS OF AWE)

At Rosh HaShanah a ten-day period of penitence begins, a solemn time of contemplation, self-examination, personal and national cleansing, and preparation to meet God. These are the "Days of Awe" (*Yamim Nora'im*). The actual period is a holy **seven** days, the intermediate period between Rosh HaShanah and *Yom Kippur*, the "Day of Atonement" on the tenth of Tishrei. **God reviews his books** at the beginning of this period, and he **metes out judgment** at the end.

> "And Moses returned unto the Lord, and said. . .
>
> "Yet now, if thou wilt forgive their sin — ; and if not, blot me, I pray thee, out of thy book which thou hast written.
>
> "And the Lord said unto Moses, Whosoever has sinned against me, him will I blot out of my book."
>
> Exodus 32:32-33

The resolutions made at Rosh HaShanah meet the tests of everyday life during this period of penitence. For those who believe in Christ as the Messiah, this seven-day review period hearkens to the seven seals spoken of in the Book of Revelation, where the works of men during each of the seven dispensations are revealed:

> "And I saw in the right hand of him that sat on the throne **a book** written within and on the backside **sealed with seven seals**.
>
> "And I saw a strong angel proclaiming with a loud voice, Who is worthy to open the book, and to loose the seals thereof?

And no man in heaven, nor in earth, neither under the earth, was able to open the book, neither to look thereon.

"And I wept much, because no man was found worthy to open and to read the book, neither to look thereon.

"And one of the elders saith unto me, Weep not: behold, the Lion of the tribe of Juda, the root of David, hath prevailed to open the book and to loose the seven seals thereof."

Revelation 5:1-5 (emphasis added)

At one time it was customary to fast every day during the daylight hours for the duration of the week. Now it is only required to fast on *Yom Kippur*, the Day of Atonement.[1] On the eve of Yom Kippur one should go the *mikveh* (the ritual bath), dress in Sabbath clothes, make donations to charity, prepare a meal in preparation for the High Sabbath, bless the children, and go to synagogue.

HOW DOES ONE REPENT?

The concepts of repentance in Judaism are much the same as ours. A proverb says that Wisdom would hold that Evil will persecute the sinner and lead him unto death. Prophecy would say that the soul that sinneth will die. But the Torah says, let him repent, and his sin shall be atoned. We Mormons would add only one word to the proverb — Let him repent, and his sin shall be atoned **for**. The Book of Jonah is read during the Days of Awe. Remember how the people of Ninevah, as violent and wicked as they were reputed to be, repented sincerely for their sins and were forgiven by the Lord? It is interesting that the "sign" of Jonah is a testimony of the atonement of Christ — three days and nights in the belly of the whale before his release into light and life. The sign of Jonah is referred to repeatedly in the scriptures. (See Matt.12:39-41; 16:4; and Luke 11:29-30.)

The following steps constitute the process of repentance in Judaism: First, regret the bad behavior; second, make restitution if possible,[2] and try to win the forgiveness of the person you have injured; third, confess private sins to God and public sins publically; fourth, abstain from the bad behavior. The ideal is to repent not because you fear punishment or suffering, but out of love for God.

It is important to realize that a concept of Zion hovers behind every individual act in Judaism. Repentance is never just personal repentance;

it is national as well. Every prayer is more than individual; it is a prayer for Israel. We are Israel as certainly as the tribe of Judah is. *Every time we strengthen ourselves in the faith, or strengthen our families, we bless the Church. We are ever engaged in the process of creating a nation of believers.*

The Days of Awe are days of humility, the most solemn period of the Jewish year. The rains have not yet fallen. The harvest season is nearly complete. As the Lord reaps the harvest from his fields, will we be the wheat or the tares? It is almost too late to change our lives. The final ingathering is in process. The coming of the Lord is nigh.

CHAPTER 12 ENDNOTES

[1] Meet an Israeli on the street during this period, and he will wish you, "May you be inscribed in the Book of Life," and "Easy fast."

[2] See the section regarding the Law of Moses, which is almost completely misunderstood by the Christian world (including us!). The "eye for an eye" process required by the Law is NOT a process of revenge, but a process of making **restitution** in a manner justified by the severity of the injury. Thus, if you injure a person so that he loses an eye, your own eye is not required in compensation. (Such a thing would be useless to the victim; all you would satisfy is his desire for revenge, a wicked desire.) Instead, the resulting judgment is always what we call a "civil suit." You must compensate fully for the injury. This might mean that you provide all the medical care and lost income; you might provide help in the future to make restitution for the loss. The Law requires that you make enthusiastic restitution, so that the victim is guaranteed equal compensation for the loss you caused. You might give help four-fold to cover the injury. Therefore, the victim is amply cared for, and you are aided in your repentance. And no one goes to jail. Think of that, the punishment fair rather than extreme, the victim compensated, the criminal rehabilitated, and the prisons empty. A good system, yes?

CHAPTER 13:
YOM KIPPUR
(THE DAY OF ATONEMENT)

Yom Kippur is the day of individual and national repentance. It is the High Holy Day of holy days. Experiencing Yom Kippur in Jerusalem is like no other Sabbath experience. Though the Orthodox don't drive cars on any Sabbath, on Yom Kippur <u>no one</u> drives. There is not a car on any road or highway (except in a dire emergency, a police car or ambulance). This is a day of true Sabbath rest with complete quiet everywhere. There is an air of reverence that permeates every neighborhood. Families stroll together after synagogue in the mild autumn sunshine, but no bus runs, no shop is open. It is impossible to describe the feeling of *Yom Kippur* in Israel to someone who has never experienced it. The awe one feels when entering a building of worship exists everywhere. The entire world becomes a chapel.

This is never a sad day. It is a day of hope. This is the final day of the season of repentance. Israel is hopeful that she will be accepted by the Lord. Jews remember that at the end of our Passover Feast, they said a toast: "Next year in Jerusalem rebuilt!" This is the promise of the fruition of that wish, to be accepted into God's kingdom on earth, with Jerusalem as its holy capital.

A DAY TO AFFLICT ONE'S SOUL

Nevertheless, this is the day to afflict one's soul. On this Sabbath of Sabbaths one is not to eat or drink; one is not to wash or bathe nor to perform any anointings; one is not to cohabit with one's spouse; one is not to wear leather shoes or sandals; one is to have a broken heart and a contrite spirit:

> "And the Lord spake unto Moses, saying,
>
> "Also on the tenth day of this seventh month there shall be a day of atonement: it shall be an holy convocation unto you; and **ye shall afflict your souls**, and offer an offering made by fire unto the Lord.
>
> "And ye shall do no work in that same day: for **it is a day of atonement, to make an atonement for you before the Lord your God.**
>
> "For whatsoever soul it be that shall not be afflicted in that same day, he shall be cut off from among his people.
>
> "And whatsoever soul it be that doeth any work in that same day, the same soul will I destroy from among this people.
>
> "Ye shall do no manner of work: **it shall be a statute forever throughout your generations in all your dwellings.**
>
> "It shall be unto you a sabbath of rest, and ye shall afflict your souls: in the ninth day of the month at even, from even unto even, shall ye celebrate your sabbath."
>
> Leviticus 23:26-32 (emphasis added)

Ezekiel calls the process of repentance a" turning;" we should turn away from sin, and turn towards God:

> "Therefore I will judge you, O house of Israel, every one according to his ways, saith the Lord God. Repent, and **turn yourselves** from all your transgressions; so iniquity shall not be your ruin.
>
> "Cast away from you all your transgressions, whereby ye have transgressed; and make you a new heart and a new spirit: for why will ye die, O house of Israel?
>
> For I have no pleasure in the death of him that dieth, saith the Lord God: **wherefore turn yourselves, and live ye."**
>
> Ezekiel 18:30-32 (emphasis added)

The word *kippur* comes from the word *kaphar*, which means "to cover." This Day of Atonement is meant to cover one's sins. It is an interesting concept. Something that is covered is hidden, unseen. The Lord promises us that if we repent, he will not remember our sins on the Day of Judgment; they will be covered, or hidden. The atonement of Christ "covers" our sins; it takes them all into account and makes recompense for them, if only we will repent.

BLOOD ATONEMENT

In Leviticus Aaron is commanded to make sacrifices in order to "atone" for the sins of the people. **Their sins are transferred to the offering, which is then sacrificed.**

> "And this shall be an everlasting statute unto you, to make an atonement for the children of Israel for all their sins once a year. And he [Aaron] did as the Lord commanded Moses."
> Leviticus 16:34

This sacrifice brings with it the concept of blood atonement by an innocent to save the transgressors. While the Temple still stood, on *Yom Kippur*, one of the sacrifices was the "scapegoat." Two goats were brought before the High Priest in the courtyard of the Temple. One was chosen (like the choice between Barabbas and Jesus) and marked by tying a piece of red yarn around one of its horns. The high priest laid his hands on the head of this goat and transferred the sins of the people to the scapegoat. The goat was then taken to the eastern gate and led over ten miles into the wilderness. There it was either freed, or pushed off a cliff to die. This was to keep it from wandering back into the presence of innocent people, laden with their sins. The goat, with its sins, was to be completely banished. The other goat became a sin offering upon the altar.

Another ceremony entailed the use of the ashes of a sacrificed red heifer, the perfect animal so surely representing Christ. The ashes were used by the high priest, as he made the very elaborate preparations for the main Yom Kippur sacrifice. The high priest repeatedly cleansed himself and changed vestments.[1] The prayers and recitations of the high priest were very special at this time, as it was the only time when the name of the Lord could be uttered. The high priest used the name of the Lord three times as he transferred his own sins to a sacrificial bull. The blood of the bull and the remaining goat were sprinkled by the high priest before the Ark of the Covenant in the Holy of Holies. (This was the only day the high priest entered the presence of God in the Holy of Holies.) He then sprinkled the blood on the outside of the veil and on the horns of the altar in the temple courtyard. The bull and goat then became burnt offerings. Thus, we have the image of **sacrifice by blood and fire**. Blood and fire are images of the Lord's Second Coming:

"And they shall see signs and wonders, for they shall be shown forth in the heavens above, and in the earth beneath.

"And they shall behold **blood, and fire**, and vapors of smoke."

D&C 45:40-41 *(emphasis added)*

Only in the process of making the Yom Kippur sacrifices was blood sprinkled in so many places — in the Holy of Holies, on the veil, on the altar. This is another image of the Second Coming:

"And it shall be said: Who is this that cometh down from God in heaven with dyed garments; yea, from the regions which are not known, clothed in his glorious apparel, traveling in the greatness of his strength?'

"And he shall say: I am he who spake in righteousness, mighty to save.'

"And **the Lord shall be red in his apparel,** and his garments like him that treadeth in the wine-vat.

"And so great shall be the glory of his presence that the sun shall hide his face in shame, and the moon shall withhold its light, and the stars shall be hurled from their places.

"And his voice shall be heard: I have trodden the wine-press alone, and have brought judgment upon all people; and none were with me;

"And I have trampled them in my fury, and I did tread upon them in mine anger, and **their blood have I sprinkled on my garments, and stained all my raiment**; for this was the day of vengeance which was in my heart.

"And now the year of my redeemed is come; and they shall mention the loving kindness of their Lord, and all that he has bestowed upon them according to his goodness, and according to his loving kindness, forever and ever."

D&C 133:46-52 *(emphasis added)*

The message is terrifying for the wicked and reassuring for the righteous — this is the season when the wicked shall be vanquished and the righteous shall be saved.

The scriptures refer to the Savior's sacrifice as the true blood atonement. He is the true sacrificial lamb, the only offering with the power to save us:

"Surely he hath borne our griefs, and carried our sorrows: yet we did esteem him stricken, smitten of God, and afflicted.

"But he was wounded for our transgressions, he was bruised for our iniquities: the chastisement of our peace was upon him; and with his stripes we are healed.

"All we like sheep have gone astray; we have turned every one to his own way; and the Lord hath laid on him the iniquity of us all.

". . .by his knowledge shall my righteous servant justify many; for he shall bear their iniquities."

Isaiah 53:4-6, 11

"Neither by the blood of goats and calves, but by his own blood he entered in once into the holy place, having obtained eternal redemption for us.

"For if the blood of bulls and of goats, and the ashes of an heifer sprinkling the unclean, sanctifieth to the purifying of the flesh:

"How much more shall the blood of Christ, who through the eternal Spirit offered himself without spot to God, purge your conscience from dead works to serve the living God?

"And for this cause he is the mediator of the new testament, that by means of death, for the redemption of the transgressions that were under the first testament, they which are called might receive the promise of eternal inheritance.

"So Christ was once offered to bear the sins of many; and unto them that look for him shall he appear the second time without sin unto salvation."

Hebrews 9:12-15,28[2]

COVERING SIN, CLEANSING SIN

The images conveyed in the rituals of Yom Kippur are a shadow of the true substance of the redeeming sacrifice of Jesus Christ. We must go from covering sin to cleansing our sins through repentance and the power of His blood atonement. We anticipate forgiveness; someday we will fully realize forgiveness. Each year at *Yom Kippur* the House of Israel achieves a provisional atonement for sin, but Jesus Christ achieves for us an eternal and total atonement.

Thus, the image of Yom Kippur is complete. Or is it? Interestingly enough, the rituals of the Day of Atonement relate to our own work for the dead. How can this be? — In Hebrew, the name of the festival used in the Torah is *Yom HaKippurim* — the Day of **Atonements**, in the plural form. "This," the rabbis explain, "is not only because the living receive atonement, but also the dead. A tenet of Judaism is the belief in an afterlife, when the soul continues to live and is also liable to punishment for the sins it committed on earth. The idea that the living can seek atonement for the dead is found in literary sources as early as the Book of Maccabees (second century B.C.E.). There, Judah Maccabee and his men pray for their fallen comrades and bring offerings to the Temple to atone for **their** sins."[3] The current observance of Yom Kippur includes the recitation of the *yizkor*, prayers for the forgiveness of deceased loved ones.

SEPARATION AND HOPE

This is the season of separation — the repentant from the prideful, the righteous from the wicked, the prepared from the unprepared. This is the season to remember the atonement of the Savior and to look forward to his second appearance in red garments. This is a season of hope, but also a season of fear and trembling, a time of serious introspection and purification, a time to afflict one's soul until it turns unto God. The trumpet has sounded; the call to gather has been issued; the kingdom of God is near at hand.

CHAPTER 13 ENDNOTES

[1] Linen garments were required for this ceremony.

[2] See also 2 Nephi 7 and 10; Alma 42:15, 23-24; Mosiah 3:15; 13:28-35; Alma 34:11-16;

[3] Winter, *The High Holy Days,* 79.

CHAPTER 14: SUKKOT (THE FEAST OF TABERNACLES)

Sukkot means "booths" in Hebrew. This holiday hearkens back to the Exodus, when the Israelites dwelt in flimsy, temporary structures in the wilderness. This is the most joyous holiday of the Jewish year. But why? — when at this time the Children of Israel remember the crudeness of their dwellings in the desert? Because this is the threshold of the fruition of the Exodus: the wilderness trek has been accomplished. Its many trials and afflictions have purged the weakness from God's chosen people. This is the joyful conclusion to the season of testing, **the conclusion of the covenant** at Sinai and the three ordained festivals, the threshold to the Promised Land. It is time to rejoice in the very crudeness of their dwellings — they have no need of protection from the elements nor protection from an unseen enemy — they don't even need a roof over their heads. The Lord is their protector and their security. Even as they eat and sleep in their booths, families gaze through the few branches of roofing at the starry skies, expectant. Salvation is nigh.

Pilgrimage to Jerusalem was required for The Feast of Tabernacles, as it was for Passover and The Feast of Weeks. The sacrifices were animals, meal, and drink. Tithes were paid at the Temple. *Sukkot* takes place at the autumn equinox, a mirror image holiday to Passover, which occurs at the spring equinox. *Sukkot* begins on the fifteenth day of *Tishrei*. (Refer to the zodiac chart.) See that the fifteenth of *Tishrei* is directly across from the fifteenth of Nisan when the Children of Israel were delivered from Egypt. The two holidays are meridians of the Jewish year, just as the First and Second Comings of the Messiah are the defining events in earth's history upon which all else hinges.) As with the Feast of Unleavened Bread, *Sukkot* lasts seven days, with the first and last day being Sabbaths. The day after Sukkot is *Shemeni Atzeret*, the Last Great Day. *Shemeni Atzeret* parallels the day of Passover, the offering of the Lamb, the day before the Feast of Unleavened Bread begins. At Passover, the Children of Israel were reborn; they wandered in the wilderness of life; they were given help — the scriptures and the Holy Spirit; they repented, and now they stand approved. The *Sukkah*, the booth which they are commanded to build, to eat and sleep in, becomes the image of the pavilion of the Lord into which they are invited. The booth is like a temple; they are invited to dwell in the house of the Lord. King Solomon dedicated the temple at *Sukkot* (1 Kings 8:2-21), emphasizing this image for his people.

THE FINAL INGATHERING

As far as the land is concerned, this is the final harvest, the final ingathering, of the growing season. To believers in Jesus the Messiah, the final ingathering represents the preservation and gathering in of those prepared to receive God's kingdom, while the imminent latter rains represent his Second Coming and the ushering in of the Millennial Day.

Remembering the Parable of the Ten Virgins, we can see that this is the moment of the bridegroom's arrival. The Bridegroom arrives late at night, with the trumpet's call to the virgins to "awake and arise." The five righteous and prepared virgins are "gathered in" to the wedding chamber,[1] to which the *Sukkah*, the booth, is likened.[2]

> "And angels shall fly through the midst of heaven, crying with a loud voice, sounding the trump of God, saying: Prepare ye, prepare ye, O inhabitants of the earth; for the judgment of our God is come. Behold, and lo, the Bridegroom cometh; go ye out to meet him."
>
> D&C 88:92

THE SUKKAH

The booth, then, may be likened to the temple, the Lord's pavilion, *and* to the wedding chamber or canopy, wherein the bridegroom is the Lord and the bride is Israel. Since the destruction of the Temple, the booth has become the center of the festival. In Israel, booths sprout up everywhere in preparation for the holiday. Hotels build huge ones adjacent to their restaurants, and patrons eat their meals within its joyful confines. Families build their own, often on the tiny balconies of their apartments.

Schools build booths on their playgrounds. We purchased a *sukkah* frame at the open-air market (the *suq*). The element of personal labor and construction imbue the preparations with hope for the future, when families can enjoy the fruits of their labors. The exterior walls of the booth are sheets or tarps, or some other flimsy material. Palm branches and other kinds of tree limbs are laid as a roof, so that the sky is visible (by commandment). The interior is decorated festively with harvest and spiritual items. Mini-lights might span the ceiling, and drawings by the children around spiritual holiday themes might be pinned to the walls. In representation of the bountiful harvest, "four kinds" are gathered for the booth:

> "Also in the fifteenth day of the seventh month, when ye have gathered in the fruit of the land, ye shall keep a feast unto the Lord seven days: on the first day shall be a sabbath, and on the eighth day shall be a sabbath.
>
> "And ye shall take you on the first day the boughs of goodly trees, branches of palm trees, and the boughs of thick trees, and willows of the brook; and ye shall rejoice before the Lord your God seven days."
>
> Leviticus 23:39-40

The "four kinds" are associated with the virtues of the ancient patriarchs. They are the *etrog* — a lemon-like fruit representing the "beautiful trees;" the *lulav* — the long branch of the date palm, representing the "palm trees;" *hadas* — myrtle branches, representing the "leafy trees;" and *arava* — willow branches, representing the "willows of the brook." The four kinds are samples of the flora so richly blessing the Promised Land. Again, they can be found at the *suq*. It is inspiring to watch the patriarchs of orthodox Jewish families examining the four kinds to find the most perfect offerings for the festival.

The commandment is to eat and sleep within the *sukkah*.[3] The weather is very mild this time of year with the heat of the summer waning and the rains about to begin. Prayers for rain are initiated in earnest, as the final harvests come in. The air is charged with expectancy, and the inside of the family *sukkah* is festive and magical. Families gather together on selected nights at each others' homes to sing the songs of the season and share a meal.

WATER AND FIRE

Important images in the ancient observance of *Sukkot* are **water and fire**. Both have the capability to destroy and to save. The Lord destroyed the world by water at the time of Noah. He will destroy the wicked by fire at his Second Coming. Yet, water is the symbol of baptism, and the living water a symbol of the gospel and saving graces of Christ. The receiving of the Holy Ghost and witness of gospel truths is called the baptism by fire. The destructive fire that accompanies the Second Coming will be the glory of the Lord, and will bless the righteous, even as it destroys the wicked (D&C 29:9-11). Mormon spoke of fire and water and their necessity in embracing the gospel:

> "And ye will also know that ye are a remnant of the seed of Jacob; therefore ye are numbered among the people of the first covenant; and if it so be that ye believe in Christ, and are baptized, first with **water**, then with **fire** and with the Holy Ghost, following the example of our Savior, according to that which he hath commanded us, it shall be well with you in the day of judgment. Amen."
>
> Mormon 7:10

Part of the ancient festival was the **water libation**. Though the water libation was a prayer for rains in their season, it is also a symbol of the living water Christ offers us. The ceremony was a procession, led by the High Priest to the Pool of Siloam to fetch water and carry it back to the Temple altar. This water offering represented the water brought forth from the rock in the wilderness by

Moses. (Both the water and the rock are types of Christ — Jesus called himself the "fountain of all righteousness" and the rock upon which the Church is built.) Three trumpet blasts were sounded, and Isaiah 12:3 was recited:

"Therefore with joy shall ye draw water out of the wells of salvation."

At the Temple the water was poured into a silver basin, accompanied by other symbolic rituals.

In the seventh chapter of John we find an account of Jesus and His apostles going up to Jerusalem for the Feast of Tabernacles. They entered the city clandestinely (because certain of the authorities were trying to do away with Jesus), but they still wanted to bear open testimony of the divinity of Christ. John says that in ". . .the midst of the feast Jesus went up into the temple and taught" (v.14). Then, on *Shemeni Atzeret*, the Last Great Day, He spoke to them even more aggressively:

> "In the last day, that great day of the feast, **Jesus stood and cried**, saying, If any man thirst, let him come unto me, and drink.
>
> "He that believeth on me, as the scripture hath said, out of his belly shall flow rivers of living water.
>
> "(But this spake he of the Spirit, which they that believe on him should receive: for the Holy Ghost was not yet given; because that Jesus was not yet glorified.)
>
> "Many of the people therefore, when they heard this saying, said, Of a truth this is the Prophet.
>
> "Others said, This is the Christ. . . ."
>
> John 7:37-41 *(emphasis added)*

As He would do again the following Passover, Jesus used the imagery of the holiday to testify of Himself. Here, He testified of the living **water**; but He also testified during the same holiday of **fire and light**. After the first day's Sabbath of the holiday week, and from that day on, pilgrims would ascend the steps to the Temple with music and celebration. In the courtyard were four huge *menorot*, seven-branched candlesticks, which were set alight as part of the festivities.

After calling himself the living water, Jesus had gone up to the Mount of Olives. He returned to teach at the Temple, and there the Pharisees brought to Him the "woman taken in adultery." He spoke to the Pharisees:

> "...I am the light of the world: he that followeth me shall not walk in darkness, but shall have the light of life."
>
> John 8:12

The imagery was clear; with the huge *menorot* as a backdrop, Jesus claimed to be the light of the world. (See also John 4:14).

THE HOSANNA SHOUT

Among the *Sukkot* rituals at the Temple was the **waving of palm branches** and the recitation of Psalm 118:25:

"Save now, I beseech thee, O Lord: O Lord, I beseech thee, send now prosperity."

The priests marched once around the altar — the similitude is the triumphal entry of the Lord into Jerusalem, when his followers waved palm branches and laid them at his feet:

"And brought the ass, and the colt, and put on them their clothes, and they set him thereon.

"And a very great multitude spread their garments in the way; others cut down branches from the trees and strewed them in the way.

"And the multitudes that went before, and that followed, cried, saying, Hosanna to the Son of David: Blessed is he that cometh in the name of the Lord; Hosanna in the highest."

Matthew 21:7-9

The chant is "Hosanna" — "O save us!" It is the Hosanna Shout performed at the dedication of our own latter-day temples, a welcome for the Son of God, he who saves us. The great hosanna performed at Sukkot, the *HoShanah Rabbah*, includes seven circuits around the altar, said to represent the "Seven Worthies"

Abraham, Isaac, Jacob, Moses, Aaron, Phineas, and David. Here is the number seven again, the number representing perfection and wholeness. This is the seventh of seven ordained, commanded festivals. Remembered on this day were the seven days of Creation, the seven lambs set aside by Abraham in covenant with Abimelech at Beersheba, Jacob's seven years of famine, and the seven-day festivals established by Moses (Unleavened Bread and Tabernacles).

This, the seventh festival, is the festival of fulfillment, of wholeness:

"We are to understand that as God made the world in six days, and on the seventh day he finished his work, and sanctified it, and also formed man out of the dust of the earth, even so, in the beginning of the seventh thousand years will the Lord God sanctify the earth, and complete the salvation of man, and judge all things, and shall redeem all things, except that which he hath not put into his power, when he shall have sealed all things, unto the end of all things; and the sounding of the trumpets of the seven angels are the preparing and finishing of his work, in the beginning of the seventh thousand years — the preparing of the way before the time of his coming."

D&C 77:12

CHAPTER 14 ENDNOTES

[1] The booth is also likened to the wedding canopy, called a *huppah*, beneath which Jewish couples are married. The celebration of the gift of the Torah, *Simchat Torah*, also relates to wedding symbolism.

[2] Jewish wedding traditions are full of imagery testifying of the Savior and familiar gospel principles. For an excellent and thorough treatment of wedding symbolisms, see the book, *Beloved Bridegroom*, by Donna B. Nielsen, published by Onyx Press.

[3] Instructions for building and decorating your own family *sukkah* can be found in the FEAST OF TABERNACLES FAMILY HOME EVENING in Appendix A.

CHAPTER 15:
THE SEVEN FESTIVALS

The shape of the Jewish year, with its festivals as milestones, is the shape of the Plan of Salvation, is the shape of the Exodus — birth (deliverance), wandering, testing, repentance, judgment, salvation. Each milestone of the year has its message, testifying that Jesus is the Christ, symbolizing his birth, ministry, death, resurrection, saving qualities, judgment, and second coming. (See the "Seven Festivals" table on the following page.)

Rabbi Eliezer, seeing Messianic imagery in the holidays, came to the conclusion that the Messiah would come to redeem Israel during the month of *Nisan* in the spring. Rabbi Joshua disagreed with him. Surely, he said, the Messiah would come in *Tishrei* — the imagery of the fall holidays proves it. We know that both Rabbis were correct. These months are the meridians of the civil and religious Jewish year. The Passover in the month of *Nisan* testifies of the birth, life, mission, crucifixion and resurrection of the Savior. The fall holidays in the month of *Tishrei* testify of his second coming. One might ask, then, can't we expect the Second Coming to occur in the fall? Not exactly. We know that Christ will make several appearances which will all be a part of the Second Coming. The event where he again partakes of the bread and wine, together with his Chosen, is a Passover fulfillment, yet it will be a Second Coming event. The imagery is what is important, and not so much the exact timing. Rest assured, the pieces will fit together tightly and exactly; every type will be fulfilled as promised. However, the entire puzzle will not be clear to us until it is finished.

SEVEN FESTIVALS

Holiday	Month	Message
Passover (Pesach)	Nisan First full moon after the spring equinox on the 14th of Nisan (Now combined with The Feast of Unleavened Bread, beginning the 15th.)	Deliverance from Egypt; the birth, mission, identity, and crucifixion of Christ as the sacrificial lamb; rebirth, renewal, redemption.
Feast of Unleavened Bread (Chag HaMatzot)	Nisan The 15th of Nisan, the day the Israelites left Egypt, and continuing one week.	Purity, willingness to serve, choosing the yoke of the Lord. Deliverance, birth of Israel as a people. Christ is the bread of life.
First Fruits (Bikkurim)	The day after the first sabbath during Unleavened Bread, now the 16th of Nisan	First Barley Harvest, offering insures future harvest; Christ is the First Fruits of the resurrection
Counting the Omer	The 49 days following Bikkurim	Wilderness; harvesting in trepidation
Feast of Weeks (Shavuot, or Pentacost)	50 days after Bikkurim	Gift of the Torah; gift of the Holy Ghost;
Feast of Trumpets (Rosh HaShanah)	1st of Tishrei (New Moon Festival, with preparations during previous month of Elul)	Call to awake, arise and gather; judgment
Days of Awe (Yamim Nora'im)	The week following the Feast of Trumpets	Sincere, humble repentance. Separation of the righteous from the wicked.
Day of Atonement (Yom Kippur)	10th of Tishrei	Afflicting one's soul; redemption of the righteous and destruction of the wicked
Feast of Tabernacles (Sukkot) Last Great Day (Shemeni Atzeret)	Tishrei (The 15th to the 21st)	Coming of the Bridegroom; Ushering in of the Millenium

OBSERVING THE FEASTS IS NOT ENOUGH

Why did the Lord say to Israel, "I hate, I despise your feast days, and I will not smell in your solemn assemblies" (Amos 5:21)? After all, the Lord Himself ordained these feasts and establish all the imagery therein. Because, as with all the commandments of the Lord, we are to do all things with clean hands and pure hearts. It is what is written in the heart that is important. Without righteousness and sincerity, no ordinance, no ritual, has any meaning for us or for the Lord:

> "And ye shall offer for a sacrifice unto me a broken heart and a contrite spirit. And whoso cometh unto me with a broken heart and a contrite spirit, him will I baptize with fire and with the Holy Ghost..."
>
> 3 Nephi 9:20

There will come a day when the pure in heart from among all peoples will meet the Messiah when he comes. Some of the pure in heart will be Jews, and many will be Israelites. When the Lord establishes his millennial reign, what holidays, what Holy Days, will we observe? I hope they will be these same seven festivals, celebrated throughout the entire, righteous world. They will be milestones of remembrance for us: the Passover Lamb of God who came to save, the resurrection on *Bikkurim*, the outpouring of the Spirit on First Fruits, the trumpets that called us to repent and gather, the final ingathering and Second Coming of the Lord, and the establishment of God's kingdom on earth.

HEARERS OF THE WORD

The final, lingering question that Latter-day Saints ask is always the same. With all this clear, testifying imagery, why didn't the Jews recognize their own Messiah? The Savior Himself answered that question with the Parable of the Sower (Matthew 13:3; Mark 4:3; Luke 8:5). Many Jews did recognize the Messiah. They were those who received the seed into fertile ground. Many of those were the valiant founders of the Lord's Church, willing to face any hardship to serve the Christ.

The Savior speaks of a second type of personality — he who receives the word, but fails to nurture it. The "fear of the world" overcomes this person, and he fails to be valiant.

When we moved to Israel in 1983, we began our sojourn there in an apartment in Jerusalem. Within a year I was more than ready to move a few kilometers outside of the city — the tension in the air was so profound, I couldn't stand the stress. The tension had absolutely nothing to do with the Arab-Israeli problem.

There is a spiritual war going on all around us, and Jerusalem is its vortex. Can we possibly imagine what the forces of Satan were drumming up in the Holy Land, while Jesus himself was ministering there? I'm amazed anyone was able to carry on any sort of daily business in the midst of that spiritual war. Confusion, intrigue, controversy, fear, and temptation must have abounded. Only a person of particular humility and quietness of spirit would be able to hear the truth in the midst of that din. And only a person of particular faith and courage would be able to remain valiant. Remember that Jesus and his followers were originally considered a branch (a twig, actually) of Judaism. How easy would it be simply to swing back to one's former traditions and live an easier, safer life?

The third personality in the Lord's parable is a hardened one who might actively fight against the truth. Such were those certain wicked priests of the Sanhedrin, desiring to protect their power and position by any means available to them. Such a person was Saul, the Pharisee and lawyer, who became the Apostle Paul when his eyes were opened.

All three of the types represented in the Parable of the Sower surround us in the world today. Our own LDS missionaries encounter them daily in the Gentile world. It was no different among the Jews. The Lord has been patient with His children. He has been willing to stretch His nurturing and teaching over

The millennia, knowing that all the imagery would become clear in due time. The Jews will see all the imagery clearly at the same time that we, ourselves, do — when the Bridegroom comes.

PART III

PRESENTATIONS

SUPPLEMENTAL MATERIALS

You have permission to reproduce anything from the presentations section or extra materials for **non-commercial** use. Included in the presentations are instructions for staging a complete Passover meal. The Passover evening includes a lengthy ritual, full of imagery testifying of the Messiah. Part of the ritual takes place before the meal, and a shorter part after. A *haggadah*, or narrative, in the form of a printed booklet, must be made available to the celebrants, so they can follow along and participate. I've included a printable *haggadah*. My *haggadah* is based on Jewish traditional texts and patterns, enhanced with messages especially for Latter-day Saints, which explain how the Passover imagery is fulfilled in Christ.

An extensive Passover recipe collection is also included, as well as directions for setting a Passover table, a pattern for table arrangements for a large group, Passover games and songs, plus materials and patterns for the other holidays. If you don't want to present a complete Passover dinner, you may choose to present the Passover Fireside, or Family Home Evening presentation instead. Family Home Evening presentations for the other feasts and holidays are included in this section of the book.

Family Home Evening lesson plans found in this section incorporate activities and recipes. I have also included two Jewish holidays which are religious, but are not part of the seven prophetic festivals. *Purim*, observed in February-March, is a celebration of the Book of Esther. This holiday is full of fun and festivity. Everyone dresses up in costume, so it's like our Halloween without any of the ghoulish overtones. The Book of Esther is read in the synagogue. Everyone arrives in costume and brings noisemakers. The reading of the scripture is like a melodrama, where everyone boos the villain and cheers for the heroes. Gifts of sweets round out the boisterous festivities.

Chanukah, or the Festival of Lights, celebrates the rededication of the Temple by the Maccabees, after it was desecrated by the invading Syrio-Greeks. There is no Messianic imagery in this holiday either, but in the Christian world it is among the best-known of Jewish holidays, and well worth studying.

Appendix A:
FAMILY HOME EVENING PRESENTATIONS

(Including recipes and activity suggestions)

This appendix contains Family Home Evening presentations for the following Jewish celebrations:

SABBATH

PASSOVER

FIRST FRUITS

THE WILDERNESS WALK

FEAST OF WEEKS (#1)

FEAST OF WEEKS (#2)

FEAST OF TRUMPETS

DAY OF ATONEMENT

FEAST OF TABERNACLES

PURIM

CHANUKAH

A SABBATH FAMILY HOME EVENING

Songs suitable for this Family Home Evening:

    Welcome, Welcome, Sabbath Morning..#280
    Gently Raise the Sacred Strain...#146
    Saturday is a Special Day.. Page 196 (Children's Songbook) Remember the Sabbath Day........................ Page 155 (Children's Songbook)

Preparation:

Bake a recipe of Jewish Sabbath Bread (*Challah*).

Make a scroll. On the paper write, "The Queen is coming to visit your family at sundown tonight." Roll up the paper, and tie the scroll with a ribbon. Attach an official-looking seal to the scroll.

Locate the following:

1. A newspaper that shows the exact minute of sundown that evening (in the weather section).
2. Two tapered candles, plus matches.
3. Scriptures.

Tell the following story:

Once upon a time there was a kingdom with a very great king. The king was so good and wise, that the people kept all the laws and rules, just out of their love and respect for the king. In the kingdom lived a family just like us.

One day a messenger arrived at the family's house, and handed the father a scroll. The scroll looked very important. (Hand the scroll to Dad.) Everyone in the family gathered around, excited to see what the scroll said. They knew it came right from the king himself, because of the seal. The father unrolled the scroll very slowly and looked at the message, but he didn't show the rest of the family. (Have Dad unroll the scroll and read it without showing anyone else.) Dad said, "You all know this message came straight from the king. He has given us a great honor. He must think we are very special, to have chosen us to receive this great gift." Everyone wanted to know what was so great. Father showed the scroll to the family. (Dad shows the scroll to the children.) "The Queen is coming to visit us tonight at sundown!" he said. Sundown was not very far away! If the Queen was coming, they would want to prepare! Everyone wanted to get busy right away. They were filled with excitement and anticipation, but they didn't feel ready to welcome the Queen. First, Dad suggested, they should find out what time sundown would occur; then they would know what time she was coming.

Ask: Where can you find out the exact minute of sundown? There may be many sources (including an Internet search), but the easiest is the newspaper, usually in the weather section. Guide the family towards that discovery, and then determine the exact minute of sundown.

Ask: What should we do to prepare for a visit from the Queen? Get suggestions from the family. Some might be as follows: dress up, clean the house, prepare some good food, be on best behavior, be ready to tell the Queen how much you respect the royal house, turn off any rock-and-roll radio stations and the T.V., buy or make a gift for her, make sure no one telephones you during her visit, etc.

Ask: Who is the greatest king of all? (Heavenly Father) Where do we find his laws and rules? (In the scriptures)

We keep his laws and rules, because we love and trust him.

— But, who is the Queen that is coming to visit us?

Explain:

The Jews believe that The Queen is The Sabbath Day. Their Sabbath day is the last day of the week (Saturday), and it begins exactly at sundown on Friday night. All week they are excited about the upcoming visit of the Sabbath Queen, and all week long, they prepare to receive her. Religious Jews have a lot of rules that govern the Sabbath Day, and it takes a lot of preparation to be able to follow those rules. Very observant Jews do no work on the Sabbath, not even lighting a candle. Since using electricity and running an engine are like lighting fire, they don't turn on lights or push buttons in elevators, nor do they drive cars. They don't heat up the oven or talk on the phone. They walk short distances to the "synagogue" (the word they use for their church building), and they don't carry anything but the things they use for worship. The moment sundown arrives, and the Sabbath Queen appears, they begin to follow these rules out of their respect for the Lord. That means preparing! In Israel, at sundown, the shops close, and the buses stop running. Everyone must get their shopping done and get home before sundown. All the cooking for Friday night's dinner and all the Sabbath meals must be accomplished ahead of time. (It's OK to light the oven before Sabbath, and turn it off during Sabbath.) Just before sundown, the family gathers at the table. They say blessings and prayers to welcome the Sabbath Queen, and then they light the Sabbath lights — two candles. They say blessings over the Sabbath wine and bread (*challah*) that express gratitude to the Lord. It's almost like our sacrament.

We don't have so many rules governing our Sabbath observance. Jesus wanted us to know in our hearts how we can keep the Sabbath day holy. The Sabbath day was made for us; it's a great blessing, like a visit from a queen. (See Ezekiel 20:12; Isaiah 58:13, 14; Mark 2:27; Jarom 1:5; D&C 59:9; D&C 68:29.) When you get ready for the Sabbath, you do many of the things you were going to do to prepare for the Queen's visit.

You clean the house, get dressed-up, shop ahead for food, and behave nicely. For being so nice to his Queen, the Lord blesses you.

A RECIPE FOR JEWISH SABBATH BREAD (CHALLAH)

12 Tblsp dry yeast	12 tsp salt
2 cup lukewarm water	9 cups white or unbleached flour 1 tsp sugar
	Pinch saffron (optional)*
3 eggs	Golden raisins, sultanas or currants
¾ C. sugar	1 large egg, beaten with 1 Tblsp water
12 cups lukewarm water	Sesame or poppy seeds
2 cup vegetable oil	

**Saffron is an extremely expensive spice. It looks like tiny, deep yellow, straw-like filaments. Rub it between your fingers to crush it. It adds a nice yellow color to the dough, and a very nice, distinctive flavor.

Combine the yeast, the 2 cup warm water and the 1 tsp sugar. Set aside. In a large mixing bowl, beat together the eggs and sugar, then add the 1 2 cups warm water, oil, saffron, and salt. Stir in the frothing yeast mixture and beat well. Using a wooden spoon, beat in half the flour, adding the flour gradually and mixing in. Add raisins. Continue to mix and add flour until the dough pulls away from the sides of the bowl.

Dredge the rest of the flour onto a work surface. Knead the dough for 10 minutes. Place the dough in a greased bowl, cover, and let rise in an unheated oven for one hour, or until the dough has doubled in size. Punch down the dough and divide in half. Divide each half into 3 pieces, and roll each piece into a rope. Create 2 braids (six-strand braids are traditional). Tuck under the ends of each braided loaf. Place the loaves on a greased and floured baking sheet. Cover, and leave to rise for about 1 2 hours, or until doubled. Preheat oven to 4001. Brush each loaf gently with the egg and water mixture and sprinkle seeds on top. Bake for 25 minutes. Cool on wire rack.

A PASSOVER FAMILY HOME EVENING

(Passover occurs each year in late March—early April.)

Songs especially suitable for a Passover Family Home Evening are as follows:

Redeemer of Israel	#6
Israel, Israel, God is Calling	#7
Guide Us, O Thou Great Jehovah	#83
I'm a Pilgrim, I'm a Stranger	#121
Does the Journey Seem Long?	#127
Ye Elders of Israel	#319

Singing activity:

Learn the song "Let My People Go."

(You can print the music from Appendix B.)

Preparation:

Purchase matzah crackers from the supermarket or from a kosher foods store accessed on the Internet. Purchase a small bottle of horseradish (not creamed). Have on hand some celery or parsley, a hard-boiled egg, a chicken bone or neck, a bowl of salt water, and some grape juice.

Make a recipe of *charoset*. Or make *charoset* together as a family activity. Have **a Bible** on hand to read from Exodus and Luke and a **Book of Mormon** to read from. **Flannel board pictures** of Moses or the Exodus story can be used as visual aids.

Ask: Does anyone know the story of Moses and the "Exodus?"

Try to remember and shape the story without referring to the scriptures. Guide the discussion so that the following points are included:

1. Jacob and his sons went to Egypt, because there was a famine in Canaan.

2. The Egyptians welcomed Jacob's family, because Joseph had found honor in the court of Pharaoh. The Egyptians gave them land and food.

3. Jacob's family grew and grew into a large population. Joseph died, and the later Pharaohs forgot what he had done to help Egypt. They were afraid that the descendants of Jacob (called the Israelites) would join with their enemies and fight against Egypt. They began to oppress the Israelites and made them slaves. They had to make bricks and do other hard labor. The Israelites prayed for deliverance.

4. Moses had been raised in Pharaoh's court, but he had to run away, because he killed an Egyptian taskmaster who was beating an Israelite slave. He had been gone from Egypt for many, many years. When he was about 80 years old, the Lord appeared to him in a burning bush and commanded him to go back to Egypt and talk to Pharaoh, to tell Pharaoh to let the Israelites go free.

5. Moses went to Egypt. His brother Aaron helped him. Pharaoh wouldn't listen, so the Lord sent plagues on the Egyptians. The last plague killed all the first-born of Egypt, and Pharaoh finally let the Israelites go.

6. The armies of Pharaoh followed the Israelites to kill them. The Lord parted the Red Sea, and the Israelites fled through it on dry ground. The Egyptian soldiers followed them, but they were swallowed up in the sea.

7. The plagues and the parting of the Red Sea were great miracles. The Israelites want to remember them always, so they can remember how great the Lord is, and how he blesses and watches over us.

Ask: Was it difficult to remember the whole story? The Jews don't want to ever forget the miracles of God, so they have a holiday to help them remember. The holiday comes once a year, and it is called Passover.

1. At Passover the Jews have a big feast. They tell the story of Moses and the Israelites.

2. At the Passover feast, the Jews serve foods that represent parts of the story. The foods help them to remember:

3. **The bone** represents the lamb they sacrificed the night before they left Egypt. The Lord commanded them to sacrifice the

lamb as an offering.

4. The ***charoset*** represents the mortar the Israelites used to make bricks for the Egyptians. It is sweet, because it also represents the sweetness of hope. Even when they were slaves, the Israelites had faith and hope.
5. The **egg** represents a temple offering and new birth in the spring. The Israelites left Egypt in the spring.
6. The **celery and parsley** represent the green herbs that grow in springtime. The Israelites were grateful for their crops and harvests.
7. The **horseradish** is bitter. Eating it brings tears to your eyes. It represents the bitterness of slavery and oppression.
8. The **salt water** represents the tears of affliction.
9. The ***matzah*** is really "unleavened bread." The Israelites left Egypt so fast, that they didn't have time to allow their bread to rise. It baked in the hot sun. Now, it also represents the manna that God gave the Israelites to eat in the wilderness.
10. The **"wine"** (grape juice) is called "the fruit of the vine." It represents joy. Our joy comes from being saved.

Demonstrate that during the Passover feast, Jews dip the herbs in the salt water to eat, and they eat a piece of *matzah* with *charoset* and horseradish. They sip the wine to remember the covenants the Lord made with Israel. Let everyone try it. Doing this helps Jews to **remember** the experiences of their ancient fathers. We need to remember the way the Lord can save us with miracles. Reciting the story of the Exodus helps us remember. Nephi did this when his brothers were losing their faith. **Read 1 Nephi 17:23-29, 40, 42.**

Explain:
Jesus went to Jerusalem with his family every Passover. They took offerings to the Temple (a lamb, just like at the time of the Exodus). Jesus was born in April, so the Passover season was also the time of His birthday. When Jesus was just about to turn thirty-three years old, He went to Jerusalem. Instead of having the Passover feast with his family, He called his apostles together to have the feast with them (Luke 22:7-16). This time, Jesus wanted His apostles to remember more than the deliverance from Egypt. He wanted His disciples to remember that He was the deliverer, and that He would deliver them from sin, the way He

delivered their forefathers from slavery in Egypt. Jesus blessed the matzah (the unleavened bread) that represented manna from heaven. He passed it to His disciples and told them to eat it in remembrance of His body. Jesus is the "bread of life." This bread became the sacrament bread. When we partake of the sacrament bread, we do it in remembrance of Christ.

Then Jesus blessed the wine. This "cup of joy" would represent the blood He shed for the remission of sins. The remission of our sins brings us joy. So, the Passover symbols became the Sacrament symbols. Instead of having Passover once each year to remember, we take the Sacrament every week.

A FIRST-FRUITS (BIKKURIM) FAMILY HOME EVENING

First-fruits falls just after the first days of Passover each year.

Songs suitable for this family home evening:

He is Risen...#199
Christ the Lord Is Risen Today...#200
Jesus Has Risen .... Page 70 (Children's Songbook)
Did Jesus Really Live Again.................... Page 64 (Children's Songbook)

Preparation:

Some sheaves of wheat or other grain would make a fine visual aid for this lesson. You might be able to find a reasonable sheaf of "grain" at an arts & crafts store, in the artificial flowers section. If you can obtain a few stems of grain, also have on hand a cord to tie them together. Pictures of grain fields or harvesters would also be helpful.

Explain:

Since the beginning of time, Heavenly Father's children have made offerings to the Lord. (Read Moses 5:5-8.) During the lifetime of Jesus, the children of Israel went to the Temple in Jerusalem to make offerings. They could go anytime they wanted to, but they were commanded to go three times each year (at Passover, the Feast of Weeks, and the Feast of Tabernacles). People made offerings to help support the Priesthood, to help the poor, to repent of their own sins, and to pray for good crops and harvests. They expected to receive blessings from the Lord, when they kept the commandments and gave their offerings the way they were counseled to. When the people went to Jerusalem for the Passover in the spring, they often went up to the Temple many times.

Sometimes they went to worship and to listen to the teachings of the Rabbis, and other times they made their offerings. They were commanded to sacrifice a lamb at the Passover. A few days later, on a holiday called "*Bikkurim*," they offered sheaves of grain. These sheaves of grain were very special. They were the "**first fruits**" of the new barley harvest, the very first grain harvest of the year. The people couldn't eat any grain from their new harvest until they had made this offering. The offering (and the prayers that they said) guaranteed that the rest of the summer would bring good, healthy crops.

The Israelites couldn't bring just any old grain. They had to bring the most perfect grain from their entire field. Before they could harvest any grain for themselves, they would go out into the field and examine the grain. With a cord, they would tie off the best grain. This would **set apart** the grain, so no one would pick it or injure it. When the grain was ripe, they would harvest it and take it to the Temple. You could say that the farmer planted his field, and the field brought forth "fruit." The chosen grain was the **first fruits** of that field and that harvest.

Discuss:

What does it mean "to bear fruit?" Fruit doesn't just come from fruit trees. There are other sorts of fruit, like the "fruits of our labors." That means that we have worked hard and our work has "borne fruit" — our work bore successful results. When we live the commandments, our fruits are righteousness. The Lord says the world will recognize the righteous by their "fruits." What are some of the fruits of missionary work? Of reading the scriptures? Of being kind to others?

What does it mean to be "set apart?" It means that through the authority of the priesthood, you can receive the special gifts, blessings and protection that will help you fulfill your callings. Whenever someone is called to a position in the Church (Primary Teacher, Organist, Bishop, Relief Society President, etc.) he is set apart for that calling. Jesus was set apart for his calling as the Savior of the world.

Why does the best grain have to be used for the offering? Everything we have belongs to the Lord. We honor him by giving back the first and the best of all that we have — our earnings, our talents, our time.

The Israelites had to offer other sorts of **first fruits** — the first and best fruit from their trees and gardens, and the first-born, most perfect cattle from their flocks.

Jesus was the first born to Mary, the Only Begotten of the Father, a perfect person. He was like the lamb offered on Passover, and because he was set apart, then cut down, he was like the grain offering made on *Bikkurim*. The year that Jesus died, the holiday of *Bikkurim* , was on a Sunday, the day that Jesus rose from the dead. In 1 Corinthians 15:3,4, and 20, the scriptures explain that Jesus Christ was the **first fruits** of the resurrection. That means he was the very first person ever to be resurrected, and he was also the choicest, most perfect person. Just as the grain offering guaranteed that good harvests would come all through the summer, Jesus' offering guaranteed that resurrection would come to all of us.

Ask: **What was the offering that Jesus made?** He offered all his time to serving his mission for Father in Heaven. He offered all his material possessions — he never owned any property. He offered his life to atone for our sins.

Ask: **What kinds of offerings do we make?** We pay tithing — many Latter-day Saints pay their tithing before they spend any of the money they earned. We offer service to our brothers and sisters. We offer our time to fill callings, and to serve as missionaries. We offer humble obedience and try to do the Lord's will.

In section 110 of the Doctrine and Covenants (v. 13-16) we read that Elijah appeared to Joseph Smith and Oliver Cowdery and gave them the keys to the sealing power. The sealing power binds families together for eternity. Elijah's visit occurred on Bikkurim, during Passover week. Why do you think he came on that holiday?

A WILDERNESS WALK FAMILY HOME EVENING

Songs suitable for this Family Home Evening:

How Firm a Foundation .... #85
Come, Come Ye Saints .... #30
Jesus, Lover of My Soul... #102
The Lord is My Shepherd .... #108
Pioneer Children Sang as They Walked ** .... Page 214
(Children's Songbook)

** Try singing this song both as an opening and closing song.
When opening, substitute the words "Children of Israel"
for "Pioneer Children," and "Some days" for "Sundays."
When closing, sing the song as written.

Preparation:

You will need a **blindfold** for each member of the family. Also, write the following words on sheets of paper, one phrase per sheet:

FORMER HOME	THROUGH THE WATER
BREAD	WATER
HEALING	GIFTS OF THE SPIRIT
PLACE TO WORSHIP	PROPHET — GUIDE
PROMISED LAND	SCRIPTURES

The activity (wandering in the wilderness) will take up most of the lesson. The activity can be staged outside on the lawn, if the evening is windless, or if you have something to keep the sheets of paper from blowing away. Otherwise, stage the activity in the family room with furniture pushed out of the way. At one end of the room or yard, place the paper saying "Former Home" on the floor or the ground. In front of this sheet, place the paper saying "Through the water." At the far end, place the paper saying "Promised Land." At random spots on the way, place the other sheets of paper. Begin the evening seated somewhere.

Ask: Who knows what the "Exodus" was? An exodus is the migration of a very large group of people. Turn to Exodus in the Old Testament. The Children of Israel had lived in Egypt for over four hundred years. At the beginning the Egyptians treated them very well, but at the end, the Egyptians enslaved them and oppressed them. They had prayed for deliverance, and the Lord heard them. The Lord wanted them to go back to the land he had promised to the seed of Abraham, called Canaan. In order to get to the Promised Land, the Children had to cross a vast desert, where it was hot, and where there was very little food or water. (Use map #3 at the back of your Bible to show the family the route they followed. All the brownish land is dessert wilderness.) You can see that the Children of Israel did not go straight to the Promised Land. It took them forty years to get there.

Ask: Why did the Lord make the Israelites travel in circles and long paths before they could get to the Promised Land? They camped for long periods of time. They took detours to avoid their enemies. They looped back around, because they weren't righteous enough to finish their journey. The Lord wanted more than to get the Children of Israel home. He wanted to train them to be a nation of priests. He wanted them to be missionaries to the world. He wanted them to be obedient and to understand the gospel. He kept them in the wilderness until they had learned all the lessons the Lord wanted to teach them. That took forty years.

Explain:

The desert wilderness that the Israelites traveled through was a difficult place to live. Without the Lord's help, they would have died. Come, and I'll show you how they made it to the Promised Land.

Go to the activity area: Have everyone stand next to the paper saying "Former Home." Explain that this former home was Egypt. Point to the paper saying "Through the Water." Explain that the water was the Red Sea. The Lord parted the waters so that the Israelites could cross over on dry ground. They crossed the water into the wilderness.

Blindfold everyone: You can give each person a couple of spins to disorient him.

Tell the family to go across the wilderness to the Promised Land. Allow them to wander blindly. Bring them all back to the starting point, and tell them you're going to try something different. Select a family member and designate him/her as the "Prophet and Guide." (The prophet (Moses) was one of the blessings the Lord gave the Israelites to help them on their journey.) Take off his/her blindfold. Tell the other family members what you're doing. Have them all join hands. Tell the Prophet—Guide to lead them straight to the Promised Land. When they get there, have everyone remove their blindfolds. Explain that with the Prophet-Guide leading them, they got to their goal quickly, but they missed all the milestones on the way, and they didn't learn any of the lessons Heavenly Father wanted them to learn. They got to the Promised Land, but they were the same people they were when they left; they had arrived in the Promised Land unprepared. Have everyone return to Egypt.

This time have the Prophet-Guide lead them from paper to paper. No one is blindfolded. Everyone can see. The Prophet-Guide can explain each milestone on the way to the Promised Land and help the Children of Israel understand what the Lord wants them to learn. Without learning these things, they would not be prepared to inherit the Promised Land:

- **BREAD** — The Lord gave the Israelites "manna" from which to make flour and bread. They always had enough to eat. This taught them they could rely on the Lord for their daily sustenance. Jesus is the bread of life.

- **WATER** — The Lord led the Israelites to water. Through his prophet, Moses, bad water was made fresh, and water sprang from the desert stone. Jesus is the "living water." With this living water, we will never thirst.

- **HEALING** — The Lord healed the Israelites of sickness when they were righteous and obedient. The Lord has power to heal; the righteous can call upon the Lord to heal them.

- **PLACE TO WORSHIP** — The Lord told Moses how to build a temple in the wilderness. The temple was portable; it could be taken apart and carried to the next camp. The Lord comes to his temple. The temple is the center of our worship.

- **GIFTS OF THE SPIRIT** — The Lord gave the Israelites prophets (Moses and Aaron); He blessed them with a cloud by day and pillar of fire by night to lead them through the wilderness. He ordained the men from the tribe of Levi to serve the people as priests and teachers. He taught the Israelites to repent and learn obedience.

- **SCRIPTURES** — When they arrived at Mt. Sinai, the Lord gave the Israelites commandments and scriptures. The scriptures are like a map to guide us through this life in righteousness.

Have everyone sit down. Ask: How is the walk through the wilderness like a walk through this life on earth? Our former home was the Pre-mortal World, where we lived with Heavenly Father. We were born of water into earth-life, which is like a wilderness. There are trials; it can be dangerous; we can get lost; we can get sick. The Promised Land is the Celestial Kingdom. The Lord wants all of us to get there, but He wants us to be prepared. We have to learn to be like Him on our way through the wilderness. He gives us a prophet and scriptures to guide us. He gives us the Holy Ghost to help us know what is true. He assigns worthy men to serve us as priesthood holders. He heals us from sickness and sin through the power of the priesthood. He gave us Jesus Christ, who is the "bread of life," and the "living water." He gave us churches and temples.

Explain:

The Exodus was a great teaching tool for the Israelites. The Lord walked them through the Plan of Salvation, or the Plan of Happiness. The Lord did the same thing for our pioneer ancestors. They started in Nauvoo. They crossed the water (the Missouri River). They crossed the wilderness to the land promised to them (in Utah). They had a prophet to lead them (Brigham Young). They had scriptures (The Book of Mormon, The Doctrine and Covenants, The Pearl of Great Price, The Bible). They had miracles and gifts of the spirit to help them. (Read D&C 103:15-20.)

Conclude:

Life on earth is like a wilderness we must pass through. The Lord gives us a lot of help during our journey. Some people ignore his help. They try to find their way on their own. Some people become lost; others are injured. Some lose sight of the Promised Land and don't even remember that it's there. The Lord watches over those who will hear him. He guides them and nurtures them on their way home.

A FEAST OF WEEKS FAMILY HOME EVENING (#1)

(The Lord Gave the Israelites Scriptures.)

Songs suitable for this Family Home Evening:

As I Search the Holy Scriptures...#277
The Iron Rod ....#274
Search, Ponder, and Pray ....Page 109 (Children's Songbook)

Preparation:

Have all your scriptures handy. Each member of the family will need paper and a pencil or pen.

Explain:

When the Children of Israel were wandering in the wilderness, they came to a tall mountain called Mount Sinai. The Lord commanded Moses to ascend the mountain where he could speak with the Lord personally and receive instruction for the people. The Lord gave Moses the "Ten Commandments." Look them up in Exodus 20 (verses 3-17). These commandments are still in effect today. People all over the world look to them as a guide to moral behavior. The Lord gave Moses more than the Ten Commandments; He gave him the *"Torah,"* the laws of God contained in the first five books of the Bible, called the Five Books of Moses. We have more writings of Moses, given to Joseph Smith by revelation. Find them in the Pearl of Great Price.

The scriptures were a very great blessing to the Children of Israel. While Moses guided them through the wilderness, the scriptures guided them spiritually. By following the scriptures, they could purify themselves and become worthy to inherit the Promised Land. (Remember that the land they had come from, Egypt, had been wicked. The Israelites had a lot to learn in the wilderness.)

Explain:

Lehi had a dream about a vast wilderness. Turn to **1 Nephi 8:7,8** for a description of the wilderness Lehi saw. Do you remember the rest of his dream? If not, read on. The tree Lehi saw had marvelously wonderful fruit, representing the love of God and blessings of the gospel. The people who made it through the wilderness in the mists of darkness held on to an iron rod (**1 Nephi 8:19-24**). The iron rod in the dream represented the "word of God," the scriptures. The scriptures give us something straight and true that we can follow and hold on to. If we do, we can also be led straight through the wilderness to the Lord's kingdom.

Explain:

The Jews believe that the Lord gave scriptures to Moses at Mount Sinai, <u>letter by letter.</u> Every time the Jewish scribes copied the scriptures, they did so <u>letter by letter.</u> They were not allowed to change anything, even if a sentence didn't seem to make any sense. For that reason, the scriptures came from the Jews pure and undefiled.

Activity:

Choose a verse of scripture. Have everyone copy it, letter by letter, with every punctuation point in perfect order. Look them over for mistakes, then check them again. This might seem tedious, but the work of copying the Holy Scriptures was very tedious work. It was extremely important that everything be correct. Roll the papers up into scrolls. Explain that a Torah scroll is so sacred that a Jew is expected to give his life to protect the scroll if it is in danger. Would you give your life to protect your scriptures? It's just not necessary, is it? We have millions of copies. But what if there were only one copy? Yes, it would be that important to protect the scriptures with our lives. Torah scrolls are treated like treasures and kept in beautiful closets. How do you treat your scriptures?

Explain:

Later, translators took these scriptures and translated them into many languages. These translators were religious scholars from many religions and societies, and they had their own ideas. If something didn't make sense, they might change it so it <u>would</u> make sense. Many plain and precious truths were lost because of this practice.

Activity:

Turn to **Genesis 6:16**. Read it together:

"A window[a] shalt thou make to the ark, and in a cubit shalt thou finish it above; and the door of the ark shalt thou set in the side thereof; with lower, second, and third stories shalt thou make it."

This scripture makes fine sense. The Lord is telling Noah how to build the ark. Now look at the notes below:

"16a: HEB *tsohar:* some rabbis believed it was a precious stone that shone in the ark."

Interesting. The word *tsohar* means precious and shining, and the Jews had a tradition that a precious, shining stone lit the ark. Why did the translator change this word to "window?" Because it surely made more sense to him. But the original message was lost.

Read Ether 2:25 and 3:1-6. Why do you think The Brother of Jared chose to bring stones to the Lord? Could he have known from the scriptures, or from the stories of Noah, how the ark had been lit? Knowing the story of the Jaredites helps us understand the meaning of *tsohar* in Genesis. If the translator had known the story of the Jaredites, he might not have changed the word to mean "window."

Explain:

Our prophets have testified to us that the Book of Mormon is a pure book, the most pure of any on the earth. This is because the Lord himself guided Joseph Smith through the translation from the original, ancient records. This book was translated by pure revelation straight from the Lord himself. We should hold to it as our "iron rod," to lead us through the wilderness of life.

A FEAST OF WEEKS FAMILY HOME EVENING (#2)

(The Lord Gives His Disciples the Holy Spirit.)

Songs suitable for this Family Home Evening:

Let the Holy Spirit Guide ....#143
Thy Spirit, Lord, Has Stirred Our Souls .... #157
God is Love... #87
The Still Small Voice .... Page 106 (Children's Songbook)
I Think the World is Glorious .... Page 230 (Children's Songbook)

Preparation:

Obtain fresh fruit of your choice to create a fruit salad. If you wish to make blintzes, a traditional food for the Feast of Weeks, the recipe is found in the resource materials.

If you desire to make flower wreaths for your daughters' hair as a family activity, you will need flowers, a long, pliable vine or stem for each wreath, and very fine wire or floral tape. Instructions for making flower head-wreaths are found in the resource materials.

Explain:

The Jews celebrate Passover in the early spring to celebrate their deliverance from Egypt. A few days later, they celebrate "first fruits." Both holidays testify of Jesus as the Lamb of God, and the first fruits of the resurrection. These holidays occur just as the first crop of barley is being harvested, the very first harvest of the year. Then the Jews count forty-nine days (seven weeks) until the first wheat harvest. These forty-nine days are like the journey through the wilderness. They are full of uneasiness and prayers for help.

The reason for this is that this is the summer growing season in Canaan. The winter rains stop falling just after Passover, and then there is nothing but sunshine until the next October. That's a lot of sun. Everything becomes hot and dry. In the evening, however, the moist air from the Mediterranean Sea blows in from the west. The moisture condenses on the ground in the form of dew. This moisture helps, when there is no rain.

Sometimes the wind changes direction and blows in from the south-east, from the sandy desert areas. This wind is very hot, dirty, and dry. It can harm the crops. The Israelites would pray and pray that their crops would be safe, just like they prayed and prayed that they would walk safely through the wilderness.

When the Children of Israel were wandering in the wilderness, they came to a mountain called Sinai. The Lord was on the mountain, and Moses went up to speak with him. The Lord gave Moses commandments and scriptures, a very great blessing to the Israelites. It was like the Spirit of God poured down on them from Mt. Sinai.

This pouring out of spiritual blessings is just like the pouring out of the sweet harvests of wheat, flowers and fruit that come forth during this season in the Holy Land. On the fiftieth day (after counting seven weeks) the Jews have a festival called "The Feast of Weeks." This holiday is also called "Pentecost," which comes from the Greek word for fifty. When the temple in Jerusalem still stood, the people would go there to make offerings. They formed parades and decorated everything with boughs of greenery and flowers. They carried baskets of fruit and wore flowers in their hair. They went to the temple to give thanks for all the bounties of the land. They would eat fruit, and desserts made with milk and cheese. This was a very joyous and beautiful occasion.

Explain:

After Jesus was crucified, his disciples and followers were in a lot of danger. Certain wicked leaders thought his group of followers might get larger and larger, and they didn't want that to happen. During these many weeks, Jesus visited his apostles and followers, but they still worried what would become of them and their small group of believers. It was like walking in the wilderness; they needed to pray and have faith to survive. Then they went to Jerusalem and the temple at Pentecost. There, a wonderful thing happened. Many thousands of people had gathered at the temple for the festival, people from many lands, who spoke many different languages. As he had done at Mt. Sinai, the Lord sent an outflow of his spirit upon his apostles and followers. He gave them the Gift of the Holy Ghost. **(Read Acts 2:1-7, 14, 16-17.)** Many people were converted to the truth on Pentecost. You can almost see them rejoicing amid the flowers and fruits of the festival. The Holy Ghost gives us great comfort and witnesses of the truth.

A FEAST OF TRUMPETS FAMILY HOME EVENING

Songs suitable for this Family Home Evening:

Awake and Arise .... #8
Awake, Ye Saints of God, Awake .... #17
Come, All Ye Saints of Zion .... #38
Hope of Israel .... #259

Preparation:

If you choose to, make up a recipe of honey cake for the family. You can find photographs of *shofarim* (trumpets made of animal horns) on the Internet at Wikipedia.

Show the family the zodiac chart found earlier in this book. Explain that the Jewish calendar is luni-solar. The months are calculated more by the moon than the sun. This means that the holidays move around on the solar calendar, but stay in the same season. Find the month of *Nisan* on the calendar. Passover always falls in the middle of the Jewish month of *Nisan*, while on the calendar we use, it might fall in March or April. But Passover is always in the spring. Turn the calendar upside down. Remind the family that because Hebrew is written from right to left, the wheel of this calendar is read counter-clockwise. Now a new season, Fall, is at the top. As summer moves into fall, we find the month of *Elul*. *Elul* is a month of preparation. From the first day of Elul to the autumn High Holy Days is another 49-day period of preparation for the Final Judgment. Our wilderness journey is nearing its end. But we must be found worthy to enter the Promised Land. In this case, the Promised Land is Zion, the land of the righteous. Look at the chart again. The symbols for the months of the zodiac are representations of star clusters or constellations. Look at the drawing for *Nisan*. It is a bull. The bull can represent the ram that was substituted for Isaac when Abraham needed a sacrifice. Look at the picture under *Elul*. It is Virgo, the virgin. She is a fitting symbol for the month of *Elul*. Remember the parable of the ten virgins — they all started out prepared to meet the Lord, but only five were prepared when he actually arrived. Look at the picture under the month of *Tishri*. These are balance scales. They are the symbol of justice and judgment. Tishri is the month of final judgment. See how *Tishri* divides the year in half, with *Nisan* directly across from it. *Nisan* and *Tishri* are "meridians of time." Jesus was born in *Nisan*, and *Tishri* represents his Second Coming to judge all mankind.

Explain:

Rosh HaShanah, the Feast of Trumpets, is the time to call everyone and let them know that it's time to awake, arise, and gather to the temple. Many times in the scriptures, the Lord tells us to be watchmen on the watchtower to signal people, and warn them of danger. **(See D&C section 101.)** This time the watchman is at the Temple Mount. One hundred silver trumpets are blown by the priests with the call of the *shofar* blasting out in front of them.

Read: Alma 5:57-58 and Isaiah 51:1, 4-5, 7, 9.

Explain:

The long, dry season (wandering in the wilderness) is coming to an end. The final harvests of the year are being gathered in. The righteous are the Lord's harvest. This is the time to separate the wheat from the tares. **(See Matthew 13, and D&C 101:64-67.)** Soon the winter rains will come, always a very great blessing for the Israelites. The rains represent the Savior — the spring rains (Passover) represent his first coming; the winter rains represent his second coming. The righteous are preparing; they have the hope that they will be gathered to meet the Messiah. Therefore, this is a time of joy, as well as a time of preparation and repentance. We eat honey cake and apples dipped in honey, for acceptance by the Lord is sweet.

A DAY OF ATONEMENT FAMILY HOME EVENING

This is the High Holy Day of Yom Kippur,
observed 10 days after The Feast of Trumpets in the Fall.

Songs suitable for this Family Home Evening:

> More Holiness Give Me .... #131
> Repentance .... Page 98 (Children's Songbook)
> Help Me, Dear Father .... Page 99 (Children's Songbook)

Preparation:

Arrange a display of family records — baptismal certificates, birth certificates, report cards, bank registers. If desired, you can construct or buy three journals for illustrative purposes, to represent the three books of judgment.

Explain:

The trumpets have sounded from the temple mount in Jerusalem, calling the Children of Israel to awake, arise, and gather. The sound of the trumpet is also a call to repent.

Ask: What does it mean to repent? How do we do it? We confess; we try to make restitution; we don't commit the sin again. The Jews call this a "turning" — that is, turning away from wickedness and towards righteousness. Every year, beginning at the Feast of Trumpets, the Children of Israel would repent as a whole nation turning to God.

Ask: What would it be like if everyone in the world repented at once?

Explain:

The Israelites knew that everyone was repenting at the same time. When they met people on the street, or in a store, they would wish them "easy fast," and "good signature." Those are very strange greetings, aren't they? For ten days after the trumpets sounded, the Israelites would all repent. On the tenth day, *Yom Kippur*, or the "Day of Atonement," they would all fast and pray for forgiveness. They would also forgive each other for any offenses they might have caused. They believed that at this season, the Lord would write their names in his books.

Just like we keep records here on earth (show the items on display), the angels keep records in heaven. The Jews believe the Lord has three books, one for the names of the righteous (called the Book of Life), one for the names of the wicked, and one for the names of the people who couldn't decide whether to be good or bad and needed more time to repent. These heavenly books are mentioned in the Book of Mormon.

Read: Alma 5:57,58.

Explain:

This fall season of the year was when the final harvests of grains and fruit were being brought in. The final harvest is symbolic of the Lord's final harvest, when he gathers in the righteous and destroys the wicked just before the millennium. This holy holiday is symbolic of the last chance to repent before the Savior comes again.

In Israel, this day is a very solemn Sabbath day, even when it falls in the middle of the week. People go to worship services, but they walk. No one in the entire country drives a car on this day, unless there is a real emergency, and someone needs an ambulance or a fire truck. All the streets are completely quiet, and everyone in the country is fasting and praying. But even though the day is so solemn and quiet, the people are supposed to be happy. They are supposed to realize that the Messiah will come soon and usher in the Millennium, a time of peace and happiness, with no disease or war or death.

Ask: How can we make sure our names are written in the Lord's Book of Life, the book of the righteous? Develop the attributes of our Heavenly Father (see the chapter, "Be Thou Therefore Perfect.") Do good works. Repent of our sins and transgressions. Be kind to other people. Forgive. Pray. Keep the commandments. Listen to the Holy Ghost. Be baptized and confirmed. Take the sacrament. Go to church. Read the scriptures. Get the temple ordinances. Fulfill our callings.

A FEAST OF TABERNACLES FAMILY HOME EVENING

Including instructions for building a "Sukkah"

Songs suitable for this Family Home Evening:

O God, Our Help in Ages Past	#31
O Saints of Zion	#39
The Day Dawn Is Breaking	#52
Come, O Thou King of Kings	#59
When He Comes Again	Page 82 (Children's Songbook)

Preparation:

Assemble a number of fruits, vegetables or grain to represent the final harvest of the year. An outside-the-home activity could include a visit to a fruit stand or a grocery store. Choose fruits that are native to the state where you live. Have the children find a <u>flawless</u> example, such as a <u>perfect</u> apple, to offer to the Lord as an example of our fine harvests. This offering shows our gratitude, and our realization that all these blessings come from him. Prepare a meal or salad from the native fruits or harvest. (A search online or from a state resource can identify your state's native crops.)

Explain:

Sukkot was a pilgrimage festival, the third and last of the Jewish year, and the happiest. It began on the 15th of Tishri (in the fall) and lasted one week. There is no temple right now in Jerusalem, but the Jews still celebrate this holiday with great joy. This holiday is referred to as "The Season of Our Rejoicing." This is the time of the very final harvest of the year. The harvest has been bounteous; we have been richly blessed. Also, we have gone through a season of repentance, and our repentance has been accepted. Our names have been written in the Lord's Book of Life, and now we have the opportunity of visiting him in his house, the Temple, his kingdom. It is as if he is the bridegroom, and we are going to the wedding canopy to be sealed to him forever.

Explain:

When we were wanderers in the wilderness, the Lord commanded us to build special booths, or tabernacles. They were very flimsy. They would never protect us from our enemies, not even from the wind or rain. The Lord commanded us to leave holes in the roof! Why would He do that? He was teaching us something — that **He** would be our protection from enemies and from the weather, from anything that could harm us, if we would just be righteous. He commanded that we be able to see the stars through the roof, as if we were watching and waiting for Him to come to us. *Sukkot,* The Feast of Tabernacles, is the celebration of his coming to usher in one thousand years of peace and happiness.

Explain:

During the festival, which lasts one week, trumpets are blown, and the priests march around the temple altar, doing the "Hosanna Shout." If you have been to an LDS temple dedication, you too have participated in the Hosanna Shout. It is the acknowledgment that Jehovah is the Lord, and that he will save us. By doing the shout, we welcome him as our Savior.

The Jews are commanded to build *sukkahs (sukkot)* for their families. In Israel, the restaurants and hotels, and some schools, also build them. These booths are magical places. Being inside one is very much like being inside a Christmas tree. They are fun to build, fun to decorate, and fun to camp out in.

HOW TO BUILD A SUKKAH

I guarantee that it will be the memory of a lifetime, if you decide to build a *Sukkah* as a family.

In Israel, *Sukkot* occurs in late September or early October. These are the waning weeks of summer. The air is still very mild, with just a hint that the cool rains might be arriving soon. Ignore the Jewish calendar, and choose the week when the weather is right for your locale.

Follow the instructions for building the *Sukkah*. You can place a small table inside, if you like. Decorate with harvest drawings done by the kids — hang them from the ceiling or pin them to the walls. Mini-lights and other ornaments suitable for the harvest season can add a festive atmosphere. Examples of your state's harvest crops can be brought into the *sukkah*, if they are "perfect." (Dried squash and corn are fine. Use your Thanksgiving decorations.)

A *sukkah* can be any size, as long as you can eat in it. It is both acceptable and wise to use a portion of a fence, house, or deck as a supporting wall or two. Add supports for the other walls. Most sukkahs are rectangular in shape with 3 full walls and 1 partial wall. The opening is used for the entrance. Sukkahs are meant to be relatively flimsy, to the standards described below.

The *sukkah* does not have to have four complete walls. Use sheets or cheap tarps for the remaining walls. The roof is very important. It must be made of branches or leaves, never anything made of metal, or edible as food. No part of the roof can be attached to the ground, so you can't bend a tree over to use as a roof. Nor is a covered patio acceptable. Narrow slats of wood are acceptable as roofing material, but tree boughs lend much more atmosphere.

Be sure the walls of your *Sukkah* cannot blow away in the wind., but do not tie down the roofing materials. The roof must be sparsely filled in, so that rain can get through, and the stars can be seen through it at night. However, don't leave unfilled spaces of more than 10 inches.

The *sukkah* should be a shady place in the sunshine, just like the gourd shaded the prophet Jonah from the sun. Add decorations as mentioned above.

A PURIM FAMILY HOME EVENING

Purim is not one of the High Holy Days ordained by Jehovah during the Exodus, but the holiday still has religious meaning. Purim is the celebration of the story of Esther, bride of King Ahashverosh of ancient Persia. Esther saved her people, the Jews, from destruction because of her courageous and righteous choices. Purim is celebrated in February-March, and is a holiday of unparalleled fun and good cheer. We were more than happy to drop Halloween with its ghoulish overtones and adopt Purim as our holiday for dress-up and sweets. Purim is also more desirable than the Orthodox Christian carnival (pre-Lent) season with its tendency towards abandonment of good Christian moral behavior (think Mardi Gras). Everyone dresses in costume on Purim. Since the story of Esther is about a princess-bride, little girls most often choose bridal or princess costumes, but anything will do. (We saw a gorilla driving the streets of Jerusalem on Purim.) Instead of going "trick-or-treating," Jewish children create little packages of sweets for their classmates and friends. These are called *mishlo'ach manot*. These packages are more sumptuous and elaborate when passed adult to adult or business to business, and may be delivered by disguised messengers. Gifts to the poor are also traditional. The highlight of the holiday is going to the synagogue in full costume for the reading of the *Megillah* (The Book of Esther). Everyone brings noisemakers of any type — sticks, rattles, Purim pistols, spinners, etc. Whenever the reader (the Cantor of the synagogue) comes to the name of the wicked villain, Haman, everyone hisses, boos, and makes a general tumult with their noisemakers. The names of Esther and her good cousin, Mordechai, elicit sounds of approval from the congregation.

Songs suitable for this Family Home Evening:

> Choose the Right .... #239
> Do What is Right .... #237

Preparation:

Prepare a recipe of Hamentaschen ("Haman's Hats" or "Haman's Ears"). Set out the following supplies for making "Graggers" (noisemakers).

> Juice cans (clean and dry), with one lid in place   Contact paper
> Decorative stickers   Jingle bells

Dry beans   Scissors
Glitter   White Glue or

Activity:

- Make noisemakers according to the following directions:
- Use a juice can with one lid in place, cleaned and dried.
- Drop a few bells and dry beans into the can.
- Cut a circular pattern for the end-cover of the noisemaker by creating a circle 1" wider than the can.
- Cut one circle out of contact paper for each can.
- Using the scissors, snip ½" cuts about 1" apart around the perimeter of each circle.
- Peel off the backing of a circle, trying to leave some backing in the center (so the bells and beans won't stick to the paper), but pulling the backing off the tabs you created.
- Cover the open end of the juice can with the circle.
- Push the edges down around the side of the can, so that the circle adheres.
- Cut out another piece of contact paper, this time a rectangle the same width as the juice can is tall.
- Stick the paper to the can and press all the way around it, covering the original design on the can and sealing in the tabs of the circle you already applied.
- Decorate the covered can with stickers and glitter.

Activity:

After the noisemakers are finished, explain the holiday of Purim to the children, using the opening paragraph above. Send everyone to find elements of costumes around the house and get dressed. Return to the selected area, grab the noisemakers, and open your Bible to the Book of Esther.

The Book of Esther is read (actually, chanted or sung) in its entirety in the synagogue. If you want to use a shortened version, tell the story found in Appendix H. As you read, everyone should boo and make noise when Haman's name is mentioned, and cheer when you mention Esther or

Mordechai. After the story is finished, share some Hamentaschen with the family (recipe in the resource section).

A CHANUKAH FAMILY HOME EVENING

Chanukah is another favorite Jewish holiday that does not originate from the Exodus. Chanukah carries no Messianic symbolism. Chanukah lasts for eight days and falls around Christmas-time. In order to keep Jewish children from being so attracted to the trappings of Christmas, the celebration of Chanukah is becoming more and more elaborate. Children often receive a gift each night.

Chanukah is the celebration of a miracle that occurred about 160 years before Christ. King Antiochus had led a Greco-Syrian alliance in conquering the kingdom of Judah, taking control of the temple as well as the government. Antiochus demanded that the Jews worship the Greek gods, that they reject their religion, their customs, and their beliefs. Some Jews refused and rose up in rebellion. They were led by the Maccabee family — Judah Maccabee and his four brothers. Judah and his brothers had chosen their own last name. It means "hammerer" in Hebrew. After three years of bitter fighting, the Maccabees and their followers succeeded in driving out the Syrians and reclaiming the Temple. The Temple had been desecrated by the Syrians. They had erected statues of Greek gods there, and had sacrificed to them. On the 25th day of the month of Kislev, the Temple was cleansed and ready for rededication.

In every Jewish place of worship, and especially in the Temple, there is a light, called the *N'er Tamid*, "eternal light." Once lit, the light should never be extinguished. The Syrians had extinguished the flame, and the Maccabees wanted to relight it. Only a tiny jug of temple oil could be found. The oil lamp was filled and lit. The oil was just enough to provide light for one day, but it burned for eight, a great miracle. The holiday of Chanukah commemorates this miracle, as well as the victory over the Syrians. Chanukah is the "Festival of Lights," but the word *chanukah* means "rededication." Celebration of the holiday includes gift-giving, parties, singing, decorating, but most of all the lighting of the holiday candles.

The word for "lamp" in Hebrew is *menorah*. Remember that the Jewish every-day menorah has seven branches. A *chanukah menorah* has nine, eight for the nights of the holiday, plus one for the lighting-candle, called a *shamash*. A chanukah menorah is actually called a *chanukiyah*. On the first night the *shamash* is lit and used to light the first candle. Both candles are allowed to burn completely, while holiday festivities take place. On the second evening the burned-down candles are replaced, and the *shamash* is lit and used to light two candles, which again are allowed to burn completely. And so forth through the eight-day holiday. Remember, the candles are placed in the lamp from right to left. (Hebrew is written from right to left.)

A *chanukiyah* can look like anything. The lights can be candles or oil flames. Contests are held in Israeli schools and communities, and at Jewish community centers, to see who can create the most artistic lamp. One interesting winner at my son's school in Jerusalem was constructed from a gnarled piece of driftwood. The candle-holders were upturned walnut shells.

The most traditional game for *chanukah* is spinning the "dreydel." It is a simple game of chance.

Songs suitable for this Family Home Evening:

The Light Divine .... #305
We Love Thy House .... #247
I Love to See the Temple .... Page 95 (Children's Songbook)

Preparation:

Purchase birthday candles for the creation of a family *chanukah menorah*, or have materials on hand for each family member to create his own. Prepare a recipe of *chanukah latkes* (potato pancakes), and have applesauce on hand to serve with them, or else cook up a batch of *sufganiyot* (*chanukah* doughnuts). If desired, reproduce the pattern for the *chanukah dreydel* on stiff cardboard and make *dreydels* for an activity.

Read the history of the holiday found above.

Activity #1:

Either assign each family member to create his own *chanukah menorah*, or else brainstorm a design for one, decide what materials are available in the house, and construct one as a family. Light the candles as directed in the history.

Activity #2:

Make *dreydels* from the pattern and play the *dreydel* game as a family. You'll have to use your own judgment on this one. No *chanukah* celebration is complete without *dreydel* spinning, but it's simple gambling. Use items without value, toothpicks, candies, nuts, or raisins, or the like, for the booty. (See Appendix I for instructions and a dreydel pattern.)

Activity #3:

Using the Chanukah recipes in Appendix J, make Chanukah food as a family.

Figure 1: A seven-branched menorah

Figure 2a: This Hanukkah Menorah is made to represent the neighborhoods of Jerusalem. The Shamash is taller and on the right.

Appendix B: PASSOVER
HOW TO PRESENT A PASSOVER FEAST

The presentation of a Passover Feast can be an enlightening and enriching experience for Latter-day Saints. Various Christian organizations and churches regularly stage Passovers, because of the profound Messianic imagery found therein. Passover feasts have been presented yearly at Brigham Young University for over twenty years. However, there is always a danger inherent in presenting the rituals of another culture or religion. It is important to remain centered on sound LDS doctrine, while being as true as possible to Jewish culture. If successful, the evening can reaffirm testimonies of Christ, while educating celebrants in the culture of the Jews. How can this be achieved? First of all, I have rewritten the traditional Jewish *haggadah* (narration) outlining the ritual. My version includes notes and scriptural references relating the Jewish ritual to LDS gospel messages, as well as explaining the Last Supper as a Passover meal, at which the sacramental ordinance was introduced. Following the ritual in this *haggadah*, then, introduces the Jewish cultural and religious messages in the feast, while teaching revealed LDS doctrine. Secondly, preparations for the feast should reinforce the Jewish cultural experience. It's a learning experience to try to keep kosher to the extent that it's possible. Foods labeled "kosher for Passover" might not be available in your area, or they might be expensive to buy. In that case, at least do what you can to <u>completely</u> avoid leaven in the meal. Since the feast is traditionally a meat meal, don't use any milk products. Serve Jewish traditional foods, and enjoy tasting these new recipes. In a ward setting or for a large group, it is nice to have a large display table of Jewish art objects, books, etc. Collect these from people who have taken Holy Land tours, borrow books from the library, or download pictures from the Internet. The most difficult part of preparing for a Passover meal is setting the table properly. Many items are required on the table, and it can get a little complicated to remember them all. I have included a checklist of table items, and I've included a photograph of a table set for the meal. The recipes I've chosen are easy to make and don't require many unusual ingredients. (Remember that milk chocolate is a dairy food, and that gelatin is not kosher unless it's vegetarian and labeled with the kosher symbol.)

Presenting a Passover for a large group requires some creative planning. Luckily, it's been done before, and you can benefit from my own trial-and-error experiences.

1. Set up the tables as directed and diagramed. Be certain the presenter has a microphone. A game for seating the guests can be found in the supplementary materials.
2. Each table or set of tables should have a seder plate and ritual foods, and someone should be assigned to pass around those foods to his group.
3. Everyone should be able to read along in a *haggadah*, so those will need to be printed and photocopied. I usually allow my guests to keep theirs, and they are usually amenable to covering the cost of the printing.
4. If you are inclined to decorate the hall, Israel's colors are sky-blue and white. Symbols of Judaism and Israel are the six-pointed star (called the *Magen David*, or "Shield of David"), and the seven-branched *menorah* (candlestick). These symbols are easy to find as clip art in common word-processing software programs and in clip-art software packages. They are also easily found on the Internet.
5. Welch's makes a good, easy to obtain, red grape juice to use for the Passover wine. Yet, it is rarely found in abundance at the grocery store. Order ahead.
6. Recipes are found here and in the supplementary materials. Make assignments to the food committee. My recipes are geared to feed ten people.
7. Find books and Jewish objets d'art for a decorative table.
8. Assign someone to accompany the group on the piano when they sing the Passover songs. Piano music for two recreational songs is included here. Perhaps you would like some music to play as people arrive and as they eat dinner. Download some

ethnic Jewish music to play. Klezmer music or Middle Eastern music would both be good.

9. Assume that the presentation plus the meal will take a total of 2 1/2 to 3 hours, not including set up and clean up. That's a long evening. Make sure everyone is aware of that ahead of time. Those who leave early miss the most profound portions of the ritual.

10. Traditionally, a person hides the *afikomon* (the sacramental *matzah*) after it has been broken, blessed, and wrapped in white linen. Later, a child finds it and redeems it for a gift. In a family setting, this is easy. Be prepared to present a prize to the child. In a large group setting, this is more problematic. A small gift of sweets could be provided to the officiator at each table. The *afikomon* can be wrapped and passed under the table until it ends up in someone's lap. The person who guesses its location can receive the reward. Or tape a star under someone's chair before the festivities begin. That person can "find" the *afikomon* and gain the reward.

FOR THE PRESENTER

As a presenter, you should make yourself thoroughly familiar with the Passover section of this book. You should also familiarize yourself with the *haggadah*. Jot notes into your own copy of the *haggadah* to help you add explanatory information and answer questions which may arise during the ritual. Print out the suggested scriptures for the evening on cards or slips of paper, so the celebrants can participate by reading them, or remind people to bring their scriptures with them to the feast.

The Passover evening provides a very religious experience, but it is meant to be a lot of fun. Humor is allowed and encouraged, as long as it doesn't detract from the spiritual message. I am a believer in cultural integrity. Try to make the leap into Jewish culture. Find a fun Jewish joke as an ice-breaker, instead of something that refers to your local sports team. Here is how I begin my presentations.

1. Welcome the guests. Tell them you are going to present a Passover meal and ritual, the Passover being a celebration and memorial of the deliverance of the Israelites from Egypt under Moses' leadership. The order of the evening is **ritual, meal, ritual.** During the meal the guests can socialize as happily and

noisily as they like, but they will have to quiet down again to experience the climax of the evening and conclusion of the ritual after the meal. (Don't allow guests to bow out right after the meal — they will miss the most important and profound messages of the evening.) Explain that Passover is a festival ordained by the Lord. It lasts one week, and has become one-and-the-same with the Feast of Unleavened Bread. But anciently, the Passover referred to the one-day sacrifice of the Paschal Lamb, followed by the seven-day Feast of Unleavened Bread, a total of eight days. Tell your guests you hope they will glean many spiritual messages from the evening's festivities, and that they will also enjoy a Jewish cultural experience, as well. Ask if anyone knows what it means "to keep kosher."

2. Some people will know a little about keeping kosher. Not eating meat with milk is an important point. Explain that keeping kosher for Passover entails clearing leaven out of the household and the meal. Explain why and how. Ask the guests to define "leaven." This is where I enjoy presenting an "ice-breaking" activity called, "The Kosher Quiz." I bring with me to the dinner, a basket containing food items for the quiz. I hold each item up and invite the guests to raise their hands or shout out their judgments as to whether the item is kosher for Passover or not. Here are some items I use:

   A. **Bread** (Certainly not kosher, because it contains yeast.)

   B. **Soda crackers** (Not kosher, because of the soda **and** the flour. Flour and water together will rise even without leavening, so flour is not kosher for Passover. For flour, you must grind up baked matzo crackers as finely as possible. Once flour has been baked, it won't rise again.)

   C. **Baking Powder** (A leavening agent. Not kosher for Passover.) Baking powder also contains Cream of Tartar, which is a grape product. Jews can't buy "wine" from their enemies (see D&C 27:1-4).

   D. **Jell-O** (Never kosher. Discuss why. Gelatin is made from the bones and hooves of unclean animals.)

   E. **Potato Chips** (Fine, if labeled with Rabbinic approval.)

   F. **Matzo Crackers** (Hold up the box. They might not be kosher for Passover. Special Rabbinic approval must be stamped on the box. Some are clearly stamped "Not for Passover Use," even though they are unleavened.)

G. **Milk chocolate** (Not with this meat meal, because it contains milk. Dark chocolate is fine.)

H. **Rice and Beans** (Now you've got them! Some guests will vote yes, and some no. A discussion should ensue. Now they are getting into the Rabbinical spirit. Do rice and beans, once they get wet, rot or ferment? If they ferment, they are not kosher for Passover. If they rot, they are fine. Tell them the rabbis of various cultures disagree. In some locations rice and beans are the staff of life. In those places, they tend to be accepted.)

3. A Passover evening takes about 2 1/2 to 3 hours. That's a long time. Your introductory material, then, will have to be fairly brief, while being especially informative. You can choose your favorite points from the Passover section of this book. Here are the main points which should be made:

    A. Passover evenings are held in the home. They are family activities during which the Exodus from Egypt is remembered. The overriding theme is deliverance. As we discuss the deliverance from Egypt, you will come to see it as a type of the deliverance we receive through belief in Jesus Christ. The officiator in the Jewish home describes the deliverance from Egypt as if it actually happened to him. In this way, the story becomes more real for the children. The purpose is to teach the children that God is a God of miracles, and that he loves, protects, and delivers his children.

    B. The three main symbols of the Passover are the Paschal Lamb, the Unleavened Bread, and the "wine," or fruit of the vine. More than any other Old Testament holiday, the Passover teaches us as believers that Christ is the Messiah. Jesus was the Passover lamb; he was born in a stable on April 6th, which was the Passover. The "Last Supper," which Jesus shared with his apostles before he was arrested and crucified, was a Passover meal. Jesus used the images of the feast to testify of himself. The unleavened bread became the "bread of life," the sacramental bread. The Passover wine, or "cup of joy," became the sacramental wine. Jesus was the Passover Lamb, the Lamb of God. He was sacrificed on the Passover at the same time as the lambs were slain in the Temple.

C. Now that we are about to begin the feast, remember that we have cleaned the entire house and rid it of every last crumb of leavening. At the same time, we have cleansed and rededicated ourselves to be pure and righteous. (The leaven represents our evil inclinations.)

D. On the table are many symbolic foods. Their meanings will be explained during the feast.

E. Beside each guest at the table is a little booklet, called a *haggadah*. It contains the ritual, the order of the evening. Celebrants need to follow along, as we proceed through the Passover feast.

F. Some of you will be asked to read scriptures tonight, and there are places in the ritual where all the guests recite together.

G. Follow the *haggadah* through the order of the feast.

A PASSOVER FIRESIDE

When time or resources are limited, the Passover information can be presented to a group in a fireside setting. Use a home, a cultural hall, or a multi- purpose room — never a chapel. Set a Passover table at the front of the room, set with all the symbolic foods and items needed by the officiator. Seat the guests on chairs arranged to enhance visibility. Stand behind the display table to give your presentation. Give an introduction and then proceed through the *haggadah*. It is more of a learning experience, if the guests partake of the ritual, symbolic foods when called for by the ritual (unleavened bread, "wine," *charoset*, horseradish, greens). Servers can pass the foods to the guests as they remain in their seats. If food cannot be passed around the room without making a mess, or if time is limited, simply describe the action taking place. At the end of the presentation, invite the guests forward to taste the ceremonial foods. No meal is served.

HOW TO SET UP TABLES IN A LARGE HALL

Through trial and error, I've determined a good way to set up tables for a crowd in a cultural hall.

Set up one or two tables at the front of the hall, end-to-end, parallel with the front of the stage. This table, or tables, will seat the officiator and his special guests, such as his family members. They should be seated only on the side of the table(s) next to the stage, so all are facing the hall. These tables should be set especially well, and should have all the ritual foods and *seder* plate, plus the other items listed for the officiator.

A microphone should be provided for the officiator, preferably with a stand and swing-arm, so both his (her) hands can be free.

Set up the other tables for the guests in a sunray pattern (see diagram below) with the closer ends of the tables towards the officiator's table. You can increase the number of tables by lengthening the rays. Add another table, so each ray consists of two tables, end to end.

Seat the guests on both sides of the ray, with no guest seated on the end facing the officiator. The assistant officiator for each ray should be seated at the far end. These tables should be set so that the assistant officiators have *seder* plates and the other items necessary.

When the officiator blesses and passes certain foods, or holds up symbolic foods, the officiator for each ray of tables should do the same for the guests at those tables.

If you desire to decorate, use the Israeli colors of sky-blue and white, perhaps with a touch of gold or silver. Judaism's symbols are the "Shield of David" (*Magen David*) or six-pointed star, and the seven-branched candelabra (*menorah*). Souvenirs from Israel make good centerpieces.

At the side of the hall set up tables for serving and perhaps a table of Jewish objects and souvenirs from Israel collected from those who have toured there.

Obtain some background music from media stores or Jewish music websites.

Be certain to have a piano to accompany the Passover songs.

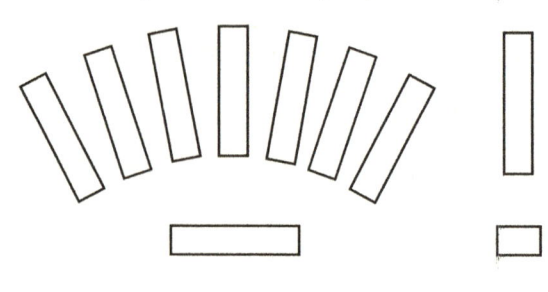

SETTING THE PASSOVER TABLE

The *seder table* is beautifully set.
- Use a formal table cloth and your best dishware and table settings.
- **Flowers** and **candles** are important to the meaning of the ceremony, representing springtime renewal and divine light.

Near the officiator at the end of the table, you will need to place a number of items:
- Stand **a small pitcher of water in an empty bowl with a napkin** at hand for ritual hand-washing.
- Buy or create a **large cloth envelope** with three compartments and insert **three whole *matzah* crackers**. Alternatively, you can layer large paper or cloth napkins.
- Most important is the ***seder plate***. You can purchase a *seder plate*, or simply use a regular plate. Small amounts of the **ceremonial foods** are placed on the *seder* plate for the presenter's use, and extra servings for the celebrants are set elsewhere. These ritual foods are:
    1) **bitter herbs** (*"maror"*), usually romaine lettuce;
    2) **horseradish** (*"chazeret"*), also a bitter herb;
    3) **a lamb shank bone or chicken neck** (*"z'roah"*);
    4) **a roasted egg** (*"baytza"*);
    5) **green herbs** (*"karpas"*), usually celery, parsley or lettuce; and
    6) **"*charoset*,"** a mash of fruit. (See *Passover Recipes*.)

Additional instructions:
- Place **a throw pillow** on the seat of the presenter.
- Be certain all celebrants have access to **bowls of salt water** and **plates of *matzah* crackers**.
- **Pitchers of red grape juice** should be available to all. Always set an extra place, or at least provide an **extra chalice-cup for Elijah** the Prophet.

- Place settings are as for a normal dinner meal with the addition of a **3 to 4 ounce cup for "wine"** at each place setting.
- **A copy of the *haggadah*** should be available for every celebrant, although two people can share. You can photocopy the *haggadah* for your own use.

The *haggadah* contains the order of the ritual, the story of the Exodus, and prayers, legends and expositions recited during the evening. The *haggadah* consists of a simple, very traditional *seder* to which I have added scriptural references and commentary meant to show how the Passover testifies of Jesus Christ, and how Christ used the Passover ritual to institute the sacrament. My commentary and scriptural references are displayed in boxes.

In our family we purchase **two prizes** (usually chocolate) for the children. One we award before the meal when we search the house for leaven. We purposely hide a piece of bread for a child to find, and declare the house free of leaven when it is discovered and discarded. In Jewish homes this search takes place the evening before the day of the *seder*.

(Remember that a Jewish day goes from sundown to sundown. If Passover in on April 6th, then your *seder* should take place on the evening of the 5th, and the search for leaven on the morning of the 5th.) The other prize is awarded to the child who finds the *afikomon*. *Afikomon* is a Greek word meaning "that which comes after." It is a piece of *matzah* which is hidden, then found, and ransomed during the *seder*.

PASSOVER TABLE-SETTING CHECKLIST

1) Flowers
2) Two candles for the lighting ceremony, others as desired
3) Matches and a headscarf for the lighting ceremony (the girl who lights the candles should cover her head).
4) For ritual hand washing – a small pitcher in a bowl with a napkin placed over the side of the bowl for drying the hands. (Place near the officiator.)
5) A special envelope made to hold three *matzah* crackers in three compartments. Or you can stack the three matzo between layers of napkins. (Place near the officiator.)
6) A pillow symbolic of reclining. (Place near the officiator.)

7) The *"seder* plate." This plate holds the ritual, symbolic foods, which may be simply put onto the plate, or contained in small bowls and then put onto the plate. You can buy a real *seder* plate on-line at Jewish (look for "Judaica") websites, or at a synagogue shop. If you cannot find a real *seder* plate, use an ordinary plate.

8) The ritual foods. Place one serving of each on the *seder* plate, then provide extra servings elsewhere on the table(s):

   A. **Bitter herbs** ("maror"), usually romaine lettuce

   B. **Horseradish** ("chazeret"), also a bitter herb. (Use ground, not creamed horseradish.)

   C. **A lamb shank bone or chicken neck** ("z'roah")

   D. **A roasted egg** ("baytza")

   E. **Green herbs** ("karpas"), usually celery, parsley, watercress, or lettuce.

   A. **A blend of chopped fruit** ("charoset"). See the Passover Recipes.

   G. **Bowls of salt water** (where the celebrants can reach them).

   A. **Plates of *matzah* crackers.** (If you can't find *matzah* crackers in your grocery store, order them on-line. Do a search for "kosher foods."

   I. Extra hard-boiled eggs.

   J. **Pitchers of red grape juice.** (Welch's makes a good red grape juice, reasonably priced. Many supermarkets, however, don't normally carry it. Order ahead.)

   K. An extra chalice-cup for Elijah the Prophet.

   L. **A 3- to 4-ounce cup** for "wine" at each place setting.

   M. **A copy of the Haggadah** for each celebrant. Or, two can share.

   N. **Two prizes.** Give one to the child who finds the piece of leavened bread before dinner, and one to the child who finds the afikomon.

A *Seder* plate with ceremonial foods

SAMPLE PASSOVER MENU

Ritual foods, including *Charoset*
and herbs (as on the *Seder* Plate)

Chazeret—ground horseradish;
hard-boiled eggs, salt water, and *matzah* crackers.

Fruit of the vine (I use red grape juice.)

Chicken soup with *matzah* balls

Roast Shoulder of Lamb or Roast Chicken
or Crusty Chicken Breasts

Potato Kugel or Passover Latkes

Choice of vegetables or salad

Passover dessert(s) of choice

HEBREW BLESSINGS FOR PASSOVER

(For use during the Passover ritual)

**Praised art Thou, O Lord our God,
King of the Universe, Creator of the fruit of the vine**

Baruch atah adonay elo-hey-nu melech ha-o-lam bo-rey p'ree ha-ga-fen.

בָּרוּךְ אַתָּה יְיָ, אֱלֹהֵינוּ מֶלֶךְ הָעוֹלָם, בּוֹרֵא פְּרִי הַגָּפֶן:

**Praised art Thou, O Lord our God, Ruler of the Universe,
Who hast given us life, kept us safely,
And brought us to this holy season**

Baruch atah adonay elo-hey-nu melech ha-o-lam sh'heh-chi-ya-nu v'ki-ma-nu v'hi-gi-ya-nu la-z'mahn ha-zeh.

בָּרוּךְ אַתָּה יְיָ, אֱלֹהֵינוּ מֶלֶךְ הָעוֹלָם, שֶׁהֶחֱיָנוּ וְקִיְּמָנוּ וְהִגִּיעָנוּ לַזְּמַן הַזֶּה.

**Praised art Thou, O Lord our God, Ruler of the Universe,
Creator of the fruit of the earth**

Baruch atah adonay elo-hey-nu melech ha-o-lam bo-rey p'ree ha-a-da-ma.

בָּרוּךְ אַתָּה יְיָ, אֱלֹהֵינוּ מֶלֶךְ הָעוֹלָם, בּוֹרֵא פְּרִי הָאֲדָמָה:

The Ten Plagues

1) Dam. 2) Tz'far-day-a.
3) Keeneem. 4) O-rov. 5) De-ver. 6) Sh'cheen. 7) Ba-rad.
8) Ar-beh. 9) Cho-shech.
10) Ma-kat B'cho-rot.

דָּם. צְפַרְדֵּעַ. כִּנִּים.
עָרוֹב. דֶּבֶר. שְׁחִין. בָּרָד.
אַרְבֶּה. חֹשֶׁךְ. מַכַּת בְּכוֹרוֹת:

Thanks for the matzah (bread)

Baruch atah adonay elo-hey-nu melech ha-o-lam asher kid' sha-nu b'mitz-vo-tav ve-tzi-va-nu al a-chi-lat ma-tzah.

בָּרוּךְ אַתָּה יְיָ, אֱלֹהֵינוּ מֶלֶךְ הָעוֹלָם, אֲשֶׁר קִדְּשָׁנוּ בְּמִצְוֹתָיו וְצִוָּנוּ עַל אֲכִילַת מַצָּה:

PASSOVER MUSIC

Let My People Go

Moderately slow
Spiritual

When Is- rael was in E- gypt's land, Let my peo- ple go. Op- ressed so hard they could not stand, Let my peo- ple go. Go down Mo- ses 'way down to E- gypt's land, Tell old Pha- raoh, to Let my peo- ple go!

Dayenu

Lively   Folk Song

Da- da- ye- nu—— da- da- da- ye- nu———

da- da- ye- nu, da- ye- nu, da- ye- nu, da- ye- nu | ye- nu, da- ye- du. *Fine*

1. Il- lu ho- tsi ho- tsi- a- nu ho- tzi- a- nu mi- mitz- ra- yim
2. Il- lu na- tan na- tan la- nu na- tan la- nu et ha- to- rah

ho- tzi- a- nu mi- mitz- ra- yim Da- ye- nu.
et ha- to- rah na- tan la- nu Da- ye- nu.

D.C. al Fine

A PASSOVER HAGGADAH
for Latter-day Saint celebrants

The Passover Ritual and Story of the Exodus from Egypt

THE PASSOVER SEDER

> Read
> **2 Nephi 11:4**
> The Law of Moses is meant to teach.
> The entire law typifies the Savior.
> **1 Corinthians 5:7**
> Jesus Christ was and is the Passover.

LIGHTING OF THE HOLIDAY CANDLES

This festival is a joyous celebration of freedom from oppression and gratitude for the Lord's care. Candles symbolize the warm glow of happiness we feel at the Passover. A girl lights the two holiday candles. She holds her hands behind the flames and recites these blessings:

Praised art thou, O Lord our God, Ruler of the universe, Who hast sanctified us by Thy commandments and commanded us to kindle the light of the holiday.

The girl continues to read:

Light is the symbol of the divine.

Light is the symbol of the divine spark in man. As it is written, the spirit of man is the light of the Lord.

Light is the symbol of the divine law. As it is written, the commandments are a lamp and the law is a light. Light is the symbol of Israel's mission. As it is written, the Lord has set Israel for a light unto the nations.

The Four Covenant Cups of Wine

The four covenants which the Lord made with Israel in the wilderness are found in **Exodus 6:6-7**. They are reverenced and remembered during the Passover *seder* by drinking four cups of wine. In shortened form they are listed thus"—I will bring you, I will deliver you, I will redeem you, and I will take you." Some scholars think there were five cups of wine in the original Passover *seder*. It seems likely, since there is another promise in **verse 8**—"I will restore you."

The temporal promises have spiritual counterparts: I will bring you out of Egypt (I will bring you out of the world); I will deliver you from slavery (I will deliver you from sin); I will redeem you (I will ransom you through the atonement); and I will take you as my people (I will take you as my spiritual sons and daughters). And for verse 8–I will restore you to the land of your inheritance (will gather you out of the world and into my kingdom). Christ did **not** partake of the final (or fifth)cup (which became the sacramental cup), because he couldn't fulfill its promise until the kingdom of God on earth was permanently established.

(See **Matthew 26:27–29**.)

Everyone at the table has a glass
of "wine" set before him.

Fill the first cup.

THE KIDDUSH
Blessing over the wine

All the celebrants hold their cups aloft
and recite together the following blessing:

Praised art Thou, O Lord our God, Ruler of the
universe, creator of the fruit of the vine.

The officiator recites:

Praised art Thou, who hast chosen us from among all peoples. Thou hast sanctified and exalted us with Thy commandments. In love Thou hast given us days of joy and seasons of gladness, even this Feast of unleavened bread, a memorial of the departure from Egypt. Thou hast chosen us for Thy service and made us sharers in the blessings of Thy holy festivals.

Praised art Thou, Who sanctified Israel and the festive seasons.

The celebrants recite together:

Praised art Thou, O Lord our God, Ruler of the
universe, Who hast given us life, kept us safely and
brought us to this holy season.

*In most Jewish homes it is traditional to recline
while drinking the covenant cups.
Just lean slightly to the left.*

*Drink the first cup of wine.
(Covenant: I will bring you out of Egypt [the world]).*

CLEANSING THE HANDS

*The leader cleanses his hands,
but he does not recite a blessing.
(Ritual cleansing is an important part of the gospel.)*

— 171 —

EATING OF THE GREENS

*This ceremony notes the greenery
that comes to life in the springtime.*

Some parsley, lettuce, or watercress is distributed to all present.

Celebrants dip it in salt water
(representing the tears of affliction).

Before partaking of the dipped greens,
Say the following in unison:

Praised art thou, O Lord our God, Ruler of the
universe, Creator of the fruit of the earth.

Partake of the greens.
[Spring renewal mingled with tears]

BREAKING OF THE MATZAH

The leader withdraws the middle matzah from the compartmented envelope.
He breaks it in two, leaving the smaller portion on the seder plate.
*The larger piece becomes the **afikomon**.*

The leader holds the afikomon aloft and says:

Behold the matzah, the bread of affliction our forefathers ate when they were slaves in the Land of Egypt. Let it remind us of people everywhere who are poor and hungry. Let it call to our minds men today who are still enslaved or oppressed. May all in need come and celebrate the Passover with us. Next year at this season, may the whole house of Israel rejoice. And may all mankind enjoy liberty, justice and peace.

The leader wraps the afikomon in a white napkin and sends someone to hide it. While the afikomon is being hidden, read the material in the following text box.

An Explanation of the Afikomon

Originally, celebrants were required to partake of a morsel of the lamb as the last food eaten during the Passover evening. During those times when there was no temple or tabernacle in which to perform animal sacrifice, the *afikomon* (a Greek word meaning "that which comes after") took the place of the lamb. The *afikomon* is the most important symbolic food of the Passover feast. It directly represents the Paschal Lamb and is absolutely mandatory in the Passover ritual. As Jesus Christ became The bread of Life and ended blood sacrifice, the *afikomon* replaced the Lamb. All celebrants are required to partake of the *afikomon* later on in the Passover ceremony (a piece at least the size of an olive). The symbolism of the Savior's suffering, burial, and resurrection is unmistakable, since the bread, already pierced and striped during its preparation, is broken, wrapped in a linen napkin, "buried" or hidden, brought forth again, then ransomed for a gift at the end of the feast. (Some Oriental Jewish families wrap the *afikomon* in red.) The position of the *afikomon* in the envelope is also significant. The upper *matzah* in the envelope represents the High Priesthood, the middle *matzah* represents the Levitical Priesthood, and the lower *matzah* represents the lay member. It was the Levites, supervised by the High Priests, who made the sacrifice in the Temple. It is the *afikomon* that Jesus used as the sacramental bread during the Last Supper.

THE RECITATION OF THE SERVICE

THE FOUR QUESTIONS
(a child asks)

Why is this night different from all other nights?

1. On all other nights we eat leavened or unleavened bread. Why on this night do we eat only matzah, the unleavened bread?
2. On all other nights we eat all kinds of herbs. Why on this night do we eat especially *maror*, the bitter herb?
3. On all other nights we do not dip the herbs even once. Why on this night do we dip the green herb into salt water, and the bitter herb into *charoset*?
4. On all other nights we may sit or recline at the table. Why on this night do we recline?

The leader replies to the child:

I am glad you asked these questions, for the story of this special night is just what I wanted you to know. Indeed, this night is different from all other nights. On this night we celebrate one of the most important events in history. On this night we celebrate the deliverance of the Hebrew people from slavery into freedom.

1. WHY do we eat only matzah tonight? When Pharaoh allowed our forefathers to depart from Egypt, they had to go in great haste. They could not prepare their bread in the usual way. They could not wait for the dough to rise. As they escaped, the hot sun baked the unleavened loaves into the flat bread we call matzah.
2. WHY do we eat bitter herbs tonight? Because our fathers were slaves in Egypt, and their lives were bitter.
3. WHY do we dip the herbs twice tonight? The sweet herbs remind us of the green that comes alive in the springtime, but we dip them into the tears of affliction, which our forefathers shed. The bitter herbs remind us of the oppression we suffered. We dip

them into the charoset, which represents the sweetness of hope.

4. WHY do we recline at the table? A slave crouches in the field to eat, but in olden times the free man reclined. Since our fathers were freed on this night, we recline.

When we perform these rituals, we ourselves taste the bitterness of slavery and the sweetness of joy that comes with deliverance. God manifests himself to us again in our day, assuring us of the right to be free, to create beauty, to perform acts of kindness, and to pursue happiness.

We celebrate tonight, because we were slaves in Egypt and the Lord delivered us in power and might. Had the Lord not redeemed our people, we and our children would still be slaves.

> At this point, the Jewish haggadah describes four kinds of children: the wise child, the wicked child, the innocent child, and the child unable to inquire. A typical haggadah instructs the leader on how to inform and encourage the child to feel the meaning of the Passover. Interestingly, Alma's counsel to his sons parallels the structure presented in the Passover ritual. This counsel begins in **Alma 36**.
>
> (I have deleted this portion of the ritual.

THE STORY OF THE OPPRESSION

The leader continues:

In every land and in every generation oppressors have sought to destroy us. We extend our gratitude to the Holy One, blessed be He, for His protection throughout eons of time. He called our father Abraham out of the bondage of idolatry to the service of truth. God led him to Canaan and began thenceforth to raise up seed unto himself. As it is written, through the seed of Abraham shall all the nations be blessed.

Abraham begat Isaac, whom the Lord saved from sacrifice. Isaac begat Jacob. And Jacob went down into Egypt to be received by the good graces of his lost son Joseph, who had risen to great power through the mercies of God. The Egyptians gave our fathers a portion of good land, and they dwelt in peace and were fruitful and multiplied.

Joseph died, and all his brethren, and all that generation. Many hundreds of years had the children of Israel sojourned in Egypt. A new Pharaoh rose up who knew not Joseph. He said unto his people, "Behold, the people of the Children of Israel are too many and too mighty for us; come, let us deal wisely with them, lest they multiply, and it come to pass that if there be a war, they join themselves unto our enemies and fight against us." Pharaoh set taskmasters over the Israelites to afflict them with terrible burdens. But the more they were afflicted, the more the children of Israel multiplied and spread abroad.

Our fathers cried unto the Lord in their afflictions, and the Lord heard our voice and saw that our burdens were great. The Holy One raised up Moses to save us, and brought us forth out of slavery and out of Egypt, with a mighty hand and with an outstretched arm, and with great terror, and with signs and wonders.

If desired, read **1 Nephi 17: 23-29, 40-42**.

Sing the song, "Let My People Go."

THE TEN PLAGUES

> The ten plagues were meant as much to instruct the Egyptians as to intimidate them into freeing the Israelites. Each plague was specific to a superstition or pagan deity of the Egyptians. For instance, they worshipped the Nile and the bull. The sacrifice of the first-born of Egypt attacked the worship of Pharaoh as a god, as well as hearkening back to Pharaoh's command to kill Israelite infants. The first Passover was celebrated exactly at the same time as the Feast of Amun, Pharaoh's personal god – It was a telling juxtaposition of righteous worship against false worship.

Fill the "wine" cups.

The leader and company then read responsively:

LEADER: When Pharaoh defied the command of God and refused to release the Israelites, he brought trouble upon himself and his people, for the Lord afflicted the Land of Egypt with plague.

COMPANY: These plagues came upon the Egyptians because of their evil; yet we do not rejoice over their downfall and defeat.

LEADER: Judaism teaches that all men are children of God, even our enemies who would seek to destroy us.

COMPANY: We cannot be glad when any man needlessly suffers. So we mourn the loss of the Egyptians and express our sorrow over their destruction.

Each person dips a spoon or a fingertip
into his cup of 'wine' and removes
a drop from this 'cup of joy' at the mention
of each of the ten plagues. He transfers
each drop of joy to his own plate.

All recite in unison:

1) Blood
2) Frogs
3) Gnats
4) Flies
5) Cattle disease
6) Boils
7) Hail.
8) Locusts
9) Darkness
10) Slaying of the First-Born

(Do not drink the 'wine', but set it down.)

DAYENU

The company repeats the refrain "Dayenu", which in Hebrew means,
"It would have been enough for us."
*The verses move from physical liberation
to spiritual freedom and covenant.*

LEADER: Had he brought us out of Egypt, and not divided the sea for us...

COMPANY: *Dayenu!*

LEADER: Had he divided the sea, and not permitted us to cross on dry land.

COMPANY: *Dayenu!*

LEADER: Had he permitted us to cross on dry land and not sustained us in the desert...

COMPANY: *Dayenu!*

LEADER: Had he sustained us in the desert and not fed us manna...

COMPANY: *Dayenu!*

LEADER: Had he fed us with manna and not ordained the Sabbath...

COMPANY: *Dayenu!*

LEADER: Had he ordained the Sabbath and not brought us to Mt. Sinai...

COMPANY: *Dayenu!*

LEADER: Had he brought us to Mt. Sinai, and not given us the Torah... (the Books of Moses)

COMPANY: *Dayenu!*

LEADER: Had he given us the Torah, and not led us to the promised land...

COMPANY: *Dayenu!*

LEADER: Had he led us to the promised land, and not built for us the Temple...

COMPANY: *Dayenu!*

LEADER: Had he built for us the Temple, and not sent us prophets of truth...

COMPANY: *Dayenu!*

LEADER: Had he sent us prophets of truth, and not made us a holy people...

COMPANY: *Dayenu!*

Sing the "Dayenu"

> How grateful we should be as Latter-day Saints that we now enjoy many of the great blessings which were lost by our ancestors – miracles, prophets, temples, and the constant presence of the Holy Ghost to lead us through the lone and dreary world. With each succeeding blessing our cups fill, until our cup of joy runs over.
>
> Our gratitude should be constant and unceasing.

All read in unison:

How grateful we must be unto the Lord for the many and wonderful favors which he bestowed upon us! Should enemies again assail us, the remembrance of the exodus of our fathers will inspire us with new courage.

THE PASSOVER SYMBOLS

The leader holds up the lamb bone and says:

This is the Passover sacrifice, offered to the Lord because he passed over the houses of the children of Israel in Egypt, smiting the Egyptians and sparing us.

The leader points to the matzah.

This represents the haste in which the children of Israel departed from Egypt. They had not made any provisions for the road.

The leader points to the bitter herb (horseradish).

This reminds us how bitter the Egyptians made the lives of our forefathers in Egypt. They made their lives bitter with forced labor, in mortar and bricks, and in all manner of work in the field.

The leader points to the salt water.

This represents the tears we shed in our affliction.

The leader points to the charoset.

The charoset represents the sweetness of hope. Even as we suffered oppression at the hands of the Egyptians, we always had hope because of our faith. It also symbolizes the mortar we used to make bricks for Pharaoh.

The leader points to the sweet herbs.

The sweet herbs remind us of the fruits of the earth which come forth in the spring.

The leader points to the roasted egg.

This reminds us of rebirth in the spring and the festival offering in the Temple.

Figure 3: A Passover Seder Plate

OTHER PASSOVER SYMBOLS

- The **romaine lettuce** is sweet at the beginning, but bitter at the end, as was our sojourn in Egypt.
- **The Lamb** represents The Lamb of God, Jesus Christ, and was to be first-born, without blemish, with no bones broken. It was to be killed between the hours of 3 to 5 p.m. on the fourteenth day of the month of Nisan, the time and date of Christ's future crucifixion.
- **The blood on the lintel** represents the blood of the Lamb of God - a protection for the household and outward show of faith.
- **Hyssop** was the branch used to apply the blood of the Lamb on the lintel. It is a healing herb, used for leprosy (Christ healed lepers). It will be used in the sacrifice of the red heifer. It was also the branch used to offer vinegar to the dying Christ.
- **Leavening** represents sin; as Paul said in 1 Corinthians 5:6-8, a little sin leavens a whole family, congregation, or society, and needs to be purged.
- **Deliverance from Egypt** represents deliverance from sin and sorrow, and from worldliness. The Israelite nation was born out of sinful Egypt, through water, into the testing ground of life (the wilderness), later to be restored to the promised land (representing eternal salvation). The Israelites were delivered on the 15th of Nisan, the date Christ was delivered from his suffering and went to minister to the spirits in Paradise.
- **Moses**, the deliverer, leader through the wilderness, was himself a type of Christ.

BLESSINGS

The "wine" cup is lifted and the leader recites:

Praised art thou, O Lord our God, Ruler of the Universe, who redeemed us, and redeemed our fathers, from Egypt. Bring us ever forward in peace to other solemn days and festivals, joyous in the building of Thy kingdom and happy in Thy service. May Thy name be sanctified in the midst of all the earth and all peoples be moved to worship Thee with one heart.

The blessing for wine is recited in unison:

Praised art Thou, O Lord our God, Ruler of the Universe, Creator of the fruit of the vine.

All drink the second cup.
[Freedom from bondage]

ALL WASH HANDS

The company recites the following blessing
as the hands are cleansed prior to the
eating of the Passover dishes.

Praised art Thou, O Lord our God, Ruler of the Universe,
Who has sanctified us by Thy commandments and commanded us
concerning the washing of the hands.

> At this point in the *seder*, since ancient times, Psalms 113 and 114 have been recited. I don't include these in my own *seders* or teaching presentations, in the interest of time.
> You may choose to read them directly from the scriptures.
> In Hebrew a psalm is called *hallel*.

EATING THE MATZAH

The upper matzah is broken and distributed.
The following two blessings are recited
in unison before eating.

Praised art Thou, O Lord our God, Ruler of the Universe, Who bringest forth bread from the earth.

Praised art Thou, O Lord our God, Ruler of the Universe, Who hast sanctified us by Thy commandments, and hast commanded us to eat matzah.

(Eat the matzah.)

TASTING THE BITTER HERB
AND A REMINDER OF THE TEMPLE

*The leader removes the lower matzah
from the envelope and breaks and
distributes it. The celebrants dip the matzah
into the charoset and the horseradish.*

It is said that Rabbi Hillel introduced this custom while the Temple still stood. (He may have invented the first sandwich.) Originally, the matzah was eaten with the charoset, horseradish, and a piece of Paschal Lamb. Since the Temple's destruction, the sacrifice of the lamb has been prohibited, so that all the symbolisms of the lamb have been transferred to the matzah, especially to the afikomon.

THE PASSOVER MEAL IS NOW EATEN.

EATING THE AFIKOMON

At the conclusion of the meal, the children are given the opportunity to search for and find the Afikomon. The leader redeems it by giving a reward to the child who finds it. The leader breaks the Afikomon and distributes pieces of it to all present. After partaking of the Afikomon, it is customary to eat nothing else during the evening.

This bread represents the Messiah. What a fitting image for Christ to use as he instituted the first sacrament, the bread representing his own flesh, the pattern of the ritual a similitude of his death, burial, and resurrection.
Read **Luke 22:19.** The afikomon became the sacrament.
Read **Hebrews 7:26–27**.
Christ was, at this one Passover, both the sacrificer and the sacrifice.
Note that nothing else is eaten after the afikomon.
It appears that the Savior ate nothing after blessing and passing this bread, but went straight to Gethsemane, trial, and death.

GRACE AFTER MEAL

(Psalm 126 can be recited here.)

UNISON: O Lord, our God, sustain and protect us. Grant us strength to bear our burdens. Let us not become dependent upon men, but let us rather trust Thy hand, which is ever open and gracious, so that we may never be put to shame.

LEADER: Our God and God of our fathers, be Thou ever mindful of us, as Thou hast been of our fathers. Grant us grace, mercy, life and peace on this Feast of Unleavened Bread. Remember us this day in kindness. Visit us this day with blessing. Preserve us this day for life.

COMPANY: Amen.

The cups are filled for the third time.
All read in unison:
Praised art Thou, O Lord Our God, King of the Universe, Creator of the fruit of the vine

Drink the third cup of wine.
[The cup of redemption; we are redeemed by Christ.]

ELIJAH THE PROPHET

The door is opened and the fourth cup of "wine" is filled.
An additional cup, the Cup of Elijah the Prophet, has been set on the table.

Fill Elijah's Cup. The company rises as if to greet him.
In Jewish tradition Elijah is the long-awaited messenger of the final redemption of mankind from all oppression.

While the company is standing, the leader
recites the following:

LEADER: Throughout our history, we have had many martyrs. But from the death of the concentration camps there has emerged in the Land of Israel a new life for the Jewish people. Now we invoke the Spirit of Elijah on behalf of all men, that they might enjoy liberty and redemption, that Elijah will turn the hearts of the fathers to their children, and the hearts of the children to their fathers. May Elijah's spirit enter this home and renew our hope. May war come to an end and men live in peace. May our hearts be united in his service and our lives sanctified by His will.

All be seated.

(Do not drink the cup of wine.)

THE FINAL BENEDICTIONS

Read **Malachi 4:5,6** – the promise of the coming of Elijah. This scripture was quoted to Joseph Smith during Moroni's visitation to him (See the Joseph Smith Story).
Read **D&C 110:13–16** – Elijah appeared to Joseph Smith at Passover (on *Bikkurim*) in 1836 to commit the keys of the fullness of time to Joseph and to announce the "great and dreadful day of the Lord"

One can only speculate which cup Jesus used as the sacramental cup. However, if it were the third cup, he could not have drunk the fourth (or fifth, if there was one), for he said he would not drink until the coming of his Father's kingdom. See Luke 22:15-20 and Matthew 26:27-29:

"Take this, and divide it among yourselves: For I say unto you, I will not drink of the fruit of the vine, until the kingdom of God shall come ....This cup is the new testament in my blood, which is shed for you."

"And he took the cup, and gave thanks, and gave it to them, saying, Drink ye all of it; for this is my blood of the new testament, which is shed for the remission of sins. But I say unto you,

I will not drink hence forth of this fruit of the vine, until that day when I drink it new with you in my Father's kingdom."

Jesus did not drink, because he was not ready to keep all five Passover covenants. One hearkens to the "Lord's prayer" – Thy kingdom come, Thy will be done, on earth, as it is in heaven.

The final covenants (represented by cups taken after dinner) have apocalyptic and eternal meanings, being redemption, becoming God's people, and inheriting the earth.

When the Messiah comes, he will redeem and judge.

When the Jews, and indeed, all the earth's inhabitants really know Jesus ("Y'shua") as the Christ, then they will be his people, and he will be their God; when the righteous inherit the earth, then will the land promised to their fathers be permanently and peacefully theirs. Only then will these covenants be fulfilled.

Jesus himself tells us under what conditions he will again partake of the fruit of the vine, completing the imagery of the Passover, in D&C 27:5-14, so important I quote it here:

Behold, this is wisdom in me; wherefore, marvel not, for the hour cometh that I will drink of the fruit of the vine with you on the earth, and with Moroni, whom I have sent unto you to reveal the Book of Mormon, containing the fulness of my everlasting gospel, to whom I have committed the keys of the record of the stick of Ephraim;

And also with Elias, to whom I have committed the keys of bringing to pass the restoration of all things spoken by the mouth of all the holy prophets since the world began, concerning the last days;

> And also John the son of Zacharias, which Zacharias he (Elias) visited and gave promise that he should have a son, and his name should be John, and he should be filled with the spirit of Elias;
>
> Which John I have sent unto you, my servants, Joseph Smith, Jun., and Oliver Cowdery, to ordain you unto the first priesthood which you have received, that you might be called and ordained even as Aaron;
>
> And also Elijah, unto whom I have committed the keys of the power of turning the hearts of the fathers to the children, and the hearts of the children to the fathers, that the whole earth may not be smitten with a curse;
>
> And also with Joseph and Jacob, and Isaac, and Abraham, your fathers, by whom the promises remain;
>
> And also with Michael, or Adam, the father of all, the prince of all, the ancient of days;
>
> And also with Peter, and James, and John, whom I have sent unto you, by whom I have ordained you and confirmed you to be apostles, and especial witnesses of my name, and bear the keys of your ministry and of the same things which I revealed unto them;
>
> Unto whom I have committed the keys of my kingdom, and a dispensation of the gospel for the last times; and for the fulness of times, in the which I will gather together in one all things, both which are in heaven, and which are on earth;
>
> And also with all those whom my Father hath given me out of the world.

Holding aloft the fourth cup of "wine,"
the leader recites the following benediction:
This festive service is now completed. Once again we have recited the glorious tale of Israel's liberation from bondage. With songs of praise, we have called upon the name of God. May he who broke Pharaoh's yoke forever shatter all fetters of oppression. May he hasten the day when swords shall, at last, be broken and wars ended. Soon may He cause glad tidings of redemption to be heard in all lands. And let us pray that all

mankind, freed from violence and from wrong, and united
in an eternal covenant of brotherhood will celebrate
a universal Passover in the name of the God of Freedom.

Before drinking the fourth cup of "wine", say:

Praised art thou, O Lord our God,
King of the Universe, Creator of the fruit
of the vine.

All drink the fourth cup.
(The cup of acceptance: You will be my people, and I will be your God.)

The 5th covenant found in Exodus is "I will restore you."
This is the cup Christ will share with all his faithful,
when he comes to gather all things in one.
This is the covenant Christ could not fulfill at the Last Supper.

The fifth cup has become a toast in the modern Passover ritual.
Everywhere in the world except Israel, celebrants say,
"Next Year in Jerusalem." In Israel, celebrants say,
"Next Year in Jerusalem Rebuilt."
Latter-day Saint celebrants can choose to shout,
"Next Year in Zion!"

Pour the fifth cup of wine.
(The cup of restoration: I will restore you
to the land of your inheritance.)

All rise for the benediction.

Hold the cup aloft.

*The leader recites
(as the company says "Amen")*

May the Lord bless us and watch over us. <u>Amen</u>.

May the Lord cause the light of his countenance to shine upon us and be gracious unto us. May he cast out of all hearts the darkness of ignorance and the blight of prejudice. <u>Amen</u>.

May the Lord lift up his countenance upon our country and render it a true home of liberty and a defender of justice. May he grant us and all mankind peace. <u>Amen</u>.

May this service thus performed be acceptable before the Lord.

Next Year in Jerusalem!

לְשָׁנָה הַבָּאָה בִּירוּשָׁלַיִם

(La-shanah ha-ba'ah biyerushalayim)

NOTES:

1. Other songs sung at Passover are "Who Knows One," "Ma Nishtana haLayla haZe," "Eliyahu haNavi," "God of Might," "Halleluyah,""Chad Gadyah," and "L'Shanah haBaah." All of these songs, as well as the two I've included in the text, are modern additions to the *seder*. The Jews normally sing the scriptures, hence the role of the cantor of the synagogue. The psalms recited at the Last Supper would have been sung.

2. The Jewish texts for this Haggadah were taken from *The Passover Seder: Pathways Through the Haggadah,* arranged by Rabbi Arthur Gilbert, Ktav Publishing House, Inc., New York, 1970, and *The Passover Haggadah*, Maxwell House, 1984.

3. A glossary of terms and bibliography can be found in *Days of Awe: Jewish Feasts and Messianic Prophecy.*

Appendix D:
PASSOVER RECIPES

"Was the food good?
Oy, don't ask!"

NOTES:

It is important to remember that absolutely no form of leavening agent may be used when cooking for Passover. This includes yeast, baking soda, baking powder, and regular flour, which can rise on its own in the presence of moisture. For Passover, Jews use ground *matzah* (unleavened bread) instead of flour. Flour made from *matzah* will not rise. Many stores in areas where few Jews live now carry *matzah* crackers, the modern equivalent for unleavened bread, but *matzah* meal and *matzah* cake meal are a bit harder to find.

To make your own cake meal, blend unsalted *matzah* crackers in a blender until as fine as possible. For *matzah* meal, grind crackers into small crumbs. A *kosher* cook, or someone following the laws of *kashrut*, will not serve meat and milk at the same meal. The Passover meal is usually a meat meal. Therefore, never serve butter, milk, cheese, or other dairy products at this meal. (Milk chocolate is a dairy food.) It is worth the effort to follow these basic rules. Those who participate in food preparation learn much from the experience.

PREPARATION SUGGESTIONS

If you prepare the chicken soup the day before and refrigerate it, you can lift off the hardened chicken fat from the top when it's cool, reducing calories. Make the *matzah* ball mixture while the chicken is boiling, so it can chill while you boil the soup. Make charoset and hard-boiled eggs the day before also. Macaroons and other Passover cookies can also be made ahead.

The following recipes should be ample for ten people.

CHAROSET

(Ashkenazic recipe)

6 tart apples (Granny Smith)	¾ Cup raisins
4 ounces walnuts or almonds	1 tsp. cinnamon
A little grape juice	Sugar to taste

Pare, then grate the apples on coarsest setting, or chop very fine. Plump the raisins by letting them sit for about 10 minutes in hot water. Drain. Mash the raisins slightly. Grind or finely chop the nuts. Mix all the ingredients together, binding them with a little juice. *(Charoset represents the mortar used to make and set the bricks the Israelites were forced to produce in Egypt. It also represents the sweetness of hope.)*

IRANIAN CHAROSET

(Not for the timid)

25 dates, pitted and diced	1 banana, sliced
½ Cup unsalted pistachio nuts	1 Cup almonds, coarsely chopped
½ -1 Cup red grape juice	1 Tblsp. Ground cloves
¼ Cup cider vinegar	1 tsp. cinnamon
½ Cup yellow raisins	1 Tblsp. pepper
1½ apples, peeled & diced	1 orange, peeled and diced
½ Tblsp. cayenne pepper	1 Tblsp ground cardamom

Mix all ingredients together. Adjust seasonings if desired. Makes about 5 cups. When I present a Passover dinner for a large group, I make one recipe of Iranian Charoset and set it on the officiator's table. I invite the bravest guests to come up and take a bit during the meal. I tell them that the good thing about Iranian charoset is that you can carry it with you on your camel from Persia to Afghanistan, and back—and when you return, it will still be good!

CARLA'S HAROSET

1 Cup peeled, diced apples   1 Cup chopped dates

1 Cup dried apricots, diced   1 Cup chopped nuts

Put fruit into saucepan and barely cover with water. Simmer 5 - 8 minutes. Fruit should not be mushy. Remove fruit from pot, draining off water. Mash fruit slightly. Cool. Add chopped nuts.

JEWISH MAMA'S CHICKEN SOUP

(Cures anything)

whole chicken   4 quarts water

carrots, sliced   1 tablespoon dill weed

2 stalks sliced celery   Chopped fresh parsley

1 large onion   Mashed garlic or garlic powder to taste

Chicken bouillon cubes

Salt & pepper to taste

Matzah balls (next recipe)

Drop chicken into water in large pot. Bring to boil with coarsely chopped onion, vegetables and seasonings. Simmer 45 minutes. Remove chicken from pot and place on a platter. Slit skin of chicken to speed cooling. Taste broth and adjust bouillon and seasonings. Remove skin and debone chicken. Pull chicken apart into bite-size pieces and put back into broth. Simmer about 15 minutes. Be certain broth is simmering strongly as you drop in *matzah* balls. Cover and simmer 20 minutes more. For lower fat, make soup the day before, chill, then skim solidified fat from the top before reheating the next day.

MATZAH BALLS

1½ Cups *matzah* meal
6 eggs
½ Cup melted shortening or oil
1½ tsp salt
Dash pepper
¾ Cup water

Beat the eggs and add the water, oil, salt and pepper. Stir in *matzah* meal. Mix well. Refrigerate at least one hour. Wet hands with cold water. Roll mixture into 1-inch balls and drop into boiling soup. Cover and simmer 20 minutes.

MATZAH STUFFING

½ Cup margarine
10 *matzah* crackers, finely broken
¼ tsp. pepper
1 Tblsp. paprika
¾ Cup minced onion
1 tsp. salt
1 egg
2½ Cups chicken broth

Sauté onion in margarine until tender but not brown. Add *matzah* crackers and toast lightly. Combine seasonings, egg and soup. Add to *matzah* mixture. Makes enough to stuff a 12-pound bird.

PASSOVER POTATO PANCAKES ("LATKES")

5 medium potatoes
1½ tsp. salt
¼ tsp. pepper
2 Tblsp. minced parsley
2 Tblsp. *matzah* cake meal
Fat for frying (not butter)
2 Tblsp. grated onion
4 eggs, beaten 'till thick

Peel potatoes and grate on a medium-fine grater. Place in a fine sieve and press out as much liquid as possible. Measure pulp. If it does not measure 4 cups, grate and strain more potato. Add cake meal, salt, pepper, onion and parsley. Fold in the well-beaten eggs. Melt margarine or fat to a depth of 1/4 inch. Heat until a drop of batter makes the fat sizzle. Drop batter by tablespoons onto the pan and flatten somewhat with spatula. When pancakes are browned on the bottom, turn over and brown on other side. Drain on paper towels and serve warm. Best served with applesauce.

POTATO KUGEL

1/4 Cup potato starch
¼ Cup oil or melted margarine
pkg. "Simply Shreds"

3 large beaten eggs
1 large onion, grated
2 tsp. salt
½ tsp. pepper Frozen potatoes, thawed

Mix all ingredients together. Grease a 2-quart casserole with margarine or chicken fat. Turn mixture into casserole dish. Bake at 375 degrees for 1 hour, until the top is brown and crusty.

CRUSTY CHICKEN BREASTS

10 Skinless, boneless chicken breasts
1½ Cups *matzah* meal
1½ tsp garlic powder

2 tsp salt
½ tsp pepper
¾ tsp oregano

In a plastic bag, toss *matzah* meal and spices together to mix. Rinse chicken breasts in tap water, dry with a paper towel, and drop one at a time into seasoned matzo meal, tossing to coat with crumbs. Fry chicken in a little olive oil until golden and cooked through.

GEFILTE FISH

Gefilte fish (fish cakes) is traditionally served at Passover meals. It is delicious when made fresh but not quite so tasty from a bottle. It is, however, elaborate and time-consuming to make, and the types of fish used are not available in some areas. Serve the bottled fish cakes, just enough for everyone to have a taste. Serve cold, with horseradish. Fish is a *parveh* food. In other words, it is neutral, neither meat nor milk, and it can be served with both.

ROAST LAMB SHOULDER ROLL

4 - 5 lb. lamb shoulder	3 Tblsp *matzah* cake meal
1 Tblsp dry mustard	½ tsp salt
½ Cup cold water	¼ tsp pepper Small jar currant jelly

Have a 4–5 pound lamb shoulder boned and rolled by your local butcher. (Supermarket butchers should be willing to special order this cut, if it's not already set out on display.) Mix flour, dry mustard, salt, and pepper; blend in cold water. Spread over meat. Place the roast on a rack in an open roasting pan. Insert a meat thermometer. Roast at 325 degrees until the thermometer registers 175–180 degrees–about 45 minutes per pound. Spread with currant jelly for the last hour of cooking, basting every 15 minutes.

Note: According to the Law of Moses, a sinew in the flank of an animal must be removed by the butcher, a time-consuming and difficult feat, which Jews can avoid by eating just the forequarters of the animal.

IRAQI MINTED SALAD

tomatoes	1 cucumber
small bunch radishes	6 spring onions
1 red bell pepper	1 green bell pepper
3 Tblsp. fresh mint leaves	1 Tblsp. chopped fresh parsley
6 Tblsp. lemon and oil dressing (below)	

Peel and dice tomatoes, cucumbers, and radishes. Dice onions and peppers. Mix all vegetables, season and dress with salad dressing. Arrange in a dish in layers, alternating with a layer of mint leaves. Sprinkle with parsley, garnish with a few mint leaves, and serve chilled. *If you don't have fresh mint, add 1½ Tblsp. dried mint to the dressing.

LEMON AND OIL DRESSING

4 Tblsp. olive oil
Pinch pprika
Pinch pepper
2 Tblsp. lemon juice
1 tsp salt

Mix oil and seasonings. Drip in lemon juice gradually, stirring all the time to form an emulsion. Best served chilled.

DENISE'S SPINACH SALAD

Fresh spinach, torn
Sliced apple (peeled)
Craisins (dried cranberries)
Spring onions, chopped
Turkey bacon, fried and broken
Poppy Seed dressing (below)

Toss all ingredients with dressing just before serving.

POPPY SEED DRESSING

¾ cup sugar
1 tsp salt
1 cup vegetable oil
1 Tblsp poppy seeds
1 tsp dry mustard
1 Tblsp minced onion
1/4 cup apple cider vinegar

Whisk sugar, vinegar, mustard, salt and onion together until sugar is dissolved. Slowly blend in oil and poppy seeds. If necessary to thin, add a little water.

ZUCCHINI CASSEROLE

4-5 cups zucchini chunks
1 onion, chopped
1/4 cup margarine
½ cup *matzah* meal
1 egg
1½ tsp salt

½ tsp pepper   1½ tsp Italian spices*

*Or add ½ tsp each garlic, oregano and basil.

Boil zucchini and onion together in salted water until tender. Dump into a colander and cut into smaller pieces with two knives or a pastry cutter, draining very well. Transfer into a casserole dish. Add margarine and stir until melted. Stir in *matzah* meal, egg, seasonings, and salt and ample pepper to taste. Bake uncovered at 350E for 45 minutes.

MATZAH CHOCOLATE TORTE

4 egg yolks, beaten	4 ounces raisins
½ Cup sugar	¼ Cup fine *matzah* meal
Juice of one orange	4 egg whites, stiffly beaten
4 ounces slivered almonds	4 ounces chocolate chips
¼ Cup grape juice	

Beat the sugar with the egg yolks until light. Add chocolate chips, almonds, raisins, *matzah* meal, orange and grape juice. Fold in egg whites. Bake in a spring-form cake pan at 350 degrees for about 1 hour.

MATZAH APPLE TORTE

8 apples, pared and grated	1 Cup *matzah* meal
8 eggs, separated	1 tsp. cinnamon
¾ Cup sugar	1 Tblsp. orange juice
¼ Cup chopped nuts	
¼ tsp. salt	

Beat egg whites with salt until very stiff. Add sugar gradually, then beaten yolks. Mix dry ingredients together and add. Stir in orange juice and nuts. Stir in apples. Bake in greased cake pan 1 to 1¼ hours at 350 degrees.

MATZAH SPONGE CAKE

8 eggs, separated	1 Cup fine *matzah* cake meal
1½ Cups sugar	½ lemon, grated rind and juice

Beat yolks until light, add sugar and beat again. Add a pinch of salt, the lemon rind, and lemon juice. Stir in the cake meal, then fold in stiffly beaten egg whites. Bake in a spring form cake pan or two 8–9 inch cake pans at 350 degrees for 35–45 minutes. Serve with sweetened strawberries or other garnish.

COCONUT KISSES

4 egg whites	½ lb. powdered sugar (2 ¼ cups)
½ lb. shredded coconut	

Grease baking sheets and line with baking paper. Beat egg whites until stiff. Gradually add sifted powdered sugar, beating mixture until very light. Stir in coconut. Drop mixture by teaspoonfuls onto **lined** baking sheet. Bake at 250–275 degrees for 45–60 minutes until golden. (Line baking sheet with baking paper.)

BROWN SUGAR MACAROONS

1 Cup light brown sugar	1¼ Cups ground pecans
1 egg white, unbeaten	

Mix all ingredients and roll into ¾ inch balls. Place on a greased pan 2 inches apart. Bake at 300 degrees for 10–15 minutes.

MATZAH COOKIES

½ cup vegetable margarine	½ cup potato flour
1 cup sugar	½ cup *matzah* meal
½ cup ground almonds	2 eggs

Cream margarine and sugar, then add other ingredients. Roll thin on a board sprinkled with potato flour and sugar. Cut into shapes and bake at 375 degrees until lightly browned.

CINNAMON DATE PASSOVER ROLL

PASTRY

Cup margarine
4 Tblsp. sugar
Cups *matzah* meal flour
1 Cup corn flour
½ tsp. salt

FILLING

½ lb. pitted dates
1 Cup sugar
1 Cup water
1½ tsp. cinnamon
¼ Cup chopped walnuts

Cream margarine and flours, sugar, and salt, then add just enough water to hold it together. Combine filling ingredients and cook over low heat for ten minutes. Remove from heat and allow to cool. Roll out dough and spread filling on it. Roll up the dough and place on a greased baking sheet or shallow pan. Bake in a 300 degree oven for 50 to 60 minutes. Sprinkle roll with sugar as soon as it comes out of the oven.

PASSOVER BANANA CAKE

7 eggs, separated
1 Cup sugar
1 cup mashed bananas
¾ Cup *matzah* meal
¼ Cup potato flour
½ Cup chopped nuts

For best results, sift the *matzah* meal to obtain the finest meal possible before measuring, or whir the *matzah* meal in a blender to crush it even finer. Mix the *matzah* meal, potato flour, and chopped nuts together.

Beat the egg whites stiff, gradually adding as much sugar as they will absorb. Beat the egg yolks, bananas, and remaining sugar together. Fold the *matzah* meal mixture into the whites, alternately with the yolk mixture. Bake in an ungreased tube pan for about 45 minutes at 325 degrees.

NOTE:

Any recipe for kisses or macaroons that does not contain flour, dairy products or leavening may be used for Passover dessert. Or just serve fruit. I like to serve **strawberries and sliced kiwi dipped in dark chocolate.** (Melt good quality semi-sweet chocolate chips in a bowl over hot water. Stir a bit of butter into the melted chocolate. Wash and **dry fruit thoroughly** before dipping. Set onto waxed paper or foil until set, peel from paper and place on a serving plate.)

Appendix E:
FEAST OF WEEKS RECIPES (SHAVUOT/PENTACOST)

It is traditional to eat dairy foods during the Feast of Weeks. The origin of this tradition is vague, so different authorities cite different reasons. Suffice it to say that the Israelites inherited a land "flowing with milk and honey." Serving sweet dairy foods seems to commemorate that gift from the Lord.

SWEET KUGEL

¾ cup butter (1½ sticks)	4 large eggs
¾ cup brown sugar	1 tsp cinnamon
½ cup pecans	½ cup sugar
16 oz. wide noodles	2 tsp salt

Melt half the butter in a casserole dish and swirl it around to coat the surfaces. Press the brown sugar and nuts onto the bottom of the dish. Cook the noodles according to the package directions. Drain very well. Beat the eggs so the yolks are broken and blended in. Melt the rest of the butter. Mix together the noodles, eggs, butter, cinnamon, sugar, and salt. Pour on top of the brown sugar and pecans. Bake at 350° for 1 hour 15 minutes. Let stand for 15 minutes. Invert onto plate or dish out with spoon.

CHEESE BLINTZES

CREPES

2 eggs	½ tsp salt
2 Tblsp vegetable oil	½ cup melted butter
1 cup milk	1½ tsp lemon juice
¾ cup flour	powdered sugar

FILLING

4 oz. cream cheese	2 Tblsp sugar
½ cup cottage cheese	1 tsp vanilla 1 egg yolk

Soften cream cheese. Mix filling ingredients together and set aside. To make the crepes, beat the eggs, oil, and milk in a medium bowl. Add the flour and salt. Beat until smooth. Cover and refrigerate batter for ½ hour. The batter should be the consistency of heavy cream. Melt a little butter in a small skillet. Pour in a little batter and quickly rotate the pan, so that the batter spreads to about a 7" circle. Cook over medium heat until the bottom of the pancake is light brown, and then slide the pancake out onto a piece of foil. Repeat until all the batter is used and pancakes are stacked between pieces of foil. To fill, take one pancake and turn browned side up. Place one tablespoon of filling in the center of the pancake. Fold the right and left side of the pancake to meet in the center over the filling. Then roll the pancake or fold it in the other direction to enclose the filling. Repeat until all the pancakes and filling have been used. Melt a little butter in a 13" pan and tilt the pan to coat the bottom. Place the blintzes seam sides down in the buttered pan. Melt the rest of the butter and blend in the lemon juice. Drizzle over the blintzes. Either serve as is, or bake for 15 minutes at 375°. Sprinkle powdered sugar on top before serving.

YOGURT COFFEE CAKE

CAKE

¾ cup sugar	1 tsp baking powder
½ cup butter, softened	1 tsp baking soda
1 tsp vanilla	¼ tsp salt

3 eggs 1 cup plain yogurt

2 cups flour

FILLING AND TOPPING

1¼ cups firmly packed brown sugar 2 tsp cinnamon

1 cup chopped walnuts 3 Tblsp butter, melted

Grease and flour a Bundt pan or angel cake pan. Mix together the topping ingredients and set aside. Combine the dry ingredients for the cake, mix well, and set aside. Cream the sugar and butter together. Blend in the vanilla and eggs. Alternately add the flour mixture and the yogurt, beginning and ending with the flour. Spread half the batter in the pan. Sprinkle with half the filling/ topping. Pour on the remaining batter, and sprinkle the remaining topping over the top. Bake at 350° for 35 to 40 minutes, or until an inserted toothpick comes out clean. Cool for 15 minutes, then invert onto a plate.

EUROPEAN JEWISH CHEESECAKE

PASTRY

1 1/3 cups flour ¼ cup butter, cut into pieces

¼ tsp salt 1 egg, slightly beaten

1/3 cup sugar

Mix the flour, salt, and sugar in a bowl. Drop the butter pieces into the flour mixture and rub the butter into the flour with your fingers. Mix in the egg. Knead the dough slightly. It should be soft, but not sticky. If the dough is sticky, add a little more flour and work in. Wrap the pastry in plastic wrap and set aside for half an hour, while you make the filling.

FILLING

16 oz tub Ricotta cheese or curd cheese	zest of 1 lemon*
2/3 cup sour cream or "fromage fraise"	juice of ½ lemon
5 eggs, separated	½ tsp vanilla extract scant
1 cup superfine sugar	

*Obtain lemon zest by finely grating the rind of a lemon.

Mix the Ricotta or curd cheese with the rest of the filling ingredients, including the yolks, but not the whites of the eggs. Beat the egg whites until stiff and fold into the cheese mixture.

Prepare the pastry shell by pressing the dough into a springform cake pan with your fingers. Press the dough onto the bottom of the pan and a little up the sides. Pour the filling over the pastry. Bake at 300° (preheat <u>oven</u>) for 90 minutes. Turn off the oven and open the door, leaving the cake inside. Allow the cake to cool in the oven.

MIDDLE EASTERN MILK PUDDING

NOTE:

Instead of rice flour, you can use corn starch, or ½ cornstarch and ½ rice flour. The rice flour is more authentic. You can buy it at health food stores.

HINT:

It's easy for milk or pudding to burn onto the bottom of a saucepan while cooking. Stir often to keep this from happening. While stirring pudding, don't scrape any burned milk off the bottom of the pan.

	¾ cup rice flour

	5½ cups cold milk (full fat)

	½ cup sugar

For flavorings, choose:

- Turkish — 1/2 tsp vanilla, or the zest of ½ lemon. Sprinkle with cinnamon.
- Iranian — 1 tsp ground cardamom
- Egyptian — 1 Tblsp orange blossom water (Buy from a store that carries imported foods.) Garnish with chopped almonds or pistachios.

Mix the rice flour with 1 cup of the cold milk in a bowl, beginning with the rice flour and drizzling in the milk. Stir constantly with a fork or whisk to prevent lumps. Bring the rest of the milk to a boil in a saucepan. Pour in the rice mixture while stirring vigorously with the whisk. Cook on very low heat until thickened. Cook gently for another 10 minutes, stirring every so often to prevent burning. Add spice or flavoring. Stir in the sugar until dissolved. Pour into a bowl. The mixture will get thicker as it cools. Chill and serve cold.

Appendix F:
FEAST OF TRUMPETS RECIPES

Sweet foods are favorite foods when celebrating *Rosh haShanah*, the civil new year, or Feast of Trumpets. Fruits are always popular. The most traditional food is apples dipped in honey. Your favorite fruit salad is a good choice to prepare as a family. Here are some other recipes for you.

APPLE UPSIDE-DOWN CAKE

½ cup (1 stick) butter or margarine
¾ cup chopped nuts
3 cups sugar
1 Tblsp ground cinnamon
medium baking apples, pared & thinly sliced
1 tsp vanilla

2 ¾ cups flour
3 tsp baking powder
½ tsp salt
2/3 cup vegetable oil
1½ cups milk
2 eggs

Melt the butter in a 13" x 9" baking pan. Combine 1 cup of the sugar, nuts, and cinnamon in a small bowl. Sprinkle evenly over the melted butter in the pan. Arrange the apple slices in the pan, overlapping slightly. Sift together the flour, the remaining sugar, the baking powder and salt into a large bowl. Mix together the oil, milk, eggs, and vanilla. Blend into the flour mixture and beat until well mixed. Pour the batter evenly over the apples. Bake at 350° for 1 hour 10 minutes, or until the top of the cake springs back when pressed with a fingertip. Cool in the pan on a wire rack for 5 minutes. Loosen around the edges of the cake with a knife. Cover with a large serving tray or cookie sheet, and invert.

APPLE KUGEL

large apples, peeled & thinly sliced   ¾ cup flour
½ cup melted butter   1 tsp cinnamon
cup sugar   1/8 tsp salt
beaten eggs

Blend all the ingredients together. Pour into a greased 9" x 9" cake pan, and bake at 375° for 50 minutes. Serve hot. Optional: top kugel with crushed corn flakes mixed with cinnamon and sugar.

ROSH HASHANAH HONEY CAKE

4 eggs   1 Tblsp baking powder
½ cup butter   ½ tsp cinnamon
1 lemon (juice & grated rind)   ½ tsp ginger
1 orange (juice & grated rind)   ½ tsp cloves
5 cups flour   ½ tsp nutmeg
1 tsp soda
1 cup hot water with 1 tsp Postum   1 cup honey
1 cup brown sugar   1 cup granulated sugar

Mix the hot Postum, brown sugar, honey, and sugar together and set aside to cool. . Sift the dry ingredients together and set aside. Beat eggs well. Add the melted and cooled butter, fruit rind (very finely grated) and juices. Add the dry ingredients alternately with the Postum mixture. Bake in two greased and floured loaf pans at 350° for 1 hour 15 minutes, or until an inserted toothpick comes out clean.

HONEY CAKE

4 eggs	½ cup melted butter or oil
Juice and grated rind of 1 lemon	Juice and grated rind of 1 orange
5 cups flour	1 tsp baking soda
3 tsp baking powder	½ tsp cinnamon
½ tsp ginger	½ tsp cloves
½ tsp nutmeg	

Bring to a boil and cool:

1 cup water	1 cup honey
cup brown sugar	1 cup granulated sugar
1 cup chopped nuts (optional)	

Beat the eggs well, add the melted butter (or oil); add the fruit rinds and juices. Sift the dry ingredients together into another bowl and add alternately with the sugar mixture. Pour into a greased angel-food cake pan, bundt pan, or large, oblong pan and bake at 350º for about 1 hour 15 minutes, or until inserted toothpick comes out clean.

Appendix G:
FEAST OF TABERNACLES RECIPES

Seasonal produce and nuts are favorites for *Sukkot*, because it is the time of the final harvest. Your favorite recipes using autumn fruits and vegetables (such as apples and pumpkins) will do. More recipes follow.

PERSIAN FRUIT SALAD

oranges, peeled and chunked	1 cup dried apricots, chopped
2 apples, peeled, cored, and diced	1 cup orange juice
2 bananas, sliced	1 cup almonds, chopped
2 cups dates, pitted and chopped	Shredded coconut

Place fruit in a serving bowl. Pour the orange juice over the fruit and mix. Garnish with coconut. Cover and chill several hours before serving, so juice will be absorbed.

ACORN SQUASH WITH APPLE STUFFING

2 acorn squash	¼ cup raisins
2 Tblsp melted butter	¼ cup red or white grape juice
salt to taste	3 medium apples
sprinkle of cinnamon	Another 2 Tblsp butter
½ cup water	¼ cup brown sugar
1 Tblsp lemon juice	

Cut the squashed in half and scoop out the seeds and stringy insides. Brush the cut surfaces with melted butter and sprinkle with salt and cinnamon. Place squash halves on a baking pan with cut sides down. Put ½ cup water in the pan, or enough to just cover the bottom of the pan. Bake the squash for 30 minutes in a preheated 350° oven.

Soak the raisins in the grape juice to plump them. Pare, core, and chop the apples. In a small frying pan, melt the remaining butter and add the chopped apples. Cook 3 to 5 minutes until the apples are slightly wilted. Stir the brown sugar and lemon juice into the apples. When the squash is done, turn the halves cut sides up. Drain the raisins and stir into the apple mixture. Then fill the squash cavities. Cover with foil and bake 20 to 30 minutes more, or until squash is very tender.

PUMPKIN SPICE CAKE WITH ORANGE SAUCE

½ cup butter or margarine	1½ cups flour
¾ cup sugar	1½ tsp baking powder
2 large eggs	¼ tsp salt
¾ cup mashed cooked pumpkin (canned is fine)	1½ tsp pumpkin pie spice
	Powdered sugar
1 tsp vanilla extract	Orange sauce (below)

Beat the butter or margarine until creamy. Gradually add the sugar, beating well. Add the eggs, one at a time, beating until blended after each addition. Stir in the pumpkin and vanilla. Combine the flour, baking powder, salt, and pie spice. Gradually beat into the sugar mixture. Pour into a greased and floured 9" x 9" pan. Bake at 350° for 20 minutes or until an inserted toothpick comes out clean. Cool in pan on wire rack for 10 minutes. Tip out of pan onto wire rack and cool. Sift the powdered sugar over the cake. Make a pattern with the sugar by placing a doily on top before sifting the sugar onto the cake. Remove doily. Serve with orange sauce.

ORANGE SAUCE

1/3 cup light brown sugar

1½ cup orange juice

1 Tblsp cornstarch

1 tsp lemon juice

Whisk together all ingredients in a heavy saucepan until blended. Bring the mixture to a boil over medium heat, stirring constantly. Boil and stir one minute. Cool. Serve over pumpkin cake.

GINGER-ALMOND SHORTBREAD

cup softened butter

1 tsp almond extract

2 tsp ground ginger

24 whole almonds

2/3 cup sifted powdered sugar

1½ cups flour

¼ cup finely ground almonds

In a large mixing bowl, cream the butter with the sugar and almond extract until smooth. Add the flour, ginger, and ground almonds and beat until well-combined. On a floured surface, roll the dough out to ½ inch thickness. Cut into 2-inch rounds and place one inch apart on an ungreased cookie sheet. Bake about 20 minutes at 350° until very lightly colored. Remove to a rack and cool. (Makes 2 dozen cookies.)

FRESH FRUIT STRUDEL

NOTE:

Find puff pastry dough in the freezer desserts department of your grocery store. In each package you will find two sheets, each folded into thirds. For this recipe, ignore the divisions, and use the two full rectangles. Be sure to fully defrost the dough before using.

1 pkg puff pastry dough

1/3 cup melted butter

4 Tblsp orange marmalade

½ tsp cinnamon

½ cup chopped almonds

½ cup matzah meal or bread

crumbs 4 cups favorite fresh fruit

¾ cups sugar

egg or oil to glaze top

Roll out each rectangle to thin the dough as much as possible. Brush each sheet with melted butter. Spread over that a thin layer of orange marmalade. Peel, core and dice fruit. Sprinkle fruit over the sheets, leaving a ½ to 1 inch space around the edges. Sprinkle with sugar, cinnamon, almonds, and bread crumbs. Roll each rectangle and fold over the ends to seal. Place on a lightly greased cookie sheet with the seam sides down. Beat an egg with a little water, or use oil to brush over the tops. Bake at 350° for about an hour, or until golden. Great with ice cream.

EDIBLE SU KKAHS

Graham crackers

Frosting or peanut butter

Celery tops and parsley

Use frosting or peanut butter to "glue" 3 graham cracker squares together, forming the three sides of a sukkah. Break one more cracker in half and attach to make the half of the fourth side, leaving a doorway. Lay celery tops and parsley over the tops of the sukkahs.

Appendix H:
PURIM

THE STORY OF ESTHER

Boo, hiss and sound noisemakers when wicked Haman's name is mentioned.
Cheer when Esther and Mordechai's names are mentioned.

A long, long time ago in very ancient times, many Jews lived in the city of Shushan in the country of Persia. The country had a great king, a very rich and powerful man named King Ahashverosh. His queen's name was Vashti.

The king loved to give huge parties at his palace. One night the king was having one of his huge parties, and he wanted Queen Vashti to dance for his guests. The king summoned her, but she refused to come. The king was very insulted. Vashti had humiliated him in front of all his guests, and soon the entire kingdom would surely hear about it. King Ahashverosh was terribly angry. He decided that Vashti would no longer be his queen, and he sent her away from the palace.

King Ahashverosh had an interesting idea to help him find a new queen. He held a sort of beauty contest to find the most beautiful young ladies in the kingdom. He was looking not just for beauty, but for poise and graciousness, too. He sent messengers throughout the country calling all the young women to the palace. One of these young women was Esther. Esther was a Jewish girl. Actually, Esther did not want to go. But her good cousin Mordechai encouraged her.

The Jews were not always treated well; it would be good to have a Jewish girl in the king's court, because she might be able to help her people someday. Esther was kind and beautiful; the king chose her to be his queen.

The king had an assistant to help him run the kingdom. The assistant was Haman. Haman was a wicked man, selfish and prideful. He was mean and greedy. He made people bow down to him wherever he went. Mordechai (Esther's cousin) would not bow down to Haman. Mordechai would only bow to God; he refused to worship this evil man. Haman was angry. He decided to punish all the Jews because of Mordechai.

Meanwhile, Mordechai went to visit Esther at the palace. While he was there, he overheard two guards whispering their plans to hurt the king. Mordechai told the king about the guards. The king was so grateful that he gave Mordechai some royal clothing and told Haman to lead Mordechai through the streets of Shushan on the king's horse, so that the people could honor him.

This made Haman even angrier. He made plans to have all the Jews in the city killed. It was all up to Queen Esther. She was the only one who could save her people.

Esther found favor with the king and invited him to a party. She also invited Haman. At the party she accused Haman of trying to hurt her. Haman protested. He would never hurt his queen! Esther accused him of trying to hurt the Jewish people, and then she told everyone that she was Jewish herself. The king was shocked. He took away Haman's job and gave it to Mordechai.

The Jews were safe. They celebrated with songs; they danced and gave parties.

HAMENTASCHEN

For the **filling,** use your favorite **fruit jam**, or order the more traditional poppy seed filling from a Jewish food supplier over the Internet.

Dough

2 sticks margarine or butter	1 Tblsp oil
1½ cups sugar	4 large eggs
½ cup pineapple or orange juice	2 tsp baking powder
¼ tsp baking soda	5 to 5½ cups flour

Mix shortenings and sugar. Cream well. Add remaining ingredients and mix well. Divide the dough into three sections and chill several hours or overnight. Roll out to 1/8 inch thick, and cut with a 3 inch round cookie cutter or drinking glass. Place a teaspoon of filling on each circle, and in your hand fold over the edges to create a triangle shape. Place on a greased cookie sheet and bake for about 15 minutes (until golden) at 350º. You can brush the cookies with egg before baking, if desired. They will come out browner, if you do.

PURIM – GIFTS OF SWEETS (*MISHLO'ACH MANOT*)

Mishlo'ach Manot are always collections of treats, small for fellow school mates and large when sent business to business. Mishlo'ach Manot are also given to the poor on Purim. In the Israeli kindergartens, the teachers instruct the children as to what to bring.

The children draw names and exchange the gifts. The collection of sweets usually consists of two bags of chips or salty snacks (small, lunch-box size bags), plus a couple of candies. One can wrap the collection in cellophane for giving.

For your Family Home Evening provide a selection of treats and have family members arrange and wrap them. Draw names and exchange the gifts. Or draw names and have family members deliver the gifts secretly to each other during the week.

Appendix I:
CHANUKAH

THE CHANUKAH STORY

Chanukah is another favorite Jewish holiday that does not originate from the Exodus. Chanukah carries no Messianic symbolism. Chanukah lasts for eight days and falls around Christmas time.

In order to keep Jewish children from being so attracted to the trappings of Christmas, the celebration of Chanukah is becoming more and more elaborate. Children often receive a gift each night.

Chanukah is the celebration of a miracle that occurred about 160 years before Christ. King Antiochus had led a Greco-Syrian alliance in conquering the kingdom of Judah, taking control of the temple as well as the government.

Antiochus demanded that the Jews worship the Greek gods, that they reject their religion, their customs, and their beliefs. Some Jews refused and rose up in rebellion. They were led by the Maccabee family — Judah Maccabee and his four brothers. Judah and his brothers had chosen their own last name. It means "hammer" in Hebrew.

After three years of bitter fighting, the Maccabees and their followers succeeded in driving out the Syrians and reclaiming the Temple. The Temple had been desecrated by the Syrians. They had erected statues of Greek gods there, and had sacrificed to them. On the 25th day of the month of Kislev, the Temple was cleansed and ready for rededication.

In every Jewish place of worship, and especially in the Temple, there is a light, called the *N'er Tamid*, "eternal light." Once lit, the light should never be extinguished. The Syrians had extinguished the flame, and the Maccabees wanted to relight it. Only a tiny jug of temple oil could be found. The oil lamp was filled and lit. The oil was just enough to provide light for one day, but it burned for eight, a great miracle.

The holiday of Chanukah commemorates this miracle, as well as the victory over the Syrians. Chanukah is the "Festival of Lights," but the word *chanukah* means "rededication."

Celebration of the holiday includes gift-giving, parties, singing, decorating, but most of all the lighting of the holiday candles.

THE DREYDEL GAME

Make dreydels from stiff cardboard from the pattern found below. Glue or tape the tabs. Put a stick into the top to use as a handle. If you don't cut out the hole in the top, even a toothpick will work.

The Hebrew letters stand for the words, *Ness gadol haya sham*, "a great miracle happened there."

- A player spins the dreydel.
- When it stops spinning, it will fall with one side up.
- If the (nun) shows, nothing happens; the next player spins.

- If the # (gimmel) shows, the player takes all the tokens in the pot.

- If the % (hey) shows, the player takes half the tokens.

- If the ש (shin) shows, the player must cast in a token.

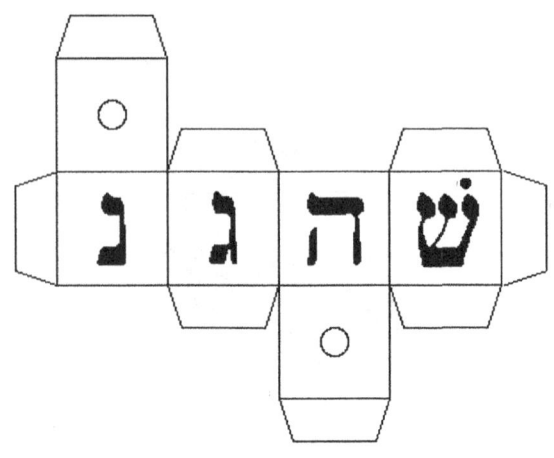

CHAUNUKAH MENORAHS

A chanukah menorah always has eight branches, plus one for the lighting candle (*shamash*). The shamash candle holder is always higher than the others. After those requirements are met, the artist has complete license to make the menorah look like they want. Here's one from Legos™.

Appendix J:
CHANUKAH RECIPES

CHANUKAH DOUGHNUTS (SUFGANIYOT)

2 packets dry yeast (2 Tblsp)	1/3 cup sugar
¾ cup warm water	¼ cup orange juice (warm)
1/3 cup margarine or butter	½ tsp salt
4 to 5 cups flour	3 egg yolks (at room temperature)
Favorite jelly or jam (not lumpy)	

Mix water, sugar, juice, and yeast. Let stand about ten minutes. Melt the shortening and add to the yeast mixture. Beat in the egg yolks and salt. Add flour, mixing with a spoon and then kneading to a soft dough. Let rise about 90 minutes or until doubled in size. (You can leave it on a floured counter-top and cover it with a clean towel, or turn it into a greased bowl and cover it to double.) Roll the dough to about ¼ inch thickness and cut out circles about 2 inches wide. Cover circles with a towel and allow to rise about 30 minutes. Deep fry in hot oil (about 400º) for about 3 minutes, turning once. Cool on paper towels. Pipe a little jelly into the center of each doughnut with a pastry piping tool. Roll in granulated sugar.

POTATO PANCAKES (LATKES)

2 large eggs + 1 yolk	½ tsp baking powder
2 small grated onions	4 medium potatoes, peeled & shredded
¼ cup minced parsley	Salt and pepper to taste
2 Tblsp flour	1/3 cup butter or margarine Applesauce

Beat the eggs and yolk and add all other ingredients except the butter. Shred the potatoes just before adding them. The mixture will look fairly strange. Heat the butter in a large skillet over medium heat. Drop the pancake mixture into the hot butter to form 3 inch rounds, slightly mounded. Flatten them with a spatula. Cook, occasionally flattening the pancakes into the butter. Turn carefully when the underside is brown and crusty, especially around the edges. Brown the second side. Keep warm in a warm oven while cooking the rest of the pancakes. Serve hot with applesauce.

CHANUKAH POTATO PANCAKES (LATKES)

(Serve with applesauce)

2 peeled potatoes	1 small peeled onion
2 eggs	3 Tblsp. milk
2 Tblsp. melted butter	¼ cup flour
½ tsp salt	Dash pepper
Butter for frying	Applesauce

Grate the potatoes and onion into a bowl. Beat together the eggs, milk and melted butter. Mix into the potatoes. Add the flour, salt and pepper, blending well. Heat a generous amount of butter in a frying pan. Drop potato mixture into hot butter by quarter-cupfuls. Spread to create 4" pancakes. Brown on both sides. Serve warm with applesauce.

HONEY AND SPICE COOKIES

COOKIES

½ cup (1 stick) butter, softened

½ cup firmly packed dark brown sugar

½ cup honey

egg

2½ cups flour

¼ tsp ground cloves

2 tsp ground ginger

1 tsp baking soda

1 tsp ground cinnamon

1 tsp ground nutmeg

½ tsp salt

ROYAL ICING

2 egg whites

1 Tblsp lemon juice

3 cups powdered sugar

1/8 tsp salt

In a large mixing bowl cream the butter and sugar together. Beat in the honey and egg until well combined. In a small bowl sift dry ingredients together. Add gradually to honey mixture. Beat until well blended. Cover dough. Refrigerate at least 1 hour or up to 3 days. Grease cookie sheets and set aside. Working quickly, with ¼ of the dough at a time, roll out onto a floured surface to ¼ inch thick. Cut into desired shapes – try a dreydel, menorah, or six pointed star. Using a spatula, place shapes on greased cookie sheets. Bake at 350° for 7 minutes. Transfer to wire rack to cool. Meanwhile, prepare royal icing.

In a large bowl, combine egg whites, powdered sugar, lemon juice, and salt. Beat on high speed until mixture holds soft peaks. Decorate cooled cookies with frosting by either smoothing on top or piping on around edges.

Appendix K:
CHILDREN'S PICTURES

The following pages contain pictures that children can color, as desired.

These pictures can be used in conjunction with the Family Home Evening presentations found in Appendix A.

The first sacrament was a Passover

First Fruits of the Earth

Counting the Omer
7x7 weeks

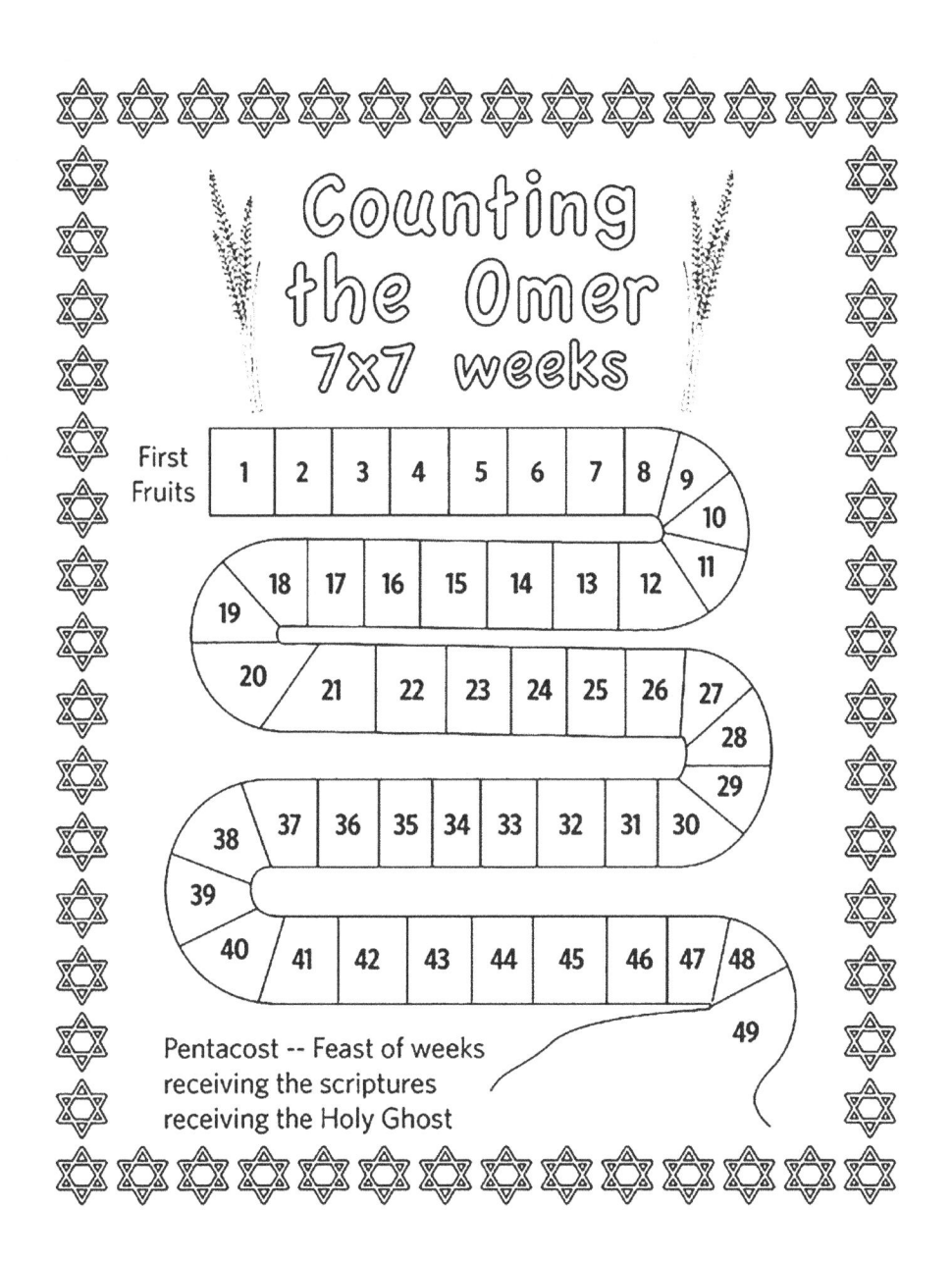

First Fruits: 1, 2, 3, 4, 5, 6, 7, 8, 9, 10, 11, 12, 13, 14, 15, 16, 17, 18, 19, 20, 21, 22, 23, 24, 25, 26, 27, 28, 29, 30, 31, 32, 33, 34, 35, 36, 37, 38, 39, 40, 41, 42, 43, 44, 45, 46, 47, 48, 49

Pentacost -- Feast of weeks
receiving the scriptures
receiving the Holy Ghost

TEN COMMANDMENTS TABLETS

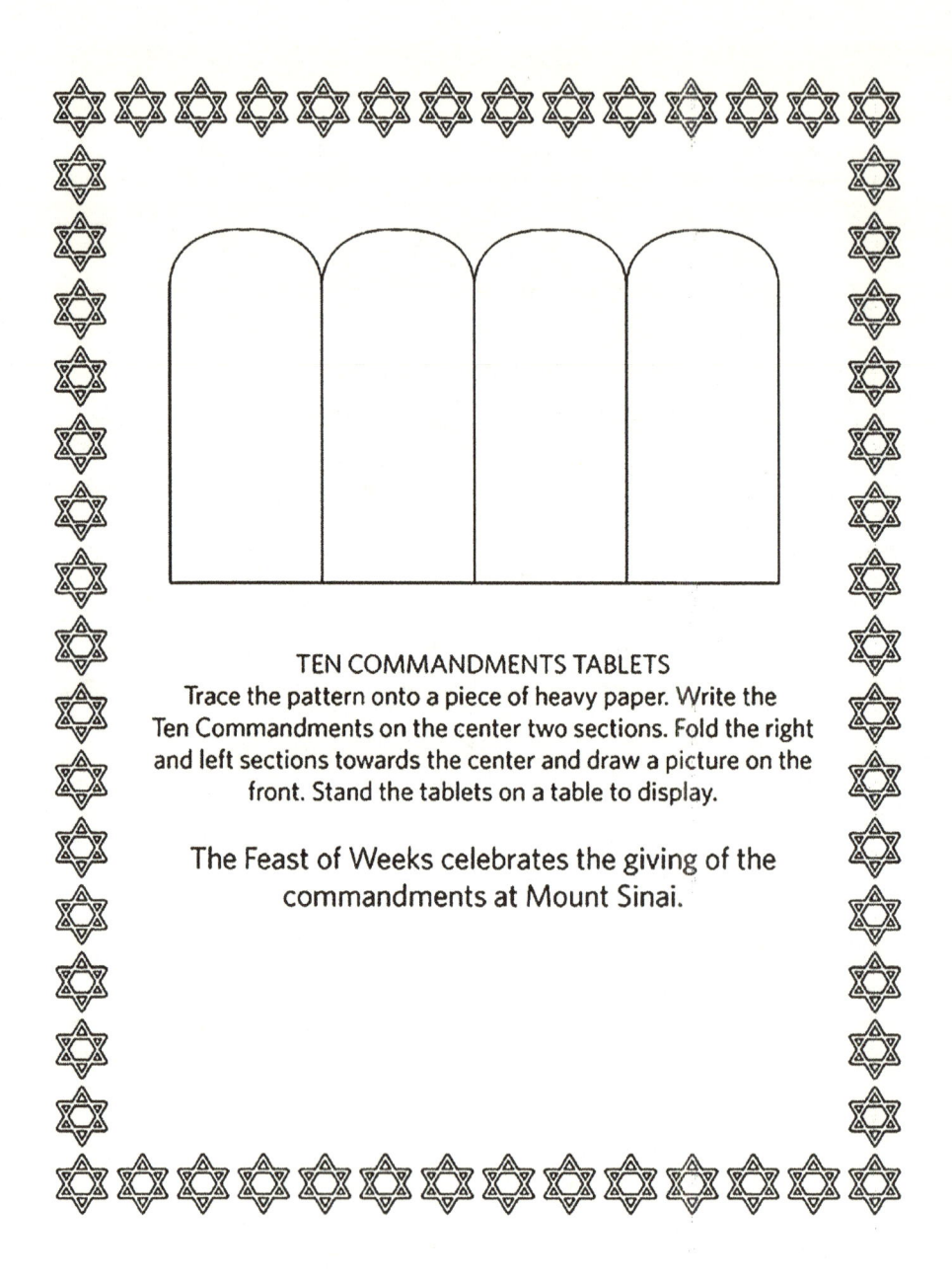

Trace the pattern onto a piece of heavy paper. Write the Ten Commandments on the center two sections. Fold the right and left sections towards the center and draw a picture on the front. Stand the tablets on a table to display.

The Feast of Weeks celebrates the giving of the commandments at Mount Sinai.

The Feast of Weeks celebrates the giving of the commandments at Mount Sinai.

DAYS OF AWE

The priests blow a ram's horn during the Feast of Trumpets (Rosh HaShanah). It calls the people to wake up, gather together, and repent, so that they will be found worthy to have their names written in the Lord's ""Book of Life.'"

SHOFAR

A "sukkah" is a booth or a tabernacle. At the Feast of Tabernacles ("sukkot") we build a sukkah in our own backyard. We decorate it with pictures, fruits of the harvest, and even lights. We eat and sleep in the sukkah and have lots of fun.

THE BOOK OF LIFE

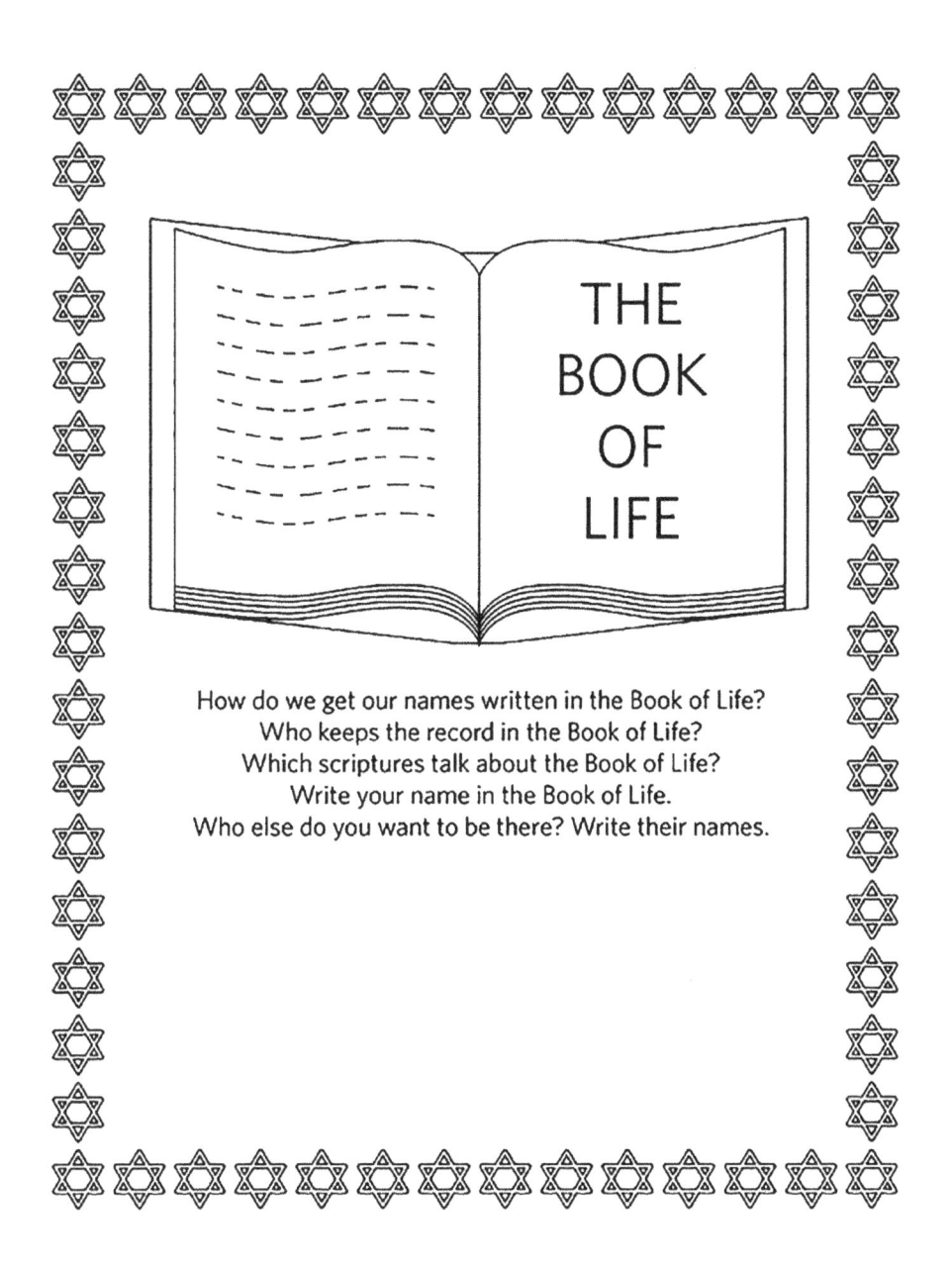

How do we get our names written in the Book of Life?
Who keeps the record in the Book of Life?
Which scriptures talk about the Book of Life?
Write your name in the Book of Life.
Who else do you want to be there? Write their names.

Purim

Brave Queen Esther saved her people by pleading with the King on their behalf.

Spinning the Dreydel

One small jug of oil lasted for 8 days

Chanukah

Appendix L:
A TORAH SCROLL

The pictures above show a Torah Scroll, pointer (*yod*), and cover (*tallit*). A Torah scroll is copied by hand letter for letter. It must contain no errors. The scroll is very carefully handled and kept in a special place in the synagogue. If it is ever in danger, a person is expected to risk his life to save it.

The picture above shows what a page from the Torah Scroll looks like. Hebrew is a phonetic language, and is read from right to left.

Appendix M:
LAG B'OMER **BONFIRE ACTIVITY**

This activity can be used for a family home evening, taking up the entire lesson time. You should already have presented the lessons on the Passover and First Fruits (*Bikkurim*). Explain what it means to "Count the Omer." Either read the chapter and summarize it, or read it with your family.

Explain that there are no numbers in Hebrew. Letters are used to represent numbers. The word *lag* is really not a word at all. It is simply the collection of letters that equals 33. The Omer is counted for forty-nine days. One time during the counting of the Omer, there was a pestilence, a sickness that afflicted many people. The people were students of a great Rabbi. On the thirty- third day the illness lifted. Now this is a holiday in Israel.

Lag B'omer usually falls in early May, so the evenings are warm. People build bonfires and spend an evening of fun with their friends and neighbors cooking food, singing songs, and relaxing. Wood is fairly scarce in Israel, so days before *Lag B'omer* children look everywhere they can for wood. Some will even take wood from construction sites, so contractors are very careful not to leave it around, if they're going to need it.

Israeli's throw raw, whole onions and raw, whole potatoes into the fire (on the edges where they can see them). They retrieve them when they are black and roasted. They remove all the blackened part and eat the insides. We didn't find this very palatable, so we cooked our traditional campfire meals – S'mores and Hobo Packs.

After studying the background of the holiday of *Lag B'omer*, send the children on a hunt for wood. If you are at home, and you have a safe corner of the yard to build a campfire, scatter wood in various places before the hunt.

If you are at a campsite or vacant lot, wood may be available to gather.

Cook your favorite campfire meal or share marshmallows or S'mores.

Appendix N:
MAKING A FLOWER HEAD WREATH

Flower head wreaths are worn in Israel for the holiday of the Feast of Weeks (*Shavuot*), and for other occasions, such as birthdays. You can make a flower head wreath from **fresh flowers** or **artificial ones**. Keep fresh flower wreaths in the refrigerator.

Begin with a **long, flexible vine**. If the wreath is artificial, buy **green wrapped heavy wire.** It comes in long stems and is available at craft stores. Twist two stems together to increase the overall length of the artificial vine. Twist the vine around itself to create a circle that will loosely lie upon the girl's head, tilted slightly downward in the back and resting just above the girl's ears. Mark the center back. A few inches from the center back place a small **cluster of leaves** with the tips pointing to the center back. Attach to the vine with **florists' tape**. Stretching the tape will make it stick. Close to the leaves, add a flower, wrapping with florists' tape as you go.

(If you are using fresh flowers, and you have twisted a long enough vine, you can insert the stems of the flowers and leaves into the twisted vine and anchor with wire, being sure not to leave wire ends where they will poke into the head of the wearer.)

Continue attaching flowers and leaves around the vine. Stop when you are a few inches from the center back and add a small cluster of leaves with the tips pointing towards the center back. If you desire, you can tie a **long piece of ribbon** to the center back.

APPENDIX 0:
RICHARD K. SCOTT PAPER

**THE CRUCIFIXION MAY HAVE OCCURRED ONE DAY
EARLIER THAN TRADITIONALLY BELIEVED**

By Richard K. Scott

TABLE OF CONTENTS

Introduction 243
The Passover Pattern Revealed In the Old Testament 244
Detailed Last Week Follows the Passover Pattern 246
Book of Mormon Clarification 251
Appendix 258
Significance of Three Days in the Bible 259
Alternative Interpretations of Ambiguous Verses 262

INTRODUCTION

The four Gospel writers devoted 1/3 of their chapters (23 of 89) to the final week before the ascension of Jesus into heaven. Subsequent Bible commentators have since spent much effort analyzing and ordering the abundance of information there recorded. Yet, the written account leaves many intriguing details unclear. From clues within the New Testament record we attempt to sequence the events and identify the corresponding day in our Sunday through Saturday calendar system. Unfortunately, the four Gospel accounts cannot be fully harmonized without compromise. The Triumphal Entry and Resurrection are generally accepted as occurring on successive Sundays, but there is less certainty as to the precise day of the midweek activities. In fact, most attempts at reconstruction work inward from the two Sundays and end up one day short of a full week. This approach requires the creation of a day of no activity, inconsistent with the characteristically detailed descriptions of this most important of all weeks. Furthermore, what about the clear promise that the crucified body of the Savior would be "three days and three nights in the heart of the earth" (Matt 12:40)? The traditionally accepted hypothesis of a Friday crucifixion allows for only a partial fulfillment of this prophecy.

There remain many questions to be answered, perspectives to be considered. From the vantage point of Old Testament pattern of the Passover week and the unique Book of Mormon account of the death of Christ, this paper will take yet another look at the final events in the mortal mission of Jesus Christ, The conclusion reached is that there is no midweek day of inactivity. Jesus was crucified on Thursday, fulfilling the Passover requirements and adding further witness that Jesus is the Lamb of God.

THE PASSOVER PATTERN REVEALED
IN THE OLD TESTAMENT

The sacrifice of a symbolic lamb (Moses 5:5) was required from the time Adam and Eve commenced mortality. To them, the angel explained, "this thing is a similitude of the sacrifice of the Only Begotten of the Father" (Moses 5:7). Thus from "the time of Adam to the time of the atoning sacrifice the lamb was a vicarious sacrifice offered by the shedding of its blood in similitude of the sacrifice that Christ would make for all men." (Joseph Fielding McConkie, *Gospel Symbolism*, p.2.) After the Exodus, the Israelites continued this focus on the Savior through the sacrificial slaying of the Passover lamb. "All that was associated with the Passover was a type of the atoning sacrifice of Christ." (ibid, p. 267, see also pp. 48-50)

In revelations to Moses, the Lord instituted the Passover and gave specific instructions as to how and when the feast was to be celebrated. There has been much written showing that all symbolisms of the Passover were fulfilled in the final week of the Savior's life. For the purposes of this paper, only facts relative to when the Passover should be celebrated will be considered.

From the 12th chapter of Exodus, we learn the Passover event should be celebrated in the "first month" (v.2) of the Israelite calendar. The selection of the lamb to be sacrificed was to be made "in the tenth day of this month." (v.3) The chosen lamb was to be kept "until the fourteenth day of the same month: and the whole assembly of the congregation of Israel shall kill it, in the evening" (v. 6). (The transition time from one day to the next, herein called "evening" or "even," was sunset (Deut. 16:6), later standardized as 6:00 p.m.). Later "that night" (Gen. 12:8) (on the next calendar day, the 15th, according to the Israelite system) the slain lamb was to be eaten along with the other symbolic foods. This "feast to the Lord" was to include "an holy convocation" wherein "no manner of work shall be done" (vv. 14, 16). This "sacrifice of the Lord's passover" (v. 27) was a "night to be much observed unto the Lord" (v. 42) and was also called "the ordinance of the Passover" (v. 43).

Relative to this very significant annual feast, Levite priests were instructed, "In the fourteenth day of the first month at even (Lev. 23:5 footnote b: between day-time and night-time) is the Lord's passover. And on the fifteenth day of the same month is the feast of the unleavened bread unto the lord: seven days ye must eat unleavened bread. In the first day ye shall have an holy convocation: ye shall do no servile work therein" (Lev 23:5-7). This fifteenth day of the month (the first day of the seven days of unleavened bread) is elsewhere referred to as a "Sabbath" (BD p. 627 Feasts) and "the feast" (Num 28:17).

The first day of the lunar month of Abib-Nisan was carefully determined by the sighting of the new moon. "In order to prevent possible confusion to the central religious authority, the chief of the Sanhedrin, in conjunction with at least two colleagues, was entrusted with the determination of new moon day for the whole nation" (*Jewish Encyclopedia* Vol. 3 p. 502). Since the major Passover activities were scheduled 14 and 15 days later, the celebration always coincided with the full moon, (see Times and Seasons, *Eardmans' Handbook To The Bible*, pp. 110-111).

Weeks, on the other hand, were calculated on the basis of seven solar days. Unfortunately, the solar year, seven day week, and twelve lunar months cannot be fully harmonized. To illustrate from our Julian calendar: if a holiday is always on a certain day of the week, such as Easter, it is celebrated on a different date each year. If a holiday is scheduled on a specific date, such as Christmas, it varies yearly as to the day of week upon which it is held. The Passover Sabbath was to be celebrated annually on 15 Abib-Nisan and, therefore, would be on various days of the week. This annual Sabbath was independent from the weekly Sabbath. The year the Lamb of God was sacrificed, Abib-Nisan 15 was on Friday, corresponding to April 7th in our calendar system. (Bruce R. McConkic, *The Mortal Messiah*, Vol. 4, p. 6, and Roger Rusk, *The Day He Died*, "Christianity Today", March 29,1974, pp. 4-6, and James E. Talmage, *Jesus the Christ*, p. 510)

PASSOVER PATTERN PROJECTED
ONTO CHRIST'S FINAL WEEK

Abib (later called Nisan)

Israelite Month Abib-Nisan	10th	14th	15th
Passover Activity	Selection of the Lamb to be sacrificed. "take to them every man a lamb" Ex. 12:3	Lord's Passover "the whole assembly of the congregation of Israel shall kill it in the evening" Ex. 12:6	Feast or Sabbath "this day shall be unto you for a memorial; and ye shall keep it a feast to the Lord throughout your

			generations; ye shall keep it a feast by an ordinance forever." Ex. 12:14
Day of Week	Sunday	Thursday	Friday
Corresponding Calendar Date	April 2	April 6	April 7

DETAILED LAST WEEK FOLLOWS THE PASSOVER PATTERN

In no other section of the Gospels is the Messiahship of Jesus more evident than in those chapters dealing with the last week of his life. The importance of these events warranted devoting a disproportionate number of chapters (28 of 89) to the account of but a single week. Correspondingly, New Testament commentators and teaching manuals typically include detailed charts and lists of each day's activities.

However, when one studies the individual Gospel accounts there remains some ambiguity as to when certain midweek activities occurred. The issue is further complicated by the differing writing styles and points of focus of the four Gospel writers. The existing lists and charts attempt to harmonize the Gospel accounts and provide a probable sequence of events. Of necessity the compilers have had to make compromises, for the Gospels don't always agree, and rely to some extent on assumptions and attempts at consistency. The challenge is emphasized by James E. Talmage who stated, "Controversy has been rife for many centuries as to the day of the passover feast in the Lord's death." (*Jesus the Christ*, pp. 617-619.) The purpose of this paper is not to refute the conclusions of other commentators, but merely to suggest that compliance to the schedule stipulated for proper Passover observance may have been followed more strictly than once thought.

The Apostle Paul stated, "Christ our Passover is sacrificed for us" (1 Cor 5:7). Let us consider then the possibility that as the Passover Lamb, Jesus, may have been slain in strict compliance with the requirements of the annual Passover schedule. The Passover schedule stipulated in the Old Testament synchronized with corresponding activities in the Savior's final week would produce the following chart:

Israelite Month of Abib-Nisan	9	10	11	12	13	14	15	16	17
Day of Week	Sat	Sun	Mon	Tues	Wed	Thur	Fri	Sat	Sun
Stipulated Passover Activity		Lamb Chosen				Lamb Slain			
Literal fulfillment by Lamb of God		Triumphal Entry				Crucifixion			
Additional Activities	Anointed		Taught	Taught	Last Supper	Interred	Rejoice with liberated dead in Spirit World		Resurrected
Julian Calendar Month of April	1	2	3	4	5	6	7	8	9

There is some question as to whether the supper at Bethany, whereat Mary anointed Jesus, occurred Saturday night (Jn 12:1-9) or in midweek (Matt 26:12-13 and Mk 14:1-9). Regarding the first day in Passion Week James E. Talmage (*Jesus the Christ*, p. 523) acknowledged, "A comparison of the accounts of the Lord's triumphant entry into Jerusalem, and of certain events following, as recorded by the three synoptists, shows at least a possibility of discrepancy as to sequence. . . . The question is admittedly an open one." However, most commentators concur that the Triumphal Entry transpired on Sunday. John mentions the significant branches of palm trees, Hosanna shout, and ass's colt then adds, "These things understood not his disciples at the first: but when Jesus was glorified, then remembered they that these things were written of him" (Jn 12:16). The very public and dramatic acceptance of Jesus as the promised Messiah (and possibly the anointing on the previous night) would be the most evident act of selecting Jesus to be the Lamb of God. As expected, the Triumphal Entry and probably the anointing took place on Abib-Nisan 10 in accordance with the Passover schedule.

The several days following the Triumphal Entry are filled with instruction and dialogue. However, the authors do not always agree or even specify the day upon which the teachings occurred. John did not even record these events. Luke, who prided himself in chronological exactness (Lk 1:1-3), merely said Jesus "taught daily" (Lk 19:47) and "on one of those days" (Lk 20:1) he taught parables. Luke used this lackadaisical approach until the "feast of unleavened bread drew nigh, which is called Passover" (Lk 22:1). Mark identifies the day after the Triumphal Entry as "on the morrow" (Mk 11:12). We are alerted to the next day with the phrase "in the morning" (Mk 11:20). Thus we can account for Sunday, Monday and Tuesday but with some ambiguity.

After the detailed record of the Sunday, Monday, and Tuesday activities, the synoptic Gospels conclude the Savior's public ministry. In this initial daily account the point of reference is how many days since the supper at Bethany and Triumphal Entry. As the focus now turns toward the final preparations of the Apostles, the point of reference for counting days shifts to the rapidly approaching Passover. This transition from a past reference point to a future one does not suggest a day of inactivity but merely a concentration of focus toward the more intimate group of devoted disciples. This small, personal group of friends were preparing for the family experience of the symbolic and final Passover celebrations.

The "first day of unleavened bread, when they killed the Passover" (Mk 14:12, see also Matt 26:17 and Lk 22:7) is the next day mentioned. If this is a daily account (which all internal evidence suggests) then preparations for the Last Supper were completed on Wednesday. Modern writers often speculate a Wednesday of inactivity, but no Gospel writer mentions such a day or even hints at a lapse in the style of detailed accounting. But why would Jesus have a Passover lamb slain on Wednesday the 13th when the Passover schedule stipulated this activity take place on the 14th? A clue may lie in the fact that Jesus ate the Passover meal (Matt 26:17, Mk 14:12, Lk 22:7-8) one day earlier than the Jews celebrated the feast (Matt 26:2-5; 27:15-26, 62; Mk 15:6-15, 42; Lk 23:15-17, 38-40; Jn 13:1-2, 29; 18:23; 19:14, 31, 42). One possible explanation for this variance is that Christ, "the real sacrifice of which all earlier altar victims had been but prototypes," had to celebrate the Passover meal one night earlier for on the official day he was committed to be the Lamb of God. Another hypothesis is that the official calendar followed by the Jewish temple leaders differed by one day from that followed by the orthodox Qumran community which Jesus may have favored. "They certainly kept festivals on different days from those observed in the temple. Practice may have varied in the days of Christ more than was once thought; this may help to explain why the last supper did not coincide with the day of Passover in the temple." (*Eardmans' Handbook To the Bible*, p. 111.) It has also been observed at the time of Christ tradition may have added an additional day of feast, the Chagigah, and possibly even an additional day of sacrificial slaying to accommodate the logistical challenge of slaying 250,000 plus lambs. (James E. Talmage, *Jesus the Christ*,

p. 618). For whatever reason, the Savior celebrated the Passover one day before the Jews and, therefore, was available to be the Lamb of God for all mankind on the official day of 14 Abib-Nisan.

The Jews plotted to kill Jesus but specifically chose not to do so "on the feast day, lest there be an uproar among the people" (Matt 26:5, also Mk 14:20). Accordingly each of the Gospel writers noted (Matt 27:62; Mk 15:42; Lk 23:54; Jn 19:14, 31, 42) that Jesus was crucified on the day of preparation before the Sabbath. This sabbath reference may have been too hastily interpreted by some to refer to the weekly Saturday Sabbath. For this reason most charts place the crucifixion day on Friday, thus putting the Last Supper on Thursday. Such a conclusion creates a vacuum of activity for Wednesday.

However, such a conclusion overlooks the fact that there is no "preparation" day before the weekly Sabbath. The preparation day was for the annual Passover Sabbath of 15 Abib-Nisan, which that year happened to be on Friday. Let us not forget that this unique week had two Sabbaths; the Friday 15 Abib-Nisan Sabbath for Passover, and the weekly Saturday Sabbath. The day on which Christ was crucified was Thursday, the day of preparation for the Friday Passover Sabbath.

John stated, "The Jews therefore, because it was the preparation, that the bodies should not remain upon the cross on Sabbath day, (for that Sabbath day was a high day) besought Pilate that their legs might be broken, and that they might be taken away" (John 19:31). Note that the Sabbath which concerned the Jews was not the weekly Sabbath, but a very special 'high' holy day. John made special note of that fact. (*Eardman's Handbook To The Bible*, p. 547) adds "the reference here is to the preparation for the Sabbath of Passover week." A footnote to John 14:31 in the LDS Edition further clarifies, "Jesus arose on the first day of the week. The previous day was the weekly Sabbath. The day before the Sabbath, being also the day after the Passover meal, could be the 'high' day." In chart form, this information is perhaps more graphic:

Preparation and Passover meal	'High' day Sabbath	Weekly Sabbath	Resurrection on first day of week
Thursday	Friday	Saturday	Sunday
14	15	16	17

Again, the commitment to the Passover schedule of killing the lamb on the 14th, followed by a special Sabbath on the 15th is evident.

It is of special interest to note that some Bible translations (Ferrar Fenton's and Scoffield) are true to the original Greek in stating (Matt 23:1) that the resurrection occurred, "In the end of the Sabbaths."

Consecutive Sabbath days would also make the period of internment and prophesies thereof more compatible.

If Christ was crucified on Thursday rather than Friday his body would have been in the tomb a full 24 hours longer than some have taught. This would be more consistent with prophecy than the traditional Friday night through Sunday morning internment. On numerous occasions (see The Significance of 'Three Days' in the Bible, located in accompanying Appendix) Jesus prophesied that he would be resurrected three days after his death. The Friday through Sunday theory only allows for about 36 hours in the tomb. True, it can be shown (and it always has to be explained because it isn't readily evident) that these hours do overlap parts (perhaps minutes) of three calendar days. However, if the hours and days must be orchestrated, it would seem to dilute the intended impact of the sign. The conspicuous inadequacy of the Friday through Sunday approach is evident when one considers the very descriptive statement by Jesus that "as Jonas was three days and three nights in the whale's belly; so shall the Son of Man be three days and three nights in the heart of the earth" (Matt 12:40). A Friday through Sunday interpretation may overlap three calendar days but there is no way it can include three days and three nights. A Thursday afternoon to Sunday morning internment of approximately 60 hours certainly approaches a more literal fulfillment of the Savior's prophecy.

The wicked Jewish leaders to whom Jesus gave the "three days and three nights" prophecy seemed to understand it to mean a full three days. The day after Jesus' body was placed in the tomb "the chief priests and Pharisees came together unto Pilate, saying, Sir, we remember that that deceiver said, while he was yet alive, after three days I will rise again. Command therefore that the sepulcher be made sure until the third day" (Matt 27:62-63). The request seems to express concern not for just one more night but for several more days.

When Matthew advanced in his narrative from the day of crucifixion to the day the guards were posted he used the phrase "Now the next day" (Matt 27:62). There is no such "next day" or "on the morrow" phrase introducing the day of resurrection. The day by day account seems to have concluded temporarily and resumes again "after the Sabbath . . . toward the first day of the week" (Matt 28:1).

That the scriptural prophesies of Christ's death and time in the tomb were important to the later Apostle Paul is evident. He said, "Christ died for our sins according to the scriptures . . . he was buried, and that he arose again the third day according to the scriptures" (1 Cor 15: 3-4). Prophecies recorded in the scriptures stipulate three days and three nights in the tomb. The preponderance of evidence considered would suggest that Jesus was slain on Thursday, resurrected on Sunday and thus satisfied all the demands of prophecy.

BOOK OF MORMON CLARIFICATION

The controversy as to the day upon which events of the Savior's last week occurred continues with no clear conclusion. Therefore, it may very well be that further dialogue using the Bible only will not bring about the desired clarification. What is needed is a fresh approach, another perspective. The Book of Mormon provides precisely that, another account of the Savior's death and resurrection. Combined, these two companion scriptures may finally provide the clarification needed to present a clear description and further increase the reader's faith in searching the scriptures to solve scriptural dilemmas.

In the very first chapter of the Book of Mormon is recorded the prophecy of Lehi concerning "the coming of a Messiah, and also the redemption of the world." (1 Nephi 1:19) As "Another Testament of' Jesus Christ," this sacred writing never diverts from its focus on Christ and, therefore, provides the reader with additional detail of his birth, life, death, and resurrection. Though thousands of miles separate the descendants of Lehi from Jerusalem, their town of origin, the focus of their family history continues to be an unquenchable interest in the fulfil- ment of prophecies relating to all aspects of the Savior's mortal mission.

That the Disciples of Christ in the Americas understood the Savior's sacrificial role is clearly evident. Nephi said of Jesus, "He offered himself a sacrifice for sin, to answer the ends of the law" (2 Nephi 2:7). Amulek taught, "Therefore, it is expedient that there should be a great and last sacrifice, and then shall there be, or it is expedient there should be, a stop to the shedding of blood; then shall the law of Moses be fulfilled; yea, it shall be all fulfilled, every jot and tittle, and none shall have passed away. And behold, this is the whole meaning of the law, every whit pointing to that great and last sacrifice; and that great and last sacrifice will be the Son of God, yea, infinite and eternal (Alma 34:13-14).

Prior to leaving Jerusalem, Lehi's family obtained the Brass Plates which contained much of our current Old Testament. These plates also contain some additional writings which have special relevance to scattered Israel and their awareness of Christ. These records included the detailed prophetic statement that the future Messiah "yieldeth himself, according to the words of the angel, as a man, into the hands of wicked men, to be lifted up, according to the words of Zenock, and to be crucified, according to the words of Neum and to be buried in a sepulchre, according to the words of Zenos, which he spake concerning the three days of darkness, which should be a sign given of his death unto those who should inherit the isles of the sea, more especially given unto those who are of the house of Israel" (1 Nephi 19:10). "A careful reading of these words of Zenos seems to indicate that the 'three days of darkness' that were to accompany the crucifixion of Christ were not to be a sign to those of the house of Israel around Jerusalem but to those who lived away from Jerusalem or on 'the isles of the sea'." (Daniel H. Ludlow, *A Companion to Your Study of the Book of Mormon*, p.120)

As we continue to read the Book of Mormon we will discover that the three days of darkness were experienced with exactness. The question then becomes, "Were the three days of darkness merely a sign of his death or also a statement of the length of time to be spent in the sepulcher?" Further analysis of Book of Mormon statements will suggest that there may in fact be a direct correlation.

The prophet Nephi, after quoting extensively from Isaiah's Messianic chapters (2 Nephi 13-24) added his own "prophecy according to . . . plainness" (Nephi 25:4). Nephi emphatically stated, ". . . they will crucify him; and after he is laid in a sepulcher for the space of three days he shall rise from the dead." (2 Nephi 25:13). It should be remembered that Nephi's intent was to speak in plainness and not in some hard to understand "manner of prophesying among the Jews" (2 Nephi 25:1).

King Benjamin's masterful discourse concerning Christ includes very detailed information regarding essential aspects of his mortal life and death. Like Nephi, Benjamin simply states, "and shall crucify him. And he shall rise the third day from the dead." (Mosiah 3:10).

Hundreds of years elapsed, but the interest of these devoted disciples in Christ did not diminish. Even before the angel Gabriel visited Zachariah, Elizabeth and Mary, the inspired Book of Mormon prophet Samuel said, 'Behold I give unto you a sign; for five years more cometh, and behold then cometh the Son of God to redeem all those who shall believe on his name.

And behold, this will I give unto you for a sign at the time of his coming; for behold, there shall be great lights in heaven, insomuch that in the night before he cometh there shall be no darkness, insomuch that it shall appear unto man as if it was day. Therefore, there shall be one day and a night and a day, as if it were one day and there were no night; and this shall be unto you for a sign; for ye shall know of the rising of the sun and also of its setting; therefore they shall know of a surety that there shall be two days and a night nevertheless the night shall not be darkened; and it shall be the night before he is born" (Helaman 14:2-4).

The day before the long awaited birth the Savior revealed himself to Nephi and said, ". . . the time is at hand, and on this night shall the sign be given, and on the morrow come I into the world, to show unto the world that I will fulfill all that which I have caused to be spoken by the mouth of my holy prophets. . . . And it came to pass that the words which came unto Nephi were fulfilled, according as they had been spoken; for behold, at the going down of the sun there was no darkness; and the people began to be astonished because there was no darkness when the night came, . . . And it came to pass that there was no darkness in all the night, but it was as light as though it was mid-day. And it came to pass that the sun did rise in the morning again, according to its proper order; and they knew that it was the day that the Lord should be born, because of the sign which had been given.... And it had come to pass, yea all things, every whit, according to the words of the prophets" (3 Nephi 1:13, 15, 19-20).

These details concerning the birth of Jesus are not directly related to the main theme of this paper - the final week, death, and resurrection of Jesus. They are quoted here because they evidence three truths about Book of Mormon prophecies. First, prophetic details and equally detailed fulfillment are recorded "every whit, according to the words of the prophets" (3 Nephi 1:20). We can, therefore, conclude that prophesied details will occur precisely and not in some generalized manner requiring later commentators to theorize inconclusively for centuries to come. Second, the concept of "day" and "night" as perceived by the Nephite observer seemed to correspond to the apparent rising and setting of the sun rather than to the 6 p.m. (Jewish) or 12 p.m. (Roman) methods of counting "days." Since it was for these very same Nephite observers that the sign of "three days of darkness" was designed, it seems probable that we should expect the fulfillment to involve three full solar days and not merely parts of three calendar days. Third, Jesus stated, "this night shall the sign be given, and on the morrow come I into the world" (3 Nephi l:13). "And it came to pass that the sun did rise in the morning again according to its proper order;

and they knew that it was the day that the Lord should be born, because of the sign which had been given" (3 Nephi 1:19).   Jesus was to be born at a moment in time which to the Nephites would follow their night and, therefore, be during day-light hours. Yet the New Testament account (Luke 2:8) implies that Jesus was born at night in Bethlehem. This discrepancy in time is to be expected for time of day is relative to longitude and the Book of Mormon and New Testament locations are more than a quarter of the earth's circumference distance from each other. Therefore, an event occurring in Bethlehem in the night would easily coincide with day-light hours in the Americas. More will be said of this interesting time distinction later for both the New Testament and the Book of Mormon writers relate events that occurred in their respective locations at the precise moment of the Savior's death.

That same Samuel, whose "one day and a night and a day" prophecy proved to be so literal, also gave a detailed sign regarding Christ's death. Said Samuel concerning " a sign of his death, behold, in that day that he shall suffer death the sun shall be darkened and refuse to give his light unto you (notice again the concept of "day" by these writers is relative to solar observations); and also the moon and the stars; and there shall be no light upon the face of this land (remember this is to be an 'isles of the sea' phenomenon); even from the time he shall suffer death, for the space of three days, to the time that he shall rise again from the dead. Yea, at the time that he shall yield up the ghost there shall be thunderings and lightnings for the space of many hours" (Helaman 14:20-21). Thus, it is clearly stated that the darkness would begin at the moment of the Savior's death in distant Jerusalem and end three days later at the resurrection. The faithful were told to look for a day (as perceived by sunrise) which would be blackened by violent storm and the attending three days of darkness.

The sign of the Savior's birth occurred precisely as predicted. Thirty-three years later "the people began to look with great earnestness for another sign which had been given by the prophet Samuel, the Lamanite, yea, for the time that there should be darkness for the space of three days over the face of the land. And it came to pass in the thirty and fourth year, in the first month, on the fourth day of the month, there arose a great storm, such an one as never had been known in all the land. . . .   And it came to pass that when the thunderings and the lightnings, and the storm, and the tempest, and the quakings of the earth did cease - for behold, they did last for about the space of three hours; and it was said by some that the time was greater; nevertheless, all these great and terrible things were done in about the space of three hours (notice how important it is to the writers that we are aware that their references to elapsed time are precise) - and behold, there was darkness upon the face of the land. . . . And it came to pass that it did last for the space of three days that there was no light seen" (3 Nephi 8:5, 19, 23).

It may be possible to deduce the approximate time of day that the prophesied three day period commenced. Samuel's statement that the sun "shall be darkened and refuse to give his light" would imply that the three day period would commence in the daylight hours. This would be consistent with the detailed New Testament account which records the time of death in Jerusalem as being the Jewish 9th hour (MK 15:33-37). Jerusalem and Central America are separated by so many longitudinal degrees that they would have approximately an eight to nine hour time difference. Thus, 3 p.m. in Jerusalem would be synchronized with about 6 a.m. Nephite time, or shortly after sunrise.

While still in the midst of the three days of darkness, the surviving Nephites heard the voice of the crucified Savior detail the various destructions which had recently befallen the less righteous inhabitants of the land. (3 Nephi 9) Through the thick darkness the Savior said to the righteous survivors, "Behold, for such I have laid down my life, and taken it up again; therefore, repent, and come unto me, ye ends of the earth, and be saved" (3 Nephi 9:22). Either the Savior was speaking prophetically or had already been resurrected for he said of his life, ". . . have taken it up again." It may be reasonable to conclude that Jesus was resurrected hours (but not days) prior to the full three days sign (3 Nephi 10:1-2).

As to the termination of the three day period the Book of Mormon account is very specific, "And it came to pass that thus did the three days pass away. And it was in the morning, and the darkness dispersed from off the face of the land" (3 Nephi 10:9). Since we have already concluded that the storm and darkness commenced soon after sunrise, the total time was in fact, a full three day period. This exactness may be very important when we consider the literalness of various signs and times associated with the Savior's death and resurrection.

Earlier, we quoted Nephi who associated the three day period with the length of time Jesus was to be laid in a sepulcher (2 Nephi 25:13). We have also noted that the Savior's comments from the darkness may evidence the resurrection occurred some hours prior to the conclusion of the full three days (3 Nephi 9:22). The New Testament account specifies that the slain body of the Savior was placed in the sepulcher "when even was come" (Matt 27:57) and was removed "as it began to dawn toward the first day of the week" (Matt 28:1). Considering all evidence it would thus appear that the time between the Savior's death and resurrection was approximately 1/2 day short of three full days, or a total of 2 1/2 days.

From the vantage point of Central America a 2 1/2 day period of supernatural darkness which commenced soon after sunrise would be followed by the natural darkness of night and combine to make a full three days of darkness. As prophesied, those of Israel scattered on the "isles of the sea" experienced three days of darkness which were associated with the death and resurrection of Christ.

These Israelites of the Book of Mormon who experienced the three full days of darkness were very careful to relate these events with prophetic statements. An editor of the Nephite record concluded, "And thus were the scriptures fulfilled which had been spoken by the prophets" (3 Nephi 10:11). The record keeper then draws the attention of the reader back to the initial three day prophecy (1 Nephi 19:10) recorded in the Book of Mormon with this counsel, "Whoso readeth, let him understand; he that hath the scriptures, let him search them. . . . Yea, the prophet Zenos did testify of these things, and also Zenock spake concerning these things, because they testified particularly concerning us, who are the remnant of their seed" (3 Nephi 10:14, 16).

Soon "after the ascension of Christ into heaven he did truly manifest himself" (3 Nephi 10:18) unto his disciples in the Book of Mormon lands. Of this ministry Mormon records, "I would that ye should behold that the Lord truly did teach the people, for the space of three days; and after that he did show himself unto them oft" (3 Nephi 26:13). This reference is cited only to reemphasize that Book of Mormon writers consistently use the term "day" to refer to daylight hours, or a 24 hour period commencing with the daylight hours. The three days of darkness experienced by the Nephites were literally three 24 hour periods or three periods of daylight each followed by a corresponding period of darkness. This day-followed-by-night sequence itself may be significant. Christ was quite specific in prophesying. "For as Jonas was three days and three nights in the whale's belly so shall the Son of Man be three days and three nights in the heart of the earth" (Matt 12:40). Certainly the disciples in Central America experienced a more literal fulfillment of this prophecy than did those dwelling in Jerusalem.

Since the New Testament account is not clear as to the day of the week upon which crucial events occurred, controversy of interpretation continues. Using Passover Feast days as reference points has left the question unsettled, for the Feast days can fall on any day of the week (such as our New Year's Day or Christmas). Using the Sabbath as a reference is also ambiguous for it is not clear whether Jesus was hurriedly buried before the Passover Feast (a Sabbath) or the weekly Sabbath. However, the New Testament is specific in stating that the resurrection was on the First day of the week (Matt 28:1) subsequently called the Lord's day. Thus, the New Testament provides the reliable reference point, Sunday morning, for the resurrection. The Book of Mormon provides the time frame, 2 1/2 days for length of time in the tomb. With these two bits of information, we can conclude that the crucifixion occurred on Thursday afternoon, 2 1/2 days before the Sunday morning resurrection.

Locating the crucifixion on Thursday is an intriguing idea, since it eliminates the need to speculate about an unrecorded Wednesday and more closely complies with the Passover pattern. The year Christ was killed, Thursday fell upon Nisan 14, the very day the lambs would have been sacrificed in symbolism of the Lamb of God. Therefore, the Book of Mormon supports the less traditional but defensible hypothesis that Jesus was slain on Thursday afternoon the 14th of Nisan, remained in the tomb through Friday the Passover Sabbath, Saturday the weekly Sabbath, and was resurrected Sunday morning the 17th of Nisan.

APPENDIX

Significance of Three Days in the Bible

Alternative Interpretations of Ambiguous Verses

SIGNIFICANCE OF THREE DAYS IN THE BIBLE

Christ was to be crucified and remain in the tomb three days prior to the resurrection. The repetitious reference to the three day period is an indication of the importance of this specific block of time. A review of the New Testament references would include:

Matt 12:40	". . . as Jonas was three days and three nights in the whale's belly; so shall the Son of man be three days and three nights in the heart of the earth."
Matt 16:21	". . . be killed, and be raised again the third day."
Matt 17:23	". . . the third day he shall be raised again."
Matt 20:19	". . . the third day he shall rise again."
Matt 26:61	". . . I am able to destroy the temple of God, and to build it in three days."
Matt 27:40	". . . Thou that destroyest the temple, and buildest it in three days, save thyself."
Matt 27:63	". . . After three days I will rise again."
Matt 27:64	". . . Command therefore that the sepulcher be made sure until the third day."
Mark 8:31	". . . be killed, and after three days rise again."
Mark 9:31	". . . after that he is killed, he shall rise the third day."
Mark 10:43	". . . shall kill him; and the third day he shall rise again."
Mark 14:58	". . . within three days I will build another made without hands."
Mark 15:29	". . . thou that destroyest the temple, and buildest it in three days."
Luke 9:22	". . . be slain, and be raised the third day."
Luke 13:32	". . . the third day I shall be perfected."
Luke 18:33	". . . the third day he shall rise again."
Luke 24:7	". . . the third day rise again."
Luke 24:21	". . . today is the third day since these things were done."
Luke 24:46	". . . to rise from the dead the third day."
John 2:19	". . . destroy this temple, and in three days I will raise it up."

John 2:20	"... wilt thou rear it up in three days?"
Acts 10:40	"... Him God raised up the third day."
1 Cor 15:4	"... he rose again the third day according to the scriptures."

Obviously, reference to a three day period was not casual, but considered to be an integral part of the whole atonement epic. It, therefore, seems appropriate that we search the scriptures to discover how this facet of prophecy was fulfilled in its entirety.

Since "...all things which have been given of God from the beginning of the world, unto men, are the typifying" (2 Nephi 11:4) of Christ, it is interesting to note the frequent use of the number three in the Old Testament. These passages could be alluding to the three day internment:

Gen. 22:4	"... on the third day Abraham lifted up his eyes, and saw the place afar off."
Gen. 40:12	"... Joseph said ... The three branches are three days."
Ex. 3:18	"... let us go, we beseech thee, three days journey into the wilderness, sacrifice to the Lord our God."
Ex. 10:22	"... there was a thick darkness in all the land of Egypt three days."
Ex. 19:11	"... the third day the Lord will come down in the sight of all the people."
Ex. 19:16	:... on the third day in the morning, that there were thunders and lightnings."
Lev. 7:17	"... but the remainder of the flesh of the sacrifice on the third day shall be burnt with fire."
Num 10:33	"... the ark of the covenant of the Lord went before them in the three days journey, to search out a resting place for them.
Joshua 1:11	"... within three days ye shall pass over this Jordan, to go in to possess the land."
Hosea 6:2	"... After two days will he revive us: in the third day he will raise us up."
Jonah 1:17	"... Now the Lord had prepared a great fish to swallow up Jonah. And Jonah was in the belly of the fish three days and three nights."

The precise wording varies slightly and may create a degree of ambiguity: "the third day," "in three days," "after three days," "within three days," "on the third day," "three days," "in the third day." However, both the final Old Testament reference and the initial New Testament reference explicitly state "three days and three nights." Only if Christ's body was in the tomb the "three days and three nights" of Thursday, Friday, and Saturday would the prophecy be fulfilled with appropriate exactness.

ALTERNATIVE INTERPRETATIONS OF AMBIGUOUS VERSES

There are four references in the Gospel accounts which are used to determine the daily schedule of events of the Savior's final week. "Then Jesus, six days before Passover, came to Bethany" (Jn 12:1) is used to identify the beginning of the week of activities. "Ye know that after two days is the feast of the Passover" (Matt 26:2) gives some clue regarding the midweek activities. "And now when the even was come, because it was the preparation, that is, the day before the Sabbath" (Mark 15:42, see Luke 23:54, also John 19:31) locates the day of crucifixion. And "In the end of the Sabbath, as it began to dawn toward the first day of the week, came Mary Magdalene and the other Mary to see the sepulcher" (Matt 28:1, also Mark 16:1, Luke 24:1, John 20:1) identifies the day of resurrection. Of these four-day specific events, only the last, which identifies the Sunday resurrection and is mentioned by all four writers, is accepted without much diversity of interpretation. The other three dates are less certain and, therefore, have produced a variety of interpretations.

John recorded, "Then Jesus, six days before the Passover, came to Bethany" (John 12:1). There at Bethany, Jesus was anointed by Mary in preparation for the Triumphal Entry and crucifixion. On the surface, the verse seems very helpful in identifying the day of arrival. However, on closer observation several questions surface. First, what is meant by "the Passover?" Does "Passover" refer to the first day of unleavened bread, the day of preparation on Abib-Nisan 14 (Lev 25:5), or the Feast of Unleavened Bread on Abib-Nisan 15 (Lev 23:6)? Of course, the transitions from Abib-Nisan 14 to 15 at 6:00 p.m. in the evening is always a confusing factor for those of our culture trying to interpret statements from those of the New Testament culture. The year of our Lord's death, Abib-Nisan 14 was Thursday and Abib-Nisan 15 was Thursday Night. Perhaps the distinction of before or after 6:00 p.m. need not even be considered for "unlike other Gospel writers, John probably uses Roman time, counting as we do from midnight. Unless, as some believe, John dates the Passover one day later than the other Gospel writers." (*Eardmen*, p. 547)

If we could determine with certainty what John meant by "the Passover," we could then focus on the second problem: what is meant by "six days" before the Passover? Was John including the Passover day in the six days or was it six days exclusive of that day? Consider the following contemporary scenario: On December 12th, your child asks, "How many more days 'till Christmas?" If your answer includes the 12th and 25th, it would be 14. If you include either the 12th or the 25th, but not both, your answer would be 13. If you are counting only the days in between the 12th and the 25th, then the correct answer would be 12. All three differing answers are correct, simply alternative ways of counting days.

Comparing the writings of John and other Gospel writers, we gain an insight into John's manner of counting days. On another occasion, John said, "And after eight days again his disciples were within" (John 20:26). Bruce R. McConkie (*Mortal Messiah* v. 4, p. 286) explains, "John, speaking after the Jewish pattern, says 'after eight days,' meaning, to us, seven days later." Even today, our missionaries serving in many foreign lands have to adjust to this way of referring to one week later. Luke (Luke 9:28) appears to use this same inclusive system of calling one week "eight days." However, this method was not universal, for Matthew (Matt 17:1) and Mark (Mark 9:2) refer to the same period as "after six days" and thus exclude the two boundary days of the weekly spectrum. (Regarding John's method of counting all possible days, Bruce R. McConkie further stated, "Their measurement of Jesus' tenure in the tomb is also counted the same way." This logic is used to explain how a few minutes or hours on Friday, all Saturday, and part of Sunday, could continue "three days." However, it must be remembered that Matthew and Mark did not use this inclusive system and they, more than Luke and John, spoke of a "three day" burial period. It, therefore, seems that we cannot merely sweep aside all the "three day" references with a simple explanation..)

Evidence would, therefore, suggest that John's inclusive method of counting six days before the Passover would include the Passover day. Using this logic, Jesus would have arrived in Bethany Saturday or Saturday night. However, it is not totally clear and some suggest that Jesus would not have traveled on the weekly Saturday Sabbath so probably arrived one day earlier. Both James E. Talmage (*Jesus the Christ*, p. 510) and Bruce R. McConkie (*Mortal Messiah*, Vol. 3, p. 333) conclude that he probably arrived on Friday. Correlating these conclusions, we have two probable options: one, John was referring to the six inclusive days of Friday to the Wednesday Last Supper Passover meal of Jesus and his disciples; or two, he was referring to the Saturday to Thursday public Passover preparation and feast of 14 and 15 Abib-Nisan. Even if John was not using his customary (Jn 20:26) inclusive method, a Friday arrival would pinpoint a Thursday Passover rather than the traditionally accepted Friday. Since the Gospel writers clearly teach that Christ was crucified on the day of preparation prior to the Passover feast, he must have died Thursday afternoon.

In midweek, following the arrival in Bethany and Triumphal Entry, there is another day spoken of using the approaching Passover as a reference day. Matthew says, "after two days is the feast of the Passover" (Matt 26:2). If the Passover feast was on Thursday night, as required by the 15 Abib-Nisan schedule, then Jesus' statement recorded by Matthew should have occurred on Tuesday afternoon. After Jesus had taught in public and then explained in more detail the signs of his second coming, ". . . it came to pass when Jesus had finished all these sayings, he said unto his disciples, Ye know that after two days is the Feast of the Passover, and the Son of Man is betrayed to be crucified." Since this statement is the conclusion of the previously quoted "sayings," it seems most logical to believe they were said on Tuesday when the sermons were given. Some have located this saying on Wednesday. However, this seems to be more of a consequence of commitment to a Friday Passover rather than accepting the account as it is written.

In Matthew's account, the first obvious shift from the day of public sermons to the next day is recorded thus, "Now the first day of the feast of unleavened bread the disciples came to Jesus, saying unto him, "Where wilt thou that we prepare for thee to eat the Passover" (Matt 26:17)? This day, Wednesday, is the first day of unleavened bread on which the Jews began to seek out leaven in anticipation of the preparation day to follow, on which the lambs would be offered. Since Jesus and his disciples celebrated the Passover one day earlier than the public celebrations of 14 and 15 Abib-Nisan, this Wednesday was far from a day of inactivity.

No other detail is quoted as frequently to identify the day of crucifixion as the scurry to remove the body from the cross before the Sabbath. "And now when the even was come, because it was the preparation, that is, the day before the Sabbath" (Mark 15:42) Joseph of Arimathaea hastily prepared the crucified body for burial. If the reader assumes that the referred to Sabbath was the routine weekly celebrations then he is committed to a Friday afternoon crucifixion, a Thursday last supper, a Wednesday of no recorded activity, and a minimal spread of hours in the tomb to satisfy the three day prophecies.

However, the scheduled day of preparations was on Thursday 14 Abib-Nisan.(Ex 12:6) Jesus was killed on the day of preparation, (Matt 27:62) intentionally before the feast day, (Matt 26:5) before the Jews had eaten the Passover. (John 18:28) That Thursday night was the Passover feast or Sabbath of 15 Abib-Nisan. John indicated that the feast day following the crucifixion (Jn 19:31) was more than the weekly Sabbath and the footnotes in the LDS edition identify the Sabbath in question as being the Friday

Passover Sabbath which preceded the normal Saturday Sabbath. When the reader locates the crucifixion day on Thursday there is no longer any need to speculate a Wednesday of no activity, explain why the Lamb of God was not slain on the scheduled day for this sacrifice, or stretch 36 hours in the tomb into three days and three nights.

BIBLIOGRAPHY for DAYS OF AWE

Birnbaum, Phillip. *Encyclopedia of Jewish Concepts*. New York: Hebrew Publishing Company, 1995.

Brandt, Edward J. "The Priesthood Ordinance of Sacrifice," *Ensign*, December 1973, 49.

Breslov Research Institute. "Counting the Omer and Shavuot," 1997. www.breslov.org.omer.html

Chumney, Edward. *The Seven Festivals of the Messiah*. Shippensburg, PA: Treasure House, 1999.

Cohen, Shaye J.D. *From the Maccabees to the Mishnah*. Philadelphia: Westminster Press, 1987. The Dead Sea Scrolls: Temple Scroll 17:6. (See the *Biblical Archaeologist*, September, 1978, 105-120.)

Edersheim, Alfred. *The Life and Times of Jesus the Messiah*. Grand Rapids, Michigan: Wm. B. Eardmans Publishing Company, 1962 (Original copyright, 1883).

Edersheim, Alfred. *Sketches of Jewish Social Life* (Updated Edition). Peabody, MA: Hendrickson Publishers, Inc., 1994.

Edersheim, Alfred. *The Temple: Its Ministry and Services* (Updated Edition). Peabody, MA: Hendrickson Publishers, Inc., 1994.

Education Department of the Jewish Agency for Israel. "Shavuot." www.jajz-ed.org.il

The Encyclopedia of Jewish Life and Thought. Jerusalem: Carta, 1996.

Freedman, Ruth Graver. *The Passover Seder — Afikomen in Exile*. Philadelphia: The University of Pennsylvania Press, 1981.

Funk and Wagnall's Company, *The Jewish Encyclopedia*. Volume IX.

Gaster, Theodor H. *Festivals of the Jewish Year*. New York: Wm. Morrow and Company, Inc., 1952.

Gilbert, Rabbi Arthur. *The Passover Seder—Pathways Through the Haggadah*. New York: Ktav Publishing House, Inc., 1965.

Golden, Hyman E. *A Treasury of the Jewish Holidays.* New York: Twayne Publishers, 1952.

Guggenheimer, Heinrich. The Scholar's Haggadah. Northvale, NJ: Jason Aronson, Inc., 1998.

Howard, Kevin & Rosenthal, Marvin. *The Feasts of the Lord*. Orlando, Florida: Zion's Hope, Inc., 1997.

Jacobs, Louis. *The Book of Jewish Belief*. Behrman House, Inc.

Josephus. *Complete Works.* Translated by William Whiston. Grand Rapids, Michigan: Kregel Publications, 1981.

Kolatch, Alfred J.*The Jewish Book of Why*. New York: Jonathan David Publishers, Inc., 1995. Kanoff, Abram. *Jewish Ceremonial Art and Religious Observance*. New York: Harry N. Abrams, Inc.

Levin, Meyer. *An Israel Haggadah*. New York: Harry N. Abrams, Inc.

Lingle, Chris. "The Timing of Pesakh According to the Nazarene (Netzarim) System. The Society for the Advancement of Nazarene Judaism, 1998.

Lingle, Chris. "When Were the True Dates of the Crucifixion and Resurrection?" The Society for the Advancement of Nazarene Judaism, 1997.

Ludlow, Victor L., "Jewish Migrations," *Ensign*, May 1972, 18.

Ludlow, Victor L., "Major Jewish Groups in the New Testament," *Ensign*, January 1975, 26.

The Maxwell House Haggadah. prepared by a consortium of Orthodox Rabbis, 1984. McConkie, Bruce R. *Mormon Doctrine.* (2nd Edition) Salt Lake City, Utah: Bookcraft, 1966. *The Jewish Mishnah.* Translation by Herbert Danby. London: Oxford University Press, 1933.

Neusner, Jacob. *An Introduction to Judaism*. Louisville, Kentucky: Westminster/John Knox Press, 1991.

A Passover Haggadah — The New Union Haggadah prepared by the Central Conference of American Rabbis, 1987.

Ohr Somayach International, "Torah Scroll," October 13, 2001, Issue 323 Ohr Somayach International."What is *Lag B'omer*?" 1998.

www.ohr.org.il/special/omer/whatis33/html

Pratt, John P. "Passover: Was It Symbolic of His Coming?" *Ensign*, January, 1994, 38.

Raphael, Chaim. *A Feast of History — The Drama of Passover Through the Ages*. London and Jerusalem: Weidenfeld and Nicholson, 1972.

Roberts, B. H. *Outlines of Ecclesiastical History*. Salt Lake City, Utah: Canon and Sons Company, 1895.

Rosen, Ceil and Moishe. *Christ in the Passover.* Chicago, IL: Moody Press, 1978.

Rubin, Barry and Steffi. *The Messianic Passover Haggadah*. Baltimore, MD: Messianic Jewish Publishers, 1998.

Schauss, Hayyim (translation by Samuel Jaffe). *The Jewish Festivals: History and Observance*. New York: Schocken Books, 1938.

Scholem, Gershom. *Kabbalah*. Jerusalem: Keter Publishing House, 1974. Skousen, W. Cleon. *The Third Thousand Years*. Salt Lake City: Bookcraft, 1964.

Suissa, David (Founder/Editor). *Farbrengen Magazine.* Chabad of California, Nissan–Sivan 5759 (Spring 1999).

Talmage, James E. *Jesus the Christ*. Salt Lake City, Utah: Deseret Book Company, 1915. Torahtots.com: "Shavuot." www.torahtots.com

The Universal Jewish Encyclopedia. New York: Leon L Watters Company, Volume 8. Winter, Naphtali. *The High Holy Days*. Jerusalem: Keter Publishing Company, 1973.

Zeligs, Dorothy F. *The Story of Jewish Holidays and Customs for Young People*. New York: Block Publishing Co, 1951.

Made in the USA
Las Vegas, NV
05 May 2022

48435506R00173